Democracy and Civil Society in Arab Political Thought

Modern Intellectual and Political History of the Middle East
Mehrzad Boroujerdi, *Series Editor*

Other titles in Modern Intellectual and Political History of the Middle East

Corporatist Ideology in Kemalist Turkey: Progress or Order?
Taha Parla and Andrew Davison

Cultural Schizophrenia: Islamic Societies Confronting the West
Daryush Shayegan; John Howe, trans.

Factional Politics in Post-Khomeini Iran
Mehdi Moslem

Freedom, Modernity, and Islam: Toward a Creative Synthesis
Richard K. Khuri

*The Genesis of Young Ottoman Thought: A Study in the Modernization
of Turkish Political Ideas*
Serif Mardin

Globalization and the Muslim World: Culture, Religion, and Modernity
Birgit Schaebler and Leif Stenberg, eds.

God and Juggernaut: Iran's Intellectual Encounter with Modernity
Farzin Vahdat

In the Path of Hizbullah
A. Nizar Hamzeh

Iranian Intellectuals and the West: The Tormented Triumph of Nativism
Mehrzad Boroujerdi

The Kurds and the State: Evolving National Identity in Iraq, Turkey, and Iran
Denise Natali

Mohammad Mosaddeq and the 1953 Coup in Iran
Mark J. Gasiorowski and Malcolm Byrne, eds.

Mysticism and Dissent: Socioreligious Thought in Qajar Iran
Mangol Bayat

The Story of the Daughters of Quchan: Gender and National Memory in Iranian History
Afsaneh Najmabadi

Democracy and Civil Society in Arab Political Thought

Transcultural Possibilities

MICHAELLE L. BROWERS

SYRACUSE UNIVERSITY PRESS

Mohamad El-Hindi Books on Arab Culture and Islamic Civilization
are published with the assistance of a grant from the M.E.H. Foundation.

The paper used in this publication meets the minimum requirements of
American National Standard of Information Sciences—Permanence of Paper of
Printed Library Materials, ANSI Z39.48–1984∞™

Library of Congress Cataloging-in-Publication Data
Browers, Michaelle, 1968–
Democracy and civil society in Arab political thought : transcultural possibilities /
Michaelle L. Browers.—1st ed.
p. cm.
Includes bibliographical references and index.
ISBN 0–8156–3099–9 (hardcover : alk. paper)
1. Democracy—Arab countries. 2. Civil society—Arab countries. 3. Political
culture—Arab countries. 4. Political science—Arab countries. I. Title.
JQ1850.A91B76 2006
321.80917'4927—dc22   2006022320

To my husband, Dan, for his constant support and humor throughout the researching, writing, and revising of this work.

Michaelle L. Browers is an assistant professor of political science at Wake Forest University in Winston-Salem, North Carolina.

Contents

Preface

This project is in many respects the result of what Hans-Georg Gadamer sums up with the term *wirkungsgeschichtliches Bewußtsein* (historically effected consciousness or consciousness in which history is at work)— that is, something that at times seemed to have come about above and beyond my wanting and willing. Until the first Gulf war in 1990 created the employment conditions that allowed me to begin study of both the Middle East and the Arabic language, I had not considered intellectual pursuits outside of more traditional Western political theory. So too, after I left the Middle East Institute and the Middle East Research and Information Project to begin graduate study, I entered as a student of political theory, though I continued to study Arabic as a second foreign language (after German). It is quite clear, to borrow from Gadamer again, that one cannot learn a language and remain unchanged. And so it was that, although political theory in American universities, including my own, generally insists on limiting its subject matter to Western traditions of political thought, I undertook this attempt to combine training in political theory with Arabic.

So too, this particular subject matter itself was literally pressed upon me as I undertook research on a much more esoteric topic that focused on the hermeneutical approaches of a number of Arab intellectuals toward their heritage *(turath)*. A predissertation grant from the Social Science Research Council permitted me to explore the topic in Morocco, where I first encountered *civil society* in Arabic (as *al-mujtama' al-madani*). Various thinkers I interviewed managed to employ the term amidst my questions about the politics of textual interpretation, and I was struck by the fact that so many professors at the main university in Rabat alone (Muhammad 'Abid al-Jabiri, Sa'id Binsa'id, and Kamal 'Abd al-Latif in philosophy; 'Abdallah Sa'if in the faculty of law; and Fatima Mernissi in sociology) had all recently written on the topic. To some extent this focus should not have been surprising: the role of civil society in the political transformations in Central and Eastern Europe was fodder for much political discourse in the early 1990s. Yet I suspect it will at least surprise those who consider the Arab region as the quintessential "other" to liberal, democratic, and civil societies. Certainly I was impressed by the extent and level of the discourse.

Today, after war has been undertaken in Iraq with the stated aim of bringing democracy to the country and when organizations (such as the Research Triangle Institute in my home state of North Carolina) are winning contracts to teach democracy to the citizens of that war-torn country, which for its part is to become the exemplar of freedom for other countries in the region, it is important to remember that democracy and civil society have been the foci of extensive discussion and political struggles for independence, political reform, social progress, and economic prosperity throughout the region since long before the current interest in democratizing the Middle East. I hope this work at the very least attests to that fact and undermines notions that the failure to democratize and reform in the region can be simply chalked up to cultural or conceptual deficiencies.

At the end of a work that spans many years and many countries, I fear I will fall rather short in sufficiently articulating my gratitude to the many individuals and organizations who have contributed to the project's completion. Much of the research for this project was conducted during multiple visits to Morocco, Syria, Jordan, Lebanon, Egypt, and the West Bank over the past decade, with generous funding provided by the Social Science Research Council, the American Institute for Maghrebi Studies, the American Center for Oriental Research, the Consortium of American Overseas Research Centers, and the MacArthur Program for Interdisciplinary Studies at the University of Minnesota.

I would like to thank all of the intellectuals and activists who shared their ideas, experiences, friendships, and homes with me. A special thanks to Fawwaz Traboulsi, Isam al-Khafaji, Ahmed Abdalla, and Basel Burgan for their hospitality and conversation; to Mohamed Farki, Yahia El-Maghraby, and Caesar Farah for invaluable instruction and advice throughout my constant struggle with Arabic texts and translations; to Terence Ball, James Farr, Caesar Farah, August Nimtz, Michael Root, Salwa Ismail, Peter Gran, and Richard Bellamy, for their challenging comments on earlier drafts; to Mehrzad Boroujerdi, editor of the series on "Modern Intellectual and Political History of the Middle East," and two anonymous reviewers for Syracuse University Press, for their critical readings of later drafts; and to Mary Selden Evans, the executive director of Syracuse University Press, for her support and guidance in bringing this book to print. The responsibility for any shortcomings or errors, in English or Arabic, lies with the author alone.

Note on Translations and Transliterations from Arabic

Unless otherwise indicated, all the translations that appear in this work are by the author. The transliteration of Arabic words uses a simplified style. All diacritical marks have been omitted except for the *ayn* (') and the *hamza* (') when it appears in the middle of a word. Arabic words are italicized, except for those that are widely used in English, such as "Qur'an." The names of Arab individuals are transliterated according to the same system, unless the author was aware of a consistently used Latinized spelling from, for example, an individual's English or French writings. When individuals are referred to solely by their last names in transliteration, the definite article "al-" has been dropped. When this information was available to the author, nationality and dates of birth and death are provided for Arab intellectuals upon first reference.

Democracy and Civil Society in Arab Political Thought

1

Crossing the Arab Democracy Gap

Toward the Transcultural Study of Political Concepts

> I, Hasan the son of Muhammad the weigh-master, I Jean-Leon de
> Medici, circumcised at the hand of a barber and baptized at the hand of
> a pope, I am now called the African, but I am not from Africa, nor from
> Europe, nor from Arabia. I am also called the Granadan, the Fassi, the
> Zayyati but I come from no country, from no city, no tribe. I am the son
> of the road, my country is the caravan, my life the most unexpected of
> voyages.
>
> —Maalouf, *Leo Africanus*

The Arab region has long been subject to claims of "exceptionalism" to
international waves of democratization and to characterizations of the
few existing Arab democratic experiments as "poor cousins" to Western
democracies (Karatnycky 2002; Korany 1994). Many explanations have
been given for the inability of democracy to take root in the region. One
approach generalizes about political culture in the region, pointing out
propensities toward authoritarianism. A version of this explanation
holds that in the Middle East "personalities rather than ideas determine
the line of government" and "where personalism is the rule, democracy
does not correspond to twentieth-century conceptions" (Tütsch 1958,
27). A related view holds that people in the Middle East tend to rely upon
"government for the necessary guidance and initiative" in bringing
about reform and to "seek a short cut by way of a military dictatorship"
(Issawi 1956, 41).

A second set of explanations focuses on a purported imbalance between state and society in the region, and has two competing strains: either Arab society is "accustomed to . . . autocracy and passive obedience" and thus weak vis-à-vis an overbearing state (Kedourie 1992, 103) or, alternatively, the historical strength of Arab-Islamic societies have made the state unstable and hindered its ability to engage in necessary political reforms (Hall 1988, 29–31). According to either account, the delicate balance between state and society necessary to sustain democracy is said to be lacking in the Middle East.

A third set of arguments, related in differing degrees to the above two explanations, points to a number of conceptual weaknesses or absences in Arab and Islamic political thought. In regard to the history of Islamic thought, Ann K. S. Lambton maintains that the "individual and the state . . . are broadly at one in their moral purpose, and so the conception of the individual is not prominent, nor the conception of rights. Islam does not in fact recognize the legal personality of the individual in which his rights are secured to him and vested in him by law" (Lambton 1988, xv). According to this view, the region either lacks conceptions of individual autonomy and active citizenship or does not sufficiently value such notions—perhaps rejecting them as "inauthentic" or "foreign"— and this deficiency hinders the development and sustenance of democratic civil spheres of interaction in which individuals might exchange views, organize voluntary associations, and engage with political institutions. More often, this argument points to secularism or secular rationality as the missing element.

In a study of what he terms "Islamic liberalism," Leonard Binder offers a particular version of the argument that the democracy gap in the Middle East can be largely accounted for by conceptual weaknesses or absences, in maintaining that "political liberalism can only exist where and when its social and intellectual prerequisites exist" (1988, 2). Binder differs from other versions of this explanation in suggesting that "these preconditions already exist in some parts of the Islamic Middle East" (1988, 2). He also maintains a dialectical hermeneutic with the writings he engages, rather than uncritically applying Western development theory to the Middle East. Much of the evidence provided in the chapters that follow supports Binder's thesis, while attempting to avoid the ideological parameters of that earlier work in regard to what constitutes both the preconditions and outcome of projects aimed at liberation and democratization in the Arab region, as well as seeking to remain more consistently attentive to Arab intellectuals' needs to be liberated from subordination to even a democratic West.[1]

The democratic transformations that took place in Eastern Europe resonated across the globe, creating possibilities for transformations that seemed much more remote only a few years earlier. Rather than forming an "exception" to this rule, regimes in the Arab region also began adopting limited political openings in the late 1980s and early 1990s—openings that have been explored by a number of scholars seeking to undermine the thesis of exceptionalism (Schwedler forthcoming). Some of these same scholars have noted, but none has explored in any depth, the existence of an extensive and sustained engagement on the part of Arab intellectuals with the ideas of this democratic wave that reveals not only the lack of acceptance of status quo politics in the region, but also undermines the notion that conceptual shortcomings can provide an explanation for the "democracy gap" in Arab politics. The evidence provided here demonstrates that during and since that time there has been a growing interest in—as well as adoption and adaptation of—the rhetoric of civil society and democracy. While it is true that discourse aimed at democratic reform has run up against durable authoritarian regimes, political conflicts, and wars, within Arab societies there has been an expansion of ideological groupings that are participating in a shared de

---

1. Binder reveals that his book is intended as a "rational discourse with those whose consciousness has been shaped by Islamic culture" in order to "enhance the prospects for political liberalism in that region . . . where it is not indigenous" (1988, 2). At times this "rational discourse" seems a matter of the subordination of the "other" to Western liberalism. Consider the presuppositions that open his study, which suggest that the liberalism he is looking for in Islamic contexts is based on consensus and indivisible: "it will either prevail worldwide, or it will have to be defended by nondiscursive action" (1988, 2).

bate that takes issue with the conduct and character of contemporary Arab politics and states.

There is also further evidence that the appreciation of democratic forms of rule and civil forms of engagement in the Arab region is exceptionally strong. A large-scale international study, the World Values Survey, conducted between 1995–96 and 2001–2, provides enough data to compare the Arab region (based on surveys in Egypt, Algeria, Morocco, and Jordan) to eight other country groupings: other (non-Arab) Islamic countries, sub-Saharan Africa, Eastern Europe, South Asia, North America, Australia and New Zealand, Latin America, East Asia, and Western Europe. According to this survey, Arabs place high value on democratic governance. In fact, Arabs topped the list of those supporting the statement that "democracy may have problems but it's better than any other form of government" and expressed the highest level of rejection of authoritarian rule, described as a strong leader who does not have to bother with a parliament and elections (United Nations Development Programme 2003, 36).

Drawing causal relationships between intellectual discourse and popular sentiments is beyond the scope of this study. However, analysis of the debates presented here—debates that have been taking place in Arabic regarding civil society and its relation to democratization over the past several decades—does go a long way toward understanding the scope, constraints, and possibilities of democratic theorizing in the Arab context. As such, it reveals important dimensions to questions of democracy and civil society in the region that have received neither serious nor systematic attention hitherto.

The Globalization of Democracy and Civil Society

In the contemporary world, democracy is often taken for granted as the global political ideal, and almost every individual and most political regimes seek to claim the mantle of democracy. A 1999 U.S. State Department report went so far as to claim that democracy currently forms one of the "universal languages" (along with human rights, money, and the Internet) and to hail the existence of "an international civil society" that can "support democracy and promote the standards embodied in the Universal Declaration of Human Rights" (U.S. Department of State 2000). What the world has been witnessing over the past few decades does not constitute the first time that notions of democracy and civil society have circulated with great frequency. While many claim that we are living in "the age of democracy," the democratic ideal has a long history in political thought, dating back to ancient Greece, and has been subject to criticism as well as praise. Nonetheless, the general commitment to democracy is a relatively recent phenomenon: throughout history the overwhelming majority of political thinkers have been highly critical of the theory and practice of democracy.

The concept of civil society also has a long history in the Anglo-European tradition of political thought, where it has been discussed by such different thinkers as Adam Ferguson, Alexis de Tocqueville, Friedrich Hegel, Karl Marx, and Antonio Gramsci. The concept has been most recently resurrected during the latter part of the 1970s in the context of the struggles against the communist state apparatuses in Central and Eastern Europe. A decade later the civil society idea was popularized in American politics in the context of Robert Putnam's work on "civic engagement" and "social capital" (1993; 2000). Since that time, civil society has become central to political debates throughout the world in which it has been consistently linked to democracy, and almost always in a positive manner. According to much contemporary democratic theory, civil society forms the bedrock of good democratic governance—and this sentiment is echoed in more popular political discourse.

Nonetheless, the history of the civil society remains as ambiguous as that of democracy: civil society has been associated with differing sets of principles and practices by thinkers working in different political and ideological contexts. Most conceptualizations are far from innocent empirical shorthand for associational life. Rather, Quentin Skinner's assessment of democracy seems applicable to civil society as well: the use of the phrase has both denotative and evaluative aspects. Skinner argues that the lack of consensus regarding the meaning of democracy has led to "two results": "the debate about what range of circumstances should be held to count as a case of [democracy] . . . and the fact that the use of the term *democracy* performs the speech act of commending what is described" (1973, 298–99). One could replace the word *democracy* with *civil society* here as well, and Skinner's assessment would continue to ring true. Those who employ the concept often attempt to insinuate theoretical and ideological assumptions into their analysis, stressing particular aspects of the notion as well as different historical sources and traditions, as suit the writer's purposes. What draws all of the competing civil societies together is not a phrase—indeed, the idea has had at least as many names as the title character of Amin Maalouf's novel described in the passage that opens this introductory chapter—but the attempt to conceive of a self-ordered sphere of associational life that is analytically (if not always empirically) distinguishable from the state, yet transcends purely individual existence. The concept is looked to as a way of accounting for, overcoming, or bypassing problems that arise in the conflict between the individual and some greater social whole, such as the state. But few social and political concepts, as one author has noted, have "traveled so far in their life and changed their meaning so much [as civil society]" (Pelczynski 1988, 363).

Concepts do not always travel well. The path of the contemporary reemergence of civil society alongside democracy is fraught with talk of the "clash of civilizations" (Huntington 1996). The concept has been ardently applied by Western scholars in studying developing and/or democratizing regions, usually to draw attention to the deficiency or absence of this realm there. Yet, insufficient attention has been paid to how scholars from those regions are theorizing civil society in studying their own political and social situation. The focus of this study is on civil society and democracy as conceptual components of political discourse, rather than on their presumed existence (or lack thereof) as social or historical realities. Viewed as such, the fact is that neither civil society nor democracy has remained confined to any single context, political culture, or language, but both have entered into the discourse of intellectuals and activists throughout the world.

Concepts are not static or universal entities, but are, rather, hotly contested and historically mutable. Being culture- and time-sensitive, they are best understood contextually. That is, neither civil society nor democracy has ever represented truly universal notions, but rather each signals ideals that have grown out of particular historical circumstances. Both ideas have been subject to considerable variation and used—and, one might add, abused—in a variety of contexts. The word *translation* itself etymologically means "transferred or carried from one place to another," transported across the "borders" between one language and another, one culture and another, one country and another. A concept, like a text, can be said to be, in a sense, translated any time it is displaced from its original context, even when it is read in its original language by someone else. In this sense, translation between natural languages—like English and Arabic, for example—presents a rather stark form of interpretation. I am using both *translation* and *interpretation* in the sense found in the hermeneutics of Hans-Georg Gadamer. He argues that "the dialogue we enter into with the past confronts us with a fundamentally different situation from our own—we will say a 'foreign' situation—and consequently demands an interpretive approach" (1993, 384–87). In our age of globalization, such "border crossings" occur constantly and rapidly, and the boundaries themselves are increasingly blurred such that what happens in translations may be obscured, even misunderstood. How does a concept cross borders, occupy a new territory, and situate itself in a new language? We commonly speak of something being "lost in translation," but seldom analyze what is "gained": the opportunities created for purposive and fruitful change—even innovation—in such crossings. When the "crossing" involves political and social concepts, the incursion is seldom an inconsequential affair. On the contrary, such occurrences often may prove no less "political" than, for example, the introduction of a new technology into a context, the addition of "woman" to the legal category of citizen, or the migration of an ethnic minority into a new national context.

The present work examines the question of what happens when concepts travel across the boundaries of "cultures" or "languages." In answering this question, I analyze the history of the concept of democracy in Arab and Islamic political thought, the more recent emergence of a discourse on civil society, the transformations that have occurred over the past several decades as a result of Arab forays into international discussions regarding civil society, and what these transformations tell us about the status of ideological and conceptual conflicts in the region and our study of them. I attempt to provide both an assessment of what has changed (in Arab democratic discourse in general and among particular ideological traditions competing in that context in particular) and an explanation as to why the change has occurred (what circumstances and actors account for the engagement with the civil society idea and the transformations in Arab political discourse). The analysis presented here demonstrates that the translation required to talk about these concepts in Arabic is not so much a hindrance to understanding as an opportunity for different understanding—that is, for political and conceptual contestation in Arab political thought. In contrast to those who would argue that either Arab or Islamic culture offers a hindrance to political reform in the region, I suggest that a significant transformation has already occurred in thinking about a whole constellation of concepts relevant to democratic theorizing. At the same time, my intention is not to proclaim the onset of Arab democracy. Practice does not necessarily follow close upon the heels of theory, and democratic practice still remains in short supply in the region. However, it is also too simple to dismiss the changes as merely evidence that Western-oriented Arab intellectuals are hopping on the bandwagon of civil society and democracy. Examination of the debates surrounding the recent translation of civil society and its relation to democracy reveals both the central issues that divide Arab society and the growing number of shared concepts amidst persistent and often intense ideological conflict.

Studying Conceptual Contestation and Transformation Cross-Culturally

How does one study concepts, their translation, and their transformation? The theoretical grounding for such work is provided by a large body of literature that studies the historical contestation of political and social concepts. Historians of conceptual change view moral and political concepts as a central mode of shared experiences and understandings that shift in meaning over time. James Farr writes, "language should be seen as an arena of usage in and through which political actions are undertaken, above and beyond the activity of describing or referring. In speech, pamphlets, and treatises, political actors struggle to realize strategic or partisan ends of some kind by playing or preying upon the needs, interests, and powers of one another" (1988, 16). Political language provides not merely a neutral or unchanging medium for describing politics, but can itself present a veritable battleground for political life. The approach of the conceptual change literature is historical, focusing on tracing conceptual shifts over time or at crucial historical junctures where "the struggle over the 'correct' concept becomes socially and politically explosive" (Koselleck 1985, 77). In *Keywords,* Raymond Williams takes "certain words at the level at which they are used," scrutinizing their developing structures of meaning "in and through historical time" in order "to contribute certain kinds of awareness" to social and political debates (1985, 23–24). However, as Reinhart Koselleck points out, "the investigation of a concept . . . can never limit itself to the meanings of words and their changes. A *Begriffsgeschichte* (conceptual history) must always keep in view the need for findings relevant to intellectual or material history" (1985, 85–86).

The distinction and relationship between words, concepts, and meaning are fodder for much debate that has yet to be resolved to anyone's satisfaction. Koselleck argues that whereas "the meaning of words can be defined more exactly, concepts can only be interpreted" (1972, xxiii). In a similar fashion, Terence Ball maintains that "words do not have histories, but concepts do" (Ball 1998, 82). While I discuss this issue at greater length in chapter 3, I certainly do not claim to resolve the argument in any way. Rather, agreeing with Koselleck that "as long as we remain sensitive to these sorts of problems, it is . . . possible to write about conceptual change" (Koselleck 1994, 8), I attempt to work out the word-concept relationship through the analysis of Arab writings on civil society and democracy. The engagement of Arab intellectuals with these traveling concepts is intentional, self-conscious, and contentious. What is clear is that while many of the particular points of contention take place at the level of the words used to translate the terms into Arabic, the *political* aspects of translation are best analyzed at the level of the concept, because "it is through concepts that a horizon is constituted, against which structural changes are perceived, evaluated, and acted upon"

(Richter 1995, 36). So too, the Arab thinkers discussed here consciously and consistently characterize their debate over how best to appropriate, approximate, or contest civil society and democracy as not one over a word *(kalim')*, but one over a concept *(mafhum)*.

It is for this reason—to capture the event-character of the cross-cultural translations of concepts—that most of the chapters that follow open with events, usually an academic conference or public discussions convened on the subjects of civil society and democratization. Such forums are not the sole or even primary source of material within each of these chapters—my analysis draws from books, journal articles, newspaper articles, pamphlets, and party platforms, and, in all cases, discussions of the individuals who figure most prominently in the analysis draw from multiple, not single, original sources. At the same time, much of the political and public significance of the translation of civil society is captured amidst the individuals who employ the term in face-to-face dialogue. The intensity of these historical events suggests that the debate over civil society cannot be dismissed as mere academic discourse.

A number of authors have distinguished between two approaches to conceptual history: the German genre of *Begriffsgeschichte,* which investigates "key concepts" of sociopolitical language by charting their shifting usage and the consequent perspectives they created for their usage (Brunner, Conze, and Koselleck 1972–97; Reichardt and Schmidt 1985–), and an Anglo-American form of "conceptual history," or what Ball (1988; 1998) calls "critical conceptual history," which takes its bearings from the "new historians" of the "Cambridge school" in recognizing that concepts need to be interpreted within the framework of the intellectual, political, and linguistic contexts (or discourses) in which political texts appear and do their work. In discussing these two schools, one author has gone so far as to posit a choice between "Heidelberg" and "Cambridge": "students of intellectual history are wavering between German *Begriffsgeschichte* and the history of political languages as it practised between Cambridge, England and Cambridge, Massachusetts" (Van Gelderen 1998, 228). Another author further distinguishes between the two Cambridge schools and suggests that there are, in fact, three competing programs of how to understand historical changes in social and political concepts: Skinner's study of "speech acts," Pocock's history of "political languages," and Koselleck's "conceptual history." One might also draw into this mix the recent work of Michael Freeden, which analyzes the conceptual histories of ideologies. Freeden's focus on ideologies distinguishes him from the both the Cambridge and *Begriffsgeschichte* approaches to some extent. However, Freeden defines ideologies as "distinctive configurations of political concepts" that "create specific conceptual patterns from a pool of indeterminate and unlimited combinations" (1996, 4) and aims to map the contour and morphologies of various conceptual configurations or "ideological families" in historical context—an aim in keeping with the other projects.

In the analysis that follows, I attempt to work within the intersections of these various approaches. Ball acknowledges affinities between his own work and the modern German genre of *Begriffsgeschichte* (1988, 9). Melvin Richter persuasively argues that these different programs have not only much in common, but also much to learn from each other (1995).[2] Similarly, Koselleck emphasizes that a history of concepts and a history of discourse continually refer to one another: "Although basic concepts always function within a discourse, they are pivots around which all arguments turn. For this reason I do not believe that the history of concepts and the history of discourse can be viewed as incompatible and opposite. Each depends inescapably on the other. A discourse requires basic concepts in order to express what it is talking about. An analysis of concepts requires command of both linguistic and extralinguistic contexts, including those provided by discourse. Only by such knowledge of context can the analyst determine what are a concept's multiple meanings, its content, importance, and the extent to which it is

2. Richter (1995) provides the best overview to date of the differences between the various approaches to the study of concepts, as well as the best analysis of the way in which each of these different "schools" complement and could benefit from the others. For a more critical account of the "complementarity" of these approaches, see Pocock (1996).

contested" (1996, 65). Underlying all of these approaches is an attention to the analysis of discourse, the communicative set of interactions through which individuals understand and create their world. Thus, despite the differences between them, the *Begriffsgeschichte,* critical conceptual histories, the Cambridge school of new historians, and Freeden's conceptual histories of ideologies all share at least three characteristics with each other and with the approach employed here: (1) the belief that "concepts can be understood as indicators of politico-social change and historical profundity" (Koselleck 1985, 77); (2) attention to the way discourses combine and valuate various concepts; and (3) a focus on periods or points where "shifts in meaning and reference [of concepts] occur at a remarkably rapid rate [and yield] unforeseen and radical implications for future thought and action" (Ball and Pocock 1988, 1).

In regard to the first two points of intersection, the present work aims to draw out the relations among concepts (for example, civil society and democracy), discourses (the collections of statements about civil society and democracy), traditions of discourse (for example, Islam, philosophical liberalism), and ideologies (for example, Islamism, socialism, and liberalism), while at the same time maintaining a distinction among these often conflated objects of analyses. In regard to the third intersection (the focus on points of dramatic change), despite the widespread view that the Arab region alone remains impervious to the democratic wave that has struck the rest of the world, rather than constituting a stagnant and unvariegated whole, Arab political discourse over the past several decades reveals high levels of intellectual fluidity and confusion, and has been marked by intense debates among diverse and competing perspectives. As such, this period has the character of what Koselleck terms a *"Sattelzeit"*—literally "saddle-period" or "saddle-time" or, as English speakers might say, "watershed"—in the history of Arab political thought.

At the same time, the present study is distinct from each of these genres in at least one important respect: its cross-cultural focus and its transcultural approach. *Transculturation* refers to the way in which distinct cultures reciprocally impact each other—though not usually from equal positions of power—to produce not a single syncretic culture but rather heterogeneity.[3] Most previous attempts at conceptual analysis share an almost exclusive focus on conceptual change over time and within one "tradition," usually within one language, and often within a single country. The project undertaken by Otto Brunner, Werner Conze, and Reinhart Koselleck is intended to map changes in the use of political and social concepts in German-speaking Europe, though it does incorporate knowledge of political and social uses from other (classical, medieval, and modern) European languages (1972–97). The German *Handbuch politisch-sozialer Grundbegriffe* in Frankreich focuses on French political and social concepts from 1680 to 1820 as a way of studying the social history of the French Revolution *mentalités* (Reichardt and Schmidt 1985–). Similar types of projects are under way in Finland, the Netherlands, and Hungary (Melching and Velema 1994; Den Boer 1998). At least one study of Chinese political concepts has appeared in English (Schoenhals 1992). Several volumes have been published that provide conceptual histories of key political concepts in the Anglo-American tradition, or more broadly in the "Western tradition" (Williams 1985; Ball and Pocock 1988; Ball, Farr, and Hanson 1989).

Some of these authors are keen to further expand (or export) the historical study of concepts to other cultural contexts and traditions in order to permit comparative work. Ball writes that "in a very limited way some of my own work amounts, in effect, to a comparative test of several of the hypotheses about conceptual change advanced by the German conceptual historians" (1988, 78). In his review of the German works noted above, Richter proposes that "Anglophone historians of political thought" undertake "a conceptual history of political theory written in English during the time treated by the [*Geschichtliche Grundbegriffe*]." "To do so," he argues, "would make it possible to attempt a comparative analysis of concepts" (Richter 1986, 633; 1995, 6). The comparative approach was taken in a number of the essays collected in *The History of Concepts: Comparative Perspectives* (Hampsher-Monk, Tilmans, and van

3. Mary Louise Pratt notes that " 'transculturation' was coined in the 1940s by Cuban sociologist Fernando Oritz" and that "Uruguayan critic Angel Rama incorporated the term into literary studies in the 1970s" (1992, 228).

Vree 1998). In discussing the Dutch project, Pim Den Boer claims that "a comparative approach was required, and an exclusively national perspective was to be avoided" (Den Boer 1998, 21). Similarly, Freeden's breathtaking study of ideologies is attentive to parallels between, for example, British, German, and French variations of liberalism.

For the most part, such attempts to study the history of concepts in other cultures remain limited by their comparative nature; that is, they view the history of conceptual change as a study of what occurs within particular cultures, traditions, or languages, and which can then be compared to conceptual changes in other cultural contexts. As such, it lacks sufficient attention to the way some concepts cross cultures and languages, as well as to the transcultural character of those concepts that approach universal status. Even in a study of conceptual history, which does go a bit further in suggesting "the need for comparative, transnational studies of the languages and conceptual schemes created by Europeans with such enormous consequences for the rest of the world," Richter describes what he has in mind as comparative studies of the definition and application of a common store of political and social concepts (1995, 7). Such projects, albeit important and valuable, still neglect the synchronic conceptual transformations that occur across cultures, traditions, and languages. In short, while the current method of study is able to provide for comparative studies of parallel developments of concepts—that is, for the delineation of similarities and differences between a concept found, for example, in both the English and German languages—what such studies lack is a perspective on the interaction, contention, negotiation, and innovation that occur between, among, and across cultures and languages.

One rare exception to this comparative or parallel approach is provided by Hans-Jürgen Lüsebrink's essay "The Case of 'Nation' in Revolutionary France and Germany." The author tries to make some preliminary strides toward developing "both a comparative and intercultural mode of investigation in conceptual history." The transcultural (Lüsebrink prefers "intercultural") dimension of his analysis "arises at the study of the transfer of concepts and conceptual fields to other cultures" (1998, 115). As a result, he analyzes "the processes of relations between two or various cultures, taking forms like reception processes, translations, imitations, adaptations, productive reception, or, more generally, the phenomena of cultural transfer" (Lüsebrink 1998, 116). Lüsebrink sharply distinguishes his level of analysis from that of a comparative perspective, which he says involves the analysis of two or more concepts "which are not necessarily linked together by direct relationships or contacts, whereas the intercultural approach focuses on the direct interrelationships between cultures (by means of texts, human interaction, or other forms of communication)" (1998, 116).

In addition to Lüsebrink's essay, in an excellent work entitled *Translating the Enlightenment,* Fania Oz-Salzberger examines the translation of Scottish political language and ideas into German discourse in the eighteenth century (1995). However, Oz-Salzberger characterizes much of the cross-cultural engagement she studies a "misreception" rather than a conscious alteration of ideas. In general, I find the conception of misreception problematic for studies that aim at delineating what was understood. How do we distinguish between misunderstanding and different understanding? Or between purposive and accidental (mis)understanding? As a result of her focus on misreception, Oz-Salzberger fails to capture much of the productive and intentional aspects of this (mis)translation, better treated by Lüsebrink.

In one of the few writings to broach this issue, Farr identifies two potential sources of conceptual change: —the disclosure of contradictions and their criticism. He argues that "conceptual change may be understood as one imaginative consequence of political actors, in concert or in conflict, criticizing and attempting to resolve the contradictions that they either discover or generate in the complex web of their beliefs, actions, and practices as they try to understand and change the world around them" (Farr 1988, 13, 23). Building upon Farr's identification of contradiction and criticism as principal factors in conceptual change, Robert W. T. Martin draws attention to the importance of thoroughly analyzing "the many potential influential [linguistic, intellectual, political, social, and economic] contexts that may have exacerbated (or alleviated) nascent or extant contradictions." According to Martin, contextual shifts can often serve to intensify contradictions, and thus provide a third factor contributing to conditions favorable for conceptual change (1997, 429, 425).

The characterization of conceptual history as a problem-solving activity in times of conflict clarifies the *Begriffsgeschichte* project's focus on periods of crisis. Richter claims that "historians of concepts have now studied in detail how periods of crisis produce fundamental disagreements about the languages of politics and society," further noting that quite often "the agents are aware of the high stakes involved in adopting one or another concepts" (Richter 1995, 10). The focus on "contextual shifts" draws attention to the occasion of cross-cultural encounters and the juxtaposition of beliefs and practices that often characterize such an occasion.

The translation of concepts across space—that is, across cultures and languages—can constitute a political and philosophical event, often foreshadowing the rise of a new theory (of democratization, for example), usually altering the currently existing constellation of concepts (such as democracy, citizen, community, and participation), and sometimes resulting in changes in political practice (such as shifting the locus of political activity or of moral authority from the state to society). One aim of the present work is to expand the purview of previous historical work regarding conceptual change by exploring the issue of conceptual shifts across cultures and languages, and thus to augment the explanation of these sorts of transformations.

East and West, Whither the Twain Shall Meet

This study focuses on what I have characterized as a particularly stark example (or what we might better term "opportunity") for conceptual change: translation. I have chosen my example from what at least those who subscribe to the "clash of civilizations" thesis might have us believe is one of the most "uncivil" or "undemocratic" of subject matters: Arab political thought. In the words of one very prominent political scientist, "By any category I can imagine that is meaningful in the world today, there is only one set of countries that is completely undemocratic: the Arab world" (Diamond 2003, 12). Such a strong indictment of Arab and

Islamic societies for their "exceptionalism" warrants a closer look—one from a different vantage point. While a study of intellectual history will not likely convince those for whom ideas are always secondary to political behavior, at the very least it will challenge those who believe there are only two possibilities for the Arab region: Islam or democracy. As John Maynard Keynes famously observed, "The ideas of economists and political philosophers, both when they are right and when they are wrong, are more powerful than is commonly understood. Indeed the world is ruled by little else" (1965, 383). The ideas that animate contemporary Arab political discourse, both those that seem to rule the day and those that contest the status quo, form the horizon in which contemporary political actors operate. It is the polysemy of the discursive field in the Arab region that this study seeks to uncover in order to reveal the condition and myriad possibilities of both politics and resistance.

But why focus on *Arab* political thought as opposed to, for example, Islamic or Middle Eastern political thought? This work confronts claims in Western scholarship about "Arab exceptionalism" and deals with the translation of concepts into Arabic and what I take to be a varied, animated, and significant discussion taking place among Arab intellectuals, a discussion that I show is not limited to questions of Islam. As such, the present work does not attempt to account for the entirety of the Islamic world nor of the Middle East and cannot fully account for debates about democratization and civil society that are taking place in non-Arab countries such as Iran, Turkey, Pakistan, or Malaysia, each of which has its own particularities.

In a recent work, Dario Castiglione and Iain Hampsher-Monk propose that "the fact that, in the modern world, political society has coincided with communities acting within the boundaries of nation-states gives a particular significance to the way in which the national context may determine both the role and the understanding of political thought and its history" (2001, 3). I suggest that political societies have also coincided with communities acting within the boundaries of natural languages, such as Arabic, and, especially in the case of intellectual political discourse in the Middle East, Arabic still in many ways forms a more natural boundary than the nation-state. In the Arabic-speaking region, the boundaries of countries remain contested and fluid: contested, since they were drawn largely by European powers, and fluid, in part because political conflicts in the region often result in the migration, immigration, displacement, and transfer of peoples across country lines. So too, nation and state do not necessarily coincide in the region. Individuals in the region often imagine themselves as more a part of an "Arab nation" or "Islamic nation"—or even a member of an ethnic grouping that aspires to nation-state status (such as a "Berber nation" or "Kurdish nation")—than as part of a nation-state.

The Arabic delineation also better suits the discursive nature of this study. Despite myriad colloquial languages, the existence of a fairly standard written and formal spoken Arabic language makes possible communication across the entire region. A number of institutions in the region commonly bring together Arab intellectuals throughout the region for conferences and lectures, and the works of, for example, Muhammad 'Abid al-Jabiri (Morocco, b. 1936) and Hasan Hanafi (Egypt, b. 1935) are commonly found in Beirut's bookstores, just as the works of Muhammad Shahrur (Syria, b. 1938) can be bought in Cairo (and this despite having been banned there). While not denying the important influence of Turkish and Persian thought on Arab intellectuals, the language barrier (and, not insignificantly, my own deficiencies in those languages) provides justification for focusing on Arab, as opposed to Middle Eastern, thought. Focusing on Islamic political thought requires broadening the study across even larger and more diverse language and national contexts—and obscures the considerable influence of Arab Christians on political thought in the region. At the same time, Arab political thought will not be treated as a hermetically sealed "other" any more than will the "Western" tradition of political thought. Such categories are posited in the process of calling them into question, by revealing the interaction among languages, cultures, and traditions.[4] The

4. For the most part, "West" and "East" are acknowledged and maintained as descriptors in Arabic writings. However, as the coming chapters demonstrate, the boundaries between "Western" are just as commonly crossed and contested. For example, a

German philosopher Friedrich Hegel, the Italian intellectual-activist Antonio Gramsci, and the Indian/Pakistani thinker Sayyid Abu al-A'la Mawdudi (1903–1979) each make important appearances in Arab discourse. The influence of and engagement with non-Arab individuals and traditions in Arab political thought form one of the central points of inquiry in this study, even though the primary object of that inquiry is a debate taking place among intellectuals speaking and writing in Arabic. At the same time, cognizant of the fact that this work will largely be read by non-Arabic speakers, I have done my best to draw attention to translated works whenever they are available.

Despite the lack of democratic practice by Arab governments, the concept of democracy and the issue of democratization have long been hotly contested in Arab political thought. So too, Arabs have a long tradition of associative life that both is nonstate and transcends Western notions of the family. However, in the latter part of the 1980s, a literally new term entered onto the scene—civil society *(al-mujtama' al-madani)*— and with it arrived a constellation of concepts that radically altered the available tools of political discourse, opening up unforeseen possibilities for political thought and action. The most noticeable change has been a distinct shift of focus in discussions of democratization from the state to society—that is, from theories that view the state as the locus of political change to theories that see the impetus for change as arising in a nongovernmental realm. At a general level, this change in many ways resembles a similar transformation in democratic theory that has been taking place in American and European contexts. However, a closer look at this development reveals that Arab thinkers have constructed often very dif-

---

number of thinkers that have been very influential in the "West," like Ibn Khaldun and Ibn Rushd (Averroes) are claimed as definitively "Eastern." So too, Arab socialists both claim to be part of an international socialist tradition and claim such "Western" thinkers as Marx and Gramsci as their own. As Roxanne L. Euben (1997a) quite eloquently states, while these categories "are profoundly inadequate because of the way they essentialize and homogenize extraordinarily diverse areas . . . they remain useful as a device that at once evokes familiar categories and provides an occasion to problematize them."

ferent answers to questions regarding the character of the associations that comprise civil society and the role this sphere of activity can play in transforming political and social institutions, individuals, and groups.

The predominant view held in the West seems to be that individuals and groups in the Arab region view ideas such as civil society, democracy, and human rights as being premised on "Western values" that are incompatible with their own. This seems to be the view of Partha Chatterjee, who, in a critique of Charles Taylor, says that he wishes to "send back the concept of civil society" to where he thinks "it properly belongs—the provincialism of European social philosophy" (1990, 120). Certainly one can find individuals who make such rejectionist pronouncements in the Arab region, and these views are often quoted in the Western media and by Western academics. However, it would be wrong to generalize from these views.

While it is true that most Arab thinkers do associate the concept with Western traditions of political thought, rather than rejection, the more common response in the case of civil society has been that individuals and groups from a wide variety of political bents and ideological persuasions have consciously sought to make use of this "foreign" concept, while "making it their own" in the process. Islamists are those most commonly characterized as rejectionist in regard to foreign ideas. However, Ahmad Moussalli argues that, in fact, there are two reactions to civil society among Islamists: "the first, which represents the minority, looks negatively at the issue of strengthening civil society; the second, advocated by the vast majority of fundamentalist thinkers, calls for the establishment of civil society as the cornerstone of the new Islamic state. In fact, claim the latter group, civil society is precisely Islam's original and ideal form of society" (1995, 81). This Islamist appropriation of civil society forms the subject matter of chapter 5 of the present work.

In a study of the evolution of the idea of "republic" in Arab political thought, Ami Ayalon writes that the "Arab observer" who encounters "an occidental political notion" would have one of three possible responses: "the notion might strike him as utterly novel and alien; or it might appear to resemble a familiar concept in certain respects, and to differ in others; or else, it might look to him to be very much alike, even identical with, a traditional idea" (1985, 824). According to Ayalon, in the first case, the "Arab observer" would likely coin a neologism (for example, "republic" becomes *"jumhuriyya,"* and "citizen" becomes *"muwatin"*) or borrow a foreign name (for example, "bourgeois" becomes *"burjwazi"*). In the second and third types of cases, "existing political terms with traditional import offer themselves and may be applied to the new European notion." However, these three responses should not be seen as mutually exclusive. While translation of a foreign *word* might stop at the creation of a neologism, the translation of a *concept* cannot take place without some process of interpreting the word in relation to the cluster of concepts, the existing vocabulary, and the horizon of vision already available to that interpreter. In addition, that process is not uniform, even across a language context such as Arabic. Rather, interpreter/translators act within a context of (to borrow Freeden's definition) "distinctive configurations of political concepts"—that is, ideologies—that play a fundamental role in the appropriation of a "foreign" political concept. Thus, this study maps the translation of civil society and the democracy-civil society relation in constellation with other significant concepts (such as equality, unity, sovereignty, freedom, among others), with attention to the historical, material, and ideological contexts within which particular translators are working.

Structure of the Present Work

Chapters 2 and 3 lay out the context that forms the horizon that contemporary Arab intellectuals seeking to translate civil society (analyzed in chapters 4, 5, 6, and 7) inhabit.

Chapter 2 traces the history of ideas and practices relevant to contemporary discussions of democracy and civil society in Arab societies. This chapter presents a conceptual history of democracy in Arab political thought in order to critically analyze the range of possible resources a contemporary translator of civil society might draw upon: the model of *shura* (consultation) articulated in the Qur'an and practiced in early Islam; social and political institutions in the ancient (pre-Islamic) Middle East; Islam's encounter with Greek philosophy beginning in the eighth century; the constitutionalist movements of the Arab Nahda (renaissance) in the nineteenth and early twentieth centuries; and contemporary political thought. The ambiguity of the democracy idea in the history of Arab and Islamic political thought, coupled with similarly variegated considerations of civil society in the West, provided space for contemporary thinkers to rethink these concepts and their relations in different ways. The nascent democratic institutions and values in these earlier periods and early engagements with non-Arab notions of democracy also indicate how much Arab discourse on democracy and civil society has changed and developed throughout its history. An overview of these developments will be given further attention in the book's concluding chapter.

Chapter 3 analyzes those aspects of the linguistic, intellectual, and political context of contemporary Arab political thought that render the translation of civil society both problematic and pressing. I argue that that context has consistently been characterized by Arab intellectuals as one of "crisis" *(azma)* since at least the 1970s, a context fraught not only with political and economic uncertainty, but also an increased fracturing of the political ideologies that first emerged in the Arab arena in the 1920s, as one witnesses a growing clash among alternative modernities, claims of authenticity, and opposing views of religious and political life, both internal to the region and in Arab intellectuals' interactions with Western political thought and practice. "Necessity," so the proverb tells us, "is the mother of invention." Crisis, in this case, appears to provide both the necessity and the opportunity for Arab intellectuals' contestation, resistance, and reconstitution of political thought and practice.

The intellectuals whose writings from the 1990s form the basis of the final four chapters consistently articulate an awareness of and concern over the political and social implications of presenting different shades of the civil society idea. These chapters analyze the use to which the concept has been put by intellectuals working the context of competing ideological traditions in the Arab region, respectively: Arab liberals' debate over the requirements of democracy (chapter 4); the contemporary Islamist discourse on the role of religion in the state, society, and political change (chapter 5); Arab socialists who are suffering declining membership within the intellectual community and alienation from the masses in whose name they claim to struggle (chapter 6); and Arab feminists who have found themselves marginalized in much of the debate (chapter 7). For Arab liberals, civil society is most importantly tolerant and democratic. For Islamists, it is most important that society be Islamic and that an Islamic civil society be independent from the existing uncivil (secular) state. Whereas the former view civil society as a vehicle for vying for political and social reform, the latter have moved toward a more radically oppositional role for civil society. Arab socialists seek to construct a civil society that provides a progressive force able to contribute toward the creation of a socialist counterhegemony to both liberalism and Islamism.

Chapters 4, 5, and 6 provide evidence for an extensive and complex engagement with the concepts of contemporary democracy theory by Arab intellectuals from a broad range of ideological persuasions. Taking up the most recent social science finding that the greatest deficit in the Arab region is a lack of democratic values of civility and tolerance—especially for gender difference—chapter 7 examines diverse Arab feminist interventions in the debates over civil society that are attempting to fill this gap.

The book's conclusion offers an assessment of the changes that have occurred in Arab discussions of democracy as a result of the introduction of the civil society idea into the debate in relation to a number of theses that have long circulated as an explanation of the "democracy deficit" in Arab and Islamic societies. While there is no current consensus regarding many concepts that exist in constellation with democratic theorizing—including pluralism, human rights, freedom, the individual, the community, unity, sovereignty, and the state, as well as civil society—there has been an expansion of distinct ideological groupings who are participating in the debate, taking up the mantles of democracy and liberty. In short, despite the lack of democratic practice in the Arab region, it is possible to detect a broad and diverse sector of elites who are developing a shared political language, insofar as they are increasingly deploying similar concepts—even as those concepts remain contested among and differently located within the existing ideological frameworks. As Richter points out, "in cases of conflict . . . discourse depends upon possession, by the parties involved, of the same shared basic concepts. Only when this is the case is it possible to understand, to persuade, to negotiate, or to even fight" (Richter 2001, 77).

Understanding the transformations in Arab political thought and their significance requires that we build upon—and move beyond—not only studies of the historical contestation of political and social concepts, but also the approach favored in the growing number of studies in comparative political theory. While each of these approaches is able to produce comparative studies, they tend to give the impression that the traditions compared developed independently of each other and do not adequately account for the translation, appropriation, and contestation of ideas that occur *across* cultures and languages. What the transcultural approach presented here reveals is the agency and innovation on the part of those Arab intellectuals who are engaged in cross-cultural translations, as well as the multiple possibilities provided by such encounters.

2

Democracy in the History of Arab and Islamic Political Thought

Take for example the rule existing in our own country, Cordova, after 500 (A.H.) [A.D. 1106/7]. For it was almost completely democratic, (but) then after 540 (A.H.) [A.D. 1145/6] it turned into tyranny.

—Averroes, *Averroes' Commentary on Plato's Republic*

Where to Begin?

Where does one begin a history of two ideas that have traveled so far—appearing, disappearing, and reappearing under so many different guises? Since both *civil society* and *democracy* are terms associated with Western traditions of thought, how do we assess their status as concepts in Arabic? The term *transculturation* has been used by ethnographers to describe how "subordinated or marginal groups select and invent from materials transmitted to them by a dominant or metropolitan culture." Even though "subjugated peoples cannot readily control what emanates from the dominant culture, they do determine to varying extents what they absorb into their own and what they use it for" (Pratt 1992, 6). The "given" of the Arab encounter with civil society and democracy includes an intertwining of both foreign and indigenous cultural horizons, as well as a horizon of concepts that are themselves transcultural—that is, ideas that are shared across cultures so that they cannot be adequately accounted for by attention to any single cultural context.

The Jordanian-Chechen writer Murad Batl al-Shiyshani articulates at least a partial understanding of this phenomenon in his characterization of the civil society idea and its application to the Arab context: "In

light of the fact that [civil society] is an adopted concept, not one indigenous to the Arab-Islamic heritage, a precise method is necessary to deal
with it in determining its genesis and development outside the Arabic
linguistic context and it is necessary to clarify its meaning in its mother
language, after which a qualitative problematic of dealing with it in the
Arab-Islamic reality emerges" (2002, 19). Thus one finds Arab intellectuals who approach civil society or democracy by first presenting a history
of the ideas in their original context before discussing those aspects of
the idea that are best adopted, adapted, or abandoned in appropriating
the concept for the Arab context. While most contend that the contemporary concept of civil society is "a concept foreign to the Arab-Islamic
heritage of political thought" (al-Habib Janhani in Janhani and Isma'il
2003, 11), there are others who decry the "abundance and overabun-
dance of such generalizations" (Sayf al-Din 'Abd al-Fattah Isma'il in Janhani and Isma'il 2003, 267) and argue that "civil society 'as a concept' has
been present in the [Arab] intellect [as long as there has been state and
society], even if civil society 'as a term' is new" (Yasin 1999, 45). In such
cases, one finds the method of appropriating reversed, as the agent looks
first to his or her own cultural resources as a source of a more suitable or
authentic cultural approximation. Both those finding themselves dealing with democracy and civil society as "new" and those who prefer
conceptual approximation view the encounter as a process with transcultural elements. They also each view the encounter as a problematic.

The question of where to begin does not center on when the word
enters the discourse, but on when the idea becomes a topic of discussion.
When we are able to locate an equivalent word—even a direct transliteration—in another language, it does not follow that we have found the
corresponding concept therein. For example, during the Scottish Enlightenment the phrase *civil society* was used interchangeably with *political society,* even though an understanding of a distinct associative realm
that was less than "state," yet more than that traditionally suggested by
"society," was emerging. So too, when Ibn Rushd (known in Latin as
Averroes, 1128–1198) notes in his twelfth-century commentary on
Plato's *Republic* that "most of those States existing today are democratic,"
he refers not to a system in which the people govern, but rule by a single

sovereign who leaves his subjects alone to pursue whatever private interests they desire (Averroes 1969, 214).

If we understand democracy in its broadest sense, it entails a political community in which (some form of) the people can be said to (in some sense) rule.[1] The parenthetical qualifications of the definition signal that even this baseline understanding raises significant questions: Who are the people? In what sense do they rule? Delineating what counts as democracy also runs into the problem that democracy is not only spoken of as a set of political institutions (such as contested elections), but also as a set of sociopolitical values (rule of law). Democratic theorists often distinguish between "procedural democracy"—which is concerned with the basic structures and institutions that must be in place in order for a democracy to flourish—and "substantive" democracy—which is concerned with whether the outcomes of governance result in the implementation of the people's will. The emphasis in the former tends to be on rights and mechanisms of participation and on open and fair rules. No assessment of results or the actual decisions that are made is required for this measure of democracy. In contrast, substantive democracy focuses more on the question of whether the practice and policies of political leaders reflect and embody certain principles of the community, such as equality or justice. Both understandings of democracy have been debated in Arab political thought and the distinction is useful in distinguishing various competing conceptions. The greatest challenge in tracing the beginning of this discourse taking place in Arabic lies in discerning, first, when and from what sources substantive and procedural notions of "rule by the people" emerge and, second, which of these sources were significant in the more recent appropriation of "civil society."

Shura in the Time of Muhammad and the Rightly Guided Caliphs

Contemporary Islamist thinkers tend to locate a democratic notion in the Qur'anic principle of consultation. There are two passages in the

---

1. I roughly follow David Held's baseline definition in *Models of Democracy* (1996, 1).

Qur'an that address the issue of *shura*. *'Imran* (3:159) says that the prophet must "take counsel with them in the conduct of affairs *(wa shawiruhum fi al-amr)*." The chapter called *al-Shura* (42:37–38) refers to those "who avoid gross sins and indecencies, and, when angered, are willing to forgive; who obey their Lord, attend to their prayers, and conduct their affairs by mutual consent *(wa amruhum shura baynahum)*" (Dawood 1994). However, there is no indication that the consultation mentioned in the Qur'an need be understood as anything more than a system of advice. It is neither specified as binding—one need only consult, not abide by the advice given—nor as the basis of government. After Muhammad died in 632 without having named a successor, the preeminent among his followers both implemented and expanded the notion of *shura* by selecting Abu Bakr al-Siddiq (ca. 573–634) to succeed the prophet as the leader of the community in the first example of election through a consultative process of consensus in Islamic history. This historical example of succession does suggest an important model of election by elites, but unfortunately it was neither expanded along democratic principles nor regularly practiced as a governmental form after the election of Abu Bakr (ruled 632–34). The second caliph, 'Umar ibn al-Khattab (ca. 581–644, ruled 634–44), was appointed by Abu Bakr in a written testament, though he did subsequently receive the stamp of approval from other elites. Although after 'Umar's death an advisory council selected 'Uthman ibn Affan (ca. 574–656, ruled 644–56) as the third caliph, serious strains on the ability of the prophet's former companions to come to consensus *(ijma')* over a leader were beginning to show. 'Uthman was assassinated and his successor, 'Ali ibn Abi Talib (ruled 656–61), never received the full recognition of a number of important political figures, such as Yazid ibn Mu'awiya (ca. 602–80), the powerful governor of Syria, and 'Ali was also eventually assassinated.

Ahmad Moussalli assigns to Mu'awiya, the founder of the Umayyad dynasty, the blame for having broken from "the model of political rule that depended on *shura* and *ijma'* by justifying the rule of political expediency," "transformed the caliphate into an absolute and hereditary government" based on "a tribalism that marginalized the people," and founded "a new model of political rule that continued, more or less, through the centuries up to modern times" (Moussalli 2001, 41, 42–43). Although Moussalli argues that a "religious ideology of opposition was developed" that "sought justification in the doctrines of popular consensus and communal consultation, not age-old tribal ties," he provides little evidence of such a discourse beyond reference to third- and fourth-century jurists like al-Harith ibn 'Asad al-Muhasabi (ca. 781–857) and Imam Ahmad ibn Hanbal (780–855), to whom he attributes ideas such as "reason was a faculty common to all people. Therefore, there was no need for a special superior individual or a select group, since the collective reason of the community could administer its affairs, including the religious, political, social, and economic" (Moussalli 2001, 16). Further, Moussalli's reading of these jurists is based upon interpretations provided by Islamic modernists, such as Muhammad 'Abduh (Egypt, 1849–1905) and Sayyid Abu al-A'la Mawdudi, and by various contemporary Islamists who sought to justify their own oppositions to existing state powers. While the concept of *shura* has proven a very important resource for substantive models of democracy in Islamic contexts, it is not until the modern period that it is developed along such lines and not then without considerable effort.

Democratic Institutions in the Ancient Middle East

Some Arab and Western scholars have uncovered nascent democratic institutions in the Middle East prior to Islam. Patricia Springborg identifies various political institutions found in the ancient Middle East—such as "impersonal government administered by a bureaucracy," "the conception of man as citizen," "forms of political representation," and "the concept of nature as governed by rational laws" (1993, 27) that Mishal Fahm al-Sulami interprets as evidence that "some democratic political institutions . . . existed in the ancient Middle East (the ancient Mesopotamian and Egyptian cities) prior to the democratic institutions of classical Greece" (2003, 19). Sulami identifies four principles of governance indicated by the existence of these institutions that can be considered democratic: "the concept of citizenship," "political representation," "rule of law," and "a procedure of electing officials to public office" (2003, 20). However, Springborg refrains from referring to the political institutions she analyzes as democratic. She is most interested in demonstrating the link of these political institutions with the development of liberal economic institutions when correlated with urbanism. Further, she maintains that "it is true that even if the classical municipal institutions of the *polis*—assembly *(ecclesia)*, council of elders *(gerousia* or *areopagus)* and the magistracies—can be shown to have had their ancestry in the second and third millennium city-states of Mesopotamia, they did not pass on their legacy to the Islamic cities as such" (Springborg 1993, 37). And, as even Sulami acknowledges, the ancient Middle East's experience of democracy was "documentary" rather than "theoretical"—that is, the Greeks, not the ancient Mesopotamians and Egyptians, were the first to "think systematically about politics," let alone democracy (2003, 20).

As a result, commencing a conceptual history of democracy in Arab societies with the ancient Middle East is fraught with two problems. First, despite the existence of some institutions that can be described as containing elements associated with democracy, there is no real evidence that a conception of democracy as such existed in that context. Second, there is a lack of continuity with more recent notions of democracy, that is, this period is seldom looked to as a resource for democratic theory. While it is possible that the two problems are related (lack of contemporary reference to the period results from the latter's lack of theory), perhaps more significantly, pre-Islamic institutions are hampered by the fact that they are from an age ignorant of Islam *(jahiliyya)*.

Athenian Democracy in Early Islamic Philosophy

One might also look to the Arab encounter with Greek philosophy beginning in the ninth century as the locus of one of the earliest sustained interactions with political thought that is neither Arab nor Islamic. It is in this context that one begins to see a discussion of the Greek model of democracy, perhaps earliest in the works of Abu al-Nasr al-Farabi (870–950). Farabi translates democracy as *"al-madina al-jama'iyya,"* the social or collective city. Muhsin Mahdi defines Farabi's understanding of this form of polity as a "regime of corporate association . . . the main purpose of whose citizens is being free to do what they wish" (2001, 131).

Following Plato, Farabi treats the democratic city as an "ignorant city" *(al-madina al-jahiliyya)*. It is based upon the absolute freedom *(hurriyya)* of its citizens to pursue whatever aim they wish, whether base or noble, and the only recognized authority is the one who works to enhance the citizens' freedom (Farabi 1963, 50). Here Farabi closely follows book 8 of Plato's *Republic* (555b–562a). However, in another passage, Farabi seems to go beyond Plato somewhat in asserting that "the construction of virtuous cities and the establishment of the rule of virtuous men are more effective and much easier out of the indispensable and democratic cities than out of any other ignorant city" (Farabi 1963, 52), thus placing democracy in a potentially positive relation with the ideal regime, but falling far short of appreciating democracy in a substantive manner.

Ibn Rushd offers a similar discussion of democracy in his commentary on Plato's *Republic*. Plato places democracy second only to tyranny among the corrupt forms of government and suggests that "tyranny evolves from democracy" (Plato 1992, 240). Ibn Rushd maintains that the existence of freedom in a democracy permits "all arts and dispositions" found in the other forms of government and, thus, not only tyranny, but also "the Ideal State and each of the other States may come into being" (Averroes 1969, 213). While both Ibn Rushd and Farabi interpret regime change to be more a contingent than a deterministic process of evolution, their accounts are far from constituting a defense of democracy as such. Rather, their reading of the text is consistent with Plato's characterization of democracy as a variegated fabric that contains every kind of constitution. Further, by his own account, Ibn Rushd finds tyranny to be a logical offspring of democracy: the people—especially those with an interest in preserving their property—turn over power to a prominent member of their community who increasingly serves his private interests and concentrates power in his own hands until the people "either conspire against him and murder him, or he rules over them, tyrannizes them all and becomes a tyrant" (Averroes 1969, 235), though elsewhere in same treatise he repeats that out of the democratic state "will grow the Ideal State and other States of these (various) kinds, because they exist in it potentially" (Averroes 1969, 230).

While Farabi never refers to a specific state in his discussion of democracy, Ibn Rushd substantiates this understanding of regime change with reference to his own times: "Take for example the rule existing in our own country, Cordova, after 500 (A.H.) [A.D. 1106/7]. For it was almost completely democratic, (but) then after 540 (A.H.) [A.D. 1145/6] it turned into tyranny" (Averroes 1969, 235). While Richard Walzer has speculated that Ibn Rushd refers here to "the Republican phase in Cordova's history [during] the rule of the three Jauwarites [Jahwarids] from 1031–1070" (Walzer 1963, 40–60), the dates Ibn Rushd gives suggest that the key to understanding this claim seems to be found in an earlier passage, where he recounts how the Murabit Dynasty, founded by Yusuf ibn Tashfin (1061–1106), at first imitated the constitution based on the Law, then changed first to a timocratic constitution under Yusuf's son, Ali ibn Yusuf (ruled from 1106 to 1142), and after him to a hedonistic (democratic) constitution during the rule of Yusuf's grandson, Tashfin ibn 'Ali (from 1142 to 1146). Ibn Rushd's noting of 1145 as the beginning of the degeneration into tyranny corresponds to the final years of the Murabit Dynasty and the brief rule of Tashfin's son, Ibrahim ibn Tashfin (in 1146), and nephew, Ishaq ibn Ali (from 1146 to 1147), before it was succeeded by the Muwahhid Dynasty (Averroes 1969, 227). So too, when Ibn Rushd writes in even broader terms that "most of those States existing today are democratic," he seems to be referring to the disintegration of the Islamic empire by the mid-tenth century into small states called *ta'ifas* (factions) and various competing caliphates, most of which proved unstable and short-lived. As such, one must take Ibn Rushd to be using "democratic" in a very limited sense to refer to the situation characterized by freedom from duties to the state on the part of the citizenry and the existence of a ruler who is little concerned with how his citizens pursue "whatever their heart desires." In short, "it is clear that in this State the home [that is, the family as the smallest economic unit] is that which is intended in the first place, and the State exists only for its sake" (Averroes 1969, 213). In such a state, Ibn Rushd maintains, "the man who is completely master over it is he who has the power of leadership, so that every man can attain his desire and preserve it" (Averroes 1969, 214). This statement seems to be more a criticism of his contemporary political culture than an advocacy of democratic rule, as at least one author has suggested (DeLue 2002, 107). It also seems apparent that both Farabi and Ibn Rushd possess a limited understanding of the Greek concept of democracy at best, focusing on three values we might today see as more akin to liberalism than democracy: freedom from duties, equality among the variety of human goods sought, and focus on the household (private interests).

Among the other concepts lacking in early Arab engagements with classical democracy are notions of the "citizen." Although Springborg and Sulami maintain that ancient civilizations of the Middle East possessed a concept of citizenship, that notion was limited to an understanding of inhabitants of a city subject to the city's governing authorities. While the term *citizen* is commonly used in translations of early Islamic philosophical texts, the fact is that Farabi, Ibn Rushd, and others spoke not of *citizen,* but of *human (insan)* or the *inhabitant of the city (ahl al-madina).* According to Ami Ayalon (2001), "the modern Arabic word for 'citizen' [*muwatin*], in the legal sense of the term (meaning 'one holding the citizenship or nationality of a sovereign state') . . . was coined around the turn of the twentieth century." This is not surprising, nor should one necessarily see this as an indication of a "cultural deficiency" because, although the French Revolution proclaimed the rights of man as well as those of citizen, modern European notions of citizenship did not encompass the right to political participation until the nineteenth century (Marshall 1963, 65–122). What it does suggest, however, is a precursor to contemporary engagements with the idea of democracy, as well as a measure against which contemporary democratic discourse reveals its development.

Constitutionalism, Republicanism, and Democracy during the Nahda

Although the early days of Islam and even the pre-Islamic Middle East may reveal latent democratic institutions and values, and while a discussion of "democracy" has existed in the Arabic language at least since the works of Plato and Aristotle were translated into Arabic in the classical period of Islam (often said to have ended with the death of Ibn Rushd), a discourse advocating the placing of political power in the hands of the citizenry has a much more recent history in Arabic, arriving after the European Enlightenment and Industrial Revolution, at a time referred to as the Nahda (renaissance or awakening), "a vast political and cultural movement that dominate[d] the period of 1850–1914. . . . [that] sought through translation and vulgarization to assimilate the great achievements of modern European civilization, while reviving the classical Arab culture that antedates the centuries of decadence and foreign domination" (Laroui 1976, vii).[2] While one must point out that the rest of the world also had only recently reappropriated many of the concepts central to the formation of modern democracy, it is not too gross an exaggeration to say that the period in between was dominated by Ibn Taymiyya's (Syria, 1263–1328) well-known claim that sixty years under the authority of even an unjust tyrant is better than one night without a government. More significantly, "the idea of 'republic' "—so central to the early modern revival of democratic theory—"was absent from Middle Eastern political experience" until the nineteenth century (Ayalon 1985, 823). European ideas of republic, constitution, and democracy were hotly debated during the Arab Nahda. Arab thinkers during this period shared the common concerns of renewal in the face of decline, the

2. Dating of the Nahda varies, though most take Islamic modernism, one of the most productive intellectual strands of the period, to have begun at some point in the nineteenth century and to have ceased to be a predominant trend by the middle of the twentieth century (Rippin 1990; Moussalli 1999). According to Antony Black (2001), the "age of modernism" starts around 1839 with the Ottoman Tanzimat (Reform) and the writings of various Muslim thinkers, most notably those of Khayr al-Din al-Tunisi. . . , and ends around 1920 with the onset of what he terms (problematically, in my view) the "age of fundamentalism" (ca. 1920–2000). Charles Kurzman uses 1840 as "a rough marker" of when this period of Islamic modernization began and maintains that "by the 1930s the movement was in serious decline" (2002, 26). Mansoor Moaddel and Kamran Talattof (2002) date the period a bit later, between the late nineteenth and early twentieth century. This period has also been referred to as "the liberal age" (referring more to the liberal trend in Europe during the period than to a general characterization of the Arab intellectuals he discusses who were interacting with the West) by Albert Hourani (1983), who dates its beginning with Napoleon's Egyptian campaign in 1798, the first major colonial penetration in the region, and ends when World War II breaks out in 1939.

fact of Western supremacy and modernization, and the abiding role of tradition in modern society. However the character of the response to this period of renewed cross-cultural engagement varied along three broad trends: Islamic modernists, Salafiyyun (tradition-oriented Islamists), and the more secular modernists whose ideas come to dominate much of the period that followed the Nahda.

Although there were a few Islamic thinkers who advocated secularism—most notably 'Ali 'Abd al-Raziq (Egypt, 1888–1966)—most Islamic modernists (as well as the Salafiyyun, who will be discussed below) sought to revive Islamic thought and raise it to central importance in the modern age. Certainly Islamic modernism was not the first movement calling for revival, renewal, and reform of the tradition in Islamic history. As early as the eighth and ninth centuries, Muslim thinkers had been involved in disputes over how Islamic sociopolitical life could best be structured as the challenges of Shi'i, Sufi, Mu'tazila, and Kharijite movements emerged alongside the formation of an Islamic orthodoxy. In the thirteenth and fourteenth centuries, reformists sought to revive Islam amidst a waning caliphate. Fazlur Rahman (Pakistan, 1919–1988) cites a number of "pre-modernist" reformation movements that "swept over the larger part of the Muslim world in the seventeenth, eighteenth, and nineteenth centuries" and shared characteristics of a "consciousness of degeneration, and of the corresponding need to remedy social evils and raise moral standards" (1970, 641). However, the difference between the "pre-modern" and "modern" reform movements is that whereas the former owed little—Rahman goes so far as to say "nothing whatsoever"—to foreign inspiration, the latter is as much a reaction to the West as it is a continuation of the thought and activism of the premodernist Islamic reformers (1970, 641). As Charles Kurzman rightly notes, the movement that begins in the first half of the nineteenth century "was not simply 'modern' (a feature of modernity) but also 'modernist' (a proponent of modernity)" (2002, 4). Islamic modernists sought to revive Islamic thought both by affirming continuity with the past and by assimilating what they saw as the achievements of modern Europe—specifically, modern material technology, modern techniques of social organization, and mobilization, as well as modern political institutions such as parliaments. They also sought to give Islamic thought a more rationalist, futuristic, and universalistic orientation. In this *Sattelzeit,* this period of dramatic conceptual transformation and translation, many of the concepts that would later form the basis for democratic theorizing entered into the discourse of Arab intellectuals.

Intellectuals and statespersons traveled to Europe and studied European constitutions. Many, like Khayr al-Din al-Tunisi (Tunisia, 1822–1890), argued that Muslims should not hesitate in "ceaselessly emulating what they deem good in the work of others," including Europeans institutions and values compatible with the Islamic *shari'a*" (1967, 75). Some sought to infuse modern political values with Islamic notions of the state. The Islamic tradition had formulated general principles governing authority, but there were few checks on absolute authority provided by that tradition. Many modernist Muslims sought to limit the traditional authoritarian powers of rulers originally derived from Islamic sources but no longer deemed compatible with Muslim interests, by claiming a principle of equivalence between various aspects of the *shari'a* (Islamic law) and the ideals of constitutionalism. In a work aptly entitled *The Extraction of Gold, or an Overview of Paris (Tahklis al-ibriz ila talkhis Bariz),* Rifa'a Rafi' al-Tahtawi (Egypt, 1801–1873) studies the French Constitutional Charter of June 4, 1814, and argues that "that which [the French] call freedom and which they crave is what we call 'justice' [*'adl*] and 'equity' [*insaf*], in as much as 'rule by freedom' means establishing equality in judgments and laws so that the ruler cannot oppress any human being" (2004, 206). By equating liberty with the Islamic notion of justice, Tahtawi affirms the primacy of the rule of law as a way of protecting subjects from tyranny. But, as Bernard Lewis (2001) notes, "what is new and alien to traditional [Islamic] political ideas is the suggestion that the subject has a *right* to be treated justly, and that some apparatus should be set up to secure that right."

According to Sunni orthodoxy, a leader was to be chosen by an elite class referred to as *ahl al-hal wa al-'aqd* (literally, "those who loose and bind"), people of authority and stature in the community such as tribal chieftains, governors of provinces, and state dignitaries. However, modernist Islamic thinkers claimed that this privilege should now fall to representative assemblies whose members now have become the effective "people of authority." Khayr al-Din al-Tunisi asks, "Is it fitting that the physicians of the *umma* should be ignorant of its ailments?"—thus suggesting that matters that affect the public should involve consulting the public in some form (1967, 72). Tahtawi deems a "safeguard against injustice and oppression" those articles in the French constitution providing for the collective exercise of legislation by the three bodies of the king and his ministers, the Chamber of Peers, and the Chamber of Deputies, the last of whom he describes as "the proxies and representatives of the subjects," and as charged with the task of "safeguarding the interests of the people" (2004, 192–95). To provide such a safeguard, Tunisi suggested that "the people . . . elect from those possessing knowledge and virtue a group called by the Europeans the Chamber of General Deputies. We would call them those qualified to loosen and bind, even though this [latter] group is not elected by the people" (1967, 161).

Drawing from a speech given by Abu Bakr al-Siddiq in 632, when he was sworn in as the first caliph after the death of the Prophet Muhammad, 'Abd al-Hamid ibn Badis (Algeria, 1889–1940) articulates no less than thirteen "Principles of Governing in Islam" that permit the adaptation of Western institutions:

O People, I was entrusted as your ruler, although I am not better than any one of you.

Support me as long as you see me following the right path, and correct me when you see me going astray.

Obey me as long as I observe God in your affairs. If I disobey Him, you owe me no obedience.

The weak among you are powerful [in my eyes] until I get them their due. The powerful among you are weak [in my eyes] until I take away from them what is due to others.

I say this and seek God's forgiveness for myself and for you. (2002, 93–94)

Most of what Ibn Badis values in this speech reflects a liberal concern with protecting against arbitrary or unjust rule, including the principles of government based on consent; rule according to qualification (as opposed to birth); political equality among citizens and between citizens and their ruler; the right to monitor rulers; the right to recall rulers; the right to correct and advise rulers; the right to question rulers; transparency of government operations; equality before the law; protection of basic human rights; and due process regardless of economic circumstances.

Kurzman rightly points out that, although one does find discussions of democracy during this period, most Islamic modernists "did not necessarily intend constitutionalism to mean democracy, as it came to be understood over the course of the twentieth century: universal adult suffrage, reduction of monarchs to symbolic offices, and constitutional protection of a growing lists of rights" (2002, 20). Rather, the concern of intellectuals during this period was with constitutional rather than with representative forms of government, with the rule of law and limits on political power rather than with empowering the masses through their participation in the formation and conduct of government. As such, constitutional reforms often retained a distinct concern with a sense of justice (*'adala*), which denotes a harmonious arrangement, and order or unity (*tawhid*), in addition to the concern with providing legal protections. Like many of the early-modern Western liberals, such as John Locke, Jeremy Bentham, or James Madison, these thinkers tended to be in many ways "reluctant democrats" who worried that empowering the uneducated and unenlightened masses could threaten fundamental rights and liberties (Held 1996, 100). However, some, such as 'Abdullah al-Nadim (Egypt, 1845–1896/7), note that "we have been stopped from keeping up with the prudent nations by a barrier that makes us too proud to consult the poor and negotiate with the weak" (1983, 130). Further, at least two of the principles Ibn Badis articulates reflect substantive democratic concerns with the articulation of the people in legislation (the ninth principle) and "a mutual responsibility of the ruler and ruled in reforming society" (principle thirteen), arguably a form of civic activism, though the moral character of the injunction to reform may put the principle in tension with some of the more liberal ideas (2002, 94–95).

So too one finds a number of political experiments in republican forms of government in the Arab region during this period. Albert Hourani (1915–1993) identifies a peasant revolt against the nobles of the Khazin family in the Maronite district of Kisrawan in Lebanon as having led to "a 'republic government' with a rough system of popular representation" in 1859 (1983, 63). In 1860, "the first constitution to be issued in any Muslim country in modern times" was established in Tunis, characterized by Hourani as "a cautious document, admitting the principle of representation only within limits and leaving executive power in the hands of the ruler." The short-lived constitution specified: "The ruler must swear to do nothing contrary to the *'ahd al-aman* [a decree issued by Muhammad Bey in 1857 that ensured the security of Tunisians and foreigners in the country against arbitrary judicial and economic processes], and is responsible for his acts before the Supreme Council; but the Supreme Council itself is to include ministers and officials as to one-third of its members, while the other two-thirds are to be nominated by the ruler in the first instance, and then to co-opt new members at regular intervals" (Hourani 1983, 63).

In the twentieth century, a number of Arab states claiming status as a republic *(jumhuriyya)* were established. However, as Ayalon has observed, the term was applied to a wide variety of regimes: "the post-1952 Egyptian *jumhuriyya* has born[e] little resemblance to that of the younger South Yemen 'Republic,' which in turn has had little in common with the *jumhuriyya* of Lebanon." The only common element seems to be that each was "professedly non-hereditary" (though even this is no longer the case in Syria) (Ayalon 1985, 833). So too, the number of governments employing parliamentary institutions grew during this period, though to varying degrees of effectiveness and representation. Although Turkey's first parliament opened in 1877 and a constitutional revolution established a parliament in Iran in 1906, with the important exception of Egypt, which experimented with an Assembly of Delegates *(majlis shura al-nuwwab)* established by decree of Khedive Ismail in 1866, most parliamentary bodies in the Arab region did not emerge until much later. Iraq created a bicameral parliament *(majlis al-umma)* consisting of an elected Chamber of Deputies *(majlis al-nuwwab)* and king-appointed Senate *(majlis al-aʿyan)* in 1922. That same year the French Mandatory authority established a consultative Representative Council in Lebanon to be elected by two-degree voting and seats earmarked according to denominational group. A Legislative Council *(majlis tashriʿi)* was set up in Jordan in 1928, though this body had little actual power and was replaced by a bicameral National Assembly *(majlis al-umma)* in 1946, after independence. Elections to representative bodies occurred in Yemen in 1971 and Bahrain in 1972 (Robinson 2001).

Islamic modernists also began to question the language used to discuss citizenship and freedom during this time. As Ayalon points out, "until the twentieth century there had been one Arabic expression to indicate the political status of the ruled: *raʿiyya,* pl. *raʿaya*" (subject; literally "herd" or "flock") (Ayalon 1987, 44). Writers during the Nahda initially used *raʿiyya* to refer to "the populace of every country under any type of government," but became increasingly uncomfortable with the term and began exploring various alternatives—such as *ahl* (folks), *sukkan* (inhabitants), *jumhur* (multitude), and *shaʿb* (people), among others—before settling on *muwatin,* which signified a relationship to a place *(watan,* place of residence, homeland) rather than a ruler, and today is understood as equivalent to *citizen* (Ayalon 1987, 48–53). Accompanying this more democratic notion of citizenship one finds in this period a corresponding "replacement of justice by freedom as the antithesis of tyranny, and the suggestion of a constitutional restriction of the sovereign's powers" (Lewis 2001).

According to the Moroccan scholar Muhammad ʿAbid al-Jabiri, many of the thinkers writing during the Nahda period sought to equate democracy and the Qur'anic notion of *shura,* not because they were ignorant of the differences that separated them, but rather because they acted within a framework that required the pacification of the religious ideologues among the "religious scholars" and the rulers. Jabiri argues that "this ideological act aimed at the elevation of our heritage and civilization to the level of the present age . . . was an act of self-affirmation and self-defense" (1994, 42). That is, their project was joined together by their invocation of a form of democracy congruent with Western democracy while taking steps to ensure that they were not inserting a heretical doctrine into Islam. Democracy, according to this reformist argument, "is but a name that for the westerners designates something like what we talk about as *shura*." Jabiri characterizes the intended outcome of this project as the "elevation" of classical Arab-Islamic heritage (authenticity) such that it "raises" it to the level of the present age (contemporaneity).

Many of the pioneers of the Salafiyyun movement, such as Jamal al-Din al-Afghani (1838/39–1897) and Muhammad 'Abduh, also articulated a desire to extend a bridge between the Arab-Islamic tradition and the European Enlightenment tradition by incorporating these various Western concepts into Arab-Islamic discourse (Dajani 1984, 115–42). But, in general, the Salafiyyun worked in a direction opposite that of the Islamic modernists: their aim was to highlight concepts that were equivalent to, or at least approximated, the central concepts of liberal European Enlightenment thought in the Islamic tradition. Thus they sought "authentic" Islamic political concepts, often rejecting their deficient (less Islamic) counterparts in Western thought in the process. Like Islamic modernists, such equivalence was asserted between the European concept of "democracy" *(dimuqratiyya)* and Qur'anic notions of *"shura,"* which they considered to be the defining principle of the form of government advocated by the prophet Muhammad and specified in the Qur'an. There exist various other Arab-Islamic terms that have been used by Islamic thinkers to indicate "democratic values, such as *maslaha* (public interest), *'adl* (justice), and *ijma'* (consensus). However, during this period, *shura* comes to be understood to designate "Islamic democracy," and the other terms are entered into the discussion as principles that support the concept of *shura*, which in turn have been further identified with other foreign concepts, such that, for example, *maslaha* is equated with utility and *ijma'* with public opinion.

In advancing their claims, almost all Islamic thinkers point to a passage that advises Muhammad to "take counsel," interpreting it to mean, as Musa Kazim (Turkey, 1858–1920) does, that leaders are required to "consult with the *umma* in every matter" (2002, 176). In an essay that bears the verse as its title, Namik Kemal (Turkey, 1840–1888) argues that in order to 'keep the state within the limits of justice' Muslims must undertake two reforms: (1) by making government operations public and open to scrutiny, that is, by "emancipat[ing] the fundamental principles of the administration from the domain of implicit interpretation and make them public," and (2) by exercising "the method of consultation [*shura*], which takes the legislative power out of the hands of the members of the government," and placing it in that of the larger Islamic community *(umma)* (2002, 145).

While one should not underestimate the extent to which the Salafiyyun and Islamic modernists were willing to push democracy as both a process for political reform and as a form of political empowerment, the difference between the two is not only one of method. One might say that they spoke a different language and often took democracy (or *shura*) to mean quite different things. The choice of *shura* over *dimuqratiyya* and the differences between them became all the more apparent amidst the ideological conflict that characterized the period that followed.

Democracy in the Age of Ideology: National-Socialism and the Rise of Political Islam

Paul Salem describes the period following the Nahda as the "age of ideology" in the Arab world—with the 1950s marking the "heyday of ideology" and the "limited victories of the 1973 war and the dramatic oil price rises that accompanied it . . . [setting] the stage for a new phase of more pragmatic, conservative, and less ideological politics in the Arab world" (1994, 2, 6). Beginning with the collapse of the Ottoman Empire after World War I and continuing with the formation of the new political systems that emerged thereafter, the intellectual traditions that animated the Nahda period are politicized and an ideological divide opens up Arab societies. During this period, secular nationalism emerged as the dominant ideology of the independence movements in the Middle East and provided the founding ideology of many of the states set up after independence. But nationalism is in many ways a "thin" ideology, lacking in programmatic formulas beyond national liberation and political independence. Thus, many of those who had fought together under the umbrella of nationalism found themselves ideologically divided after independence, as they drew upon competing discursive traditions (socialist, liberal, and Salafiyya). By the 1950s Arab political and social thought was clearly dominated by Arab nationalist socialism. As Kamal S. Abu Jaber notes, "only rarely does an idea receive the ready and widespread acceptance gained by the idea of *Ishtirakiyya* (socialism) in the Arab world since the end of the Second World War. Indeed, as the Arabs gradually win their independence, they are turning increasingly to socialism. While some Arab nations, such as Jordan and Saudi Arabia, have not officially adopted it as a state policy, they have introduced certain aspects of the welfare state and the idea of 'social justice' is gaining ground" (1966, 1).

How does democracy fare in this context? During the period that Arab nationalist-socialism dominates, we see the modernization and nationalization of industries, the institution of sweeping land reforms, and other policies aimed at providing for the poor. However, the period also witnesses the growth of one-party, bureaucratic nation-states with little interest in expanding the power of the still young parliamentary systems. As Charles Issawi notes, "It has become commonplace that the parliamentary-democratic form of government has not functioned satisfactorily in the Middle East. During the last few years, a series of *coups d'état* have proclaimed, in no uncertain terms, the dissatisfaction of several countries with their parliamentary governments and in more than one country the army has taken over power" (1956, 27). Although the constitution of the Arab Ba'th party asserts that it "is a popular party" that "believes that sovereignty is the property of the people, who alone is the source of all authority" and that the "regime of the Arab state will be a constitutional parliamentary form" (Arab Ba'th Party 1962, 235, 236), many scholars have noted the subsuming of liberal and democratic concerns under considerations of promoting an organic unity as a means for renaissance. Salem notes that "as [Michel] Aflaq [1910–1989] saw in Syria, constitutional democracy meant little in a country where pseudo-feudalism was the dominant form of economic organization. . . . Liberty meant little for a population shackled by poverty and ignorance" (Salem 1994, 69). Similarly, the Syrian thinker Sati' al-Husri (1880–1960) took considerably less interest in forms of government than in unity (Khadduri 1970, 201; Cleveland 1971, 88–89, 162–63, 172). He was known to say, "Patriotism and nationalism above and before all else, even above and before freedom" (Cleveland 1971, 170). Some, such as Adeed Dawisha, have suggested that "the inability of Arab nationalism to survive political setbacks was at least partly due to the disinterest of its custodians in creating workable democratic institutions" (2003, 297). Dawisha points to Husri's reliance on a German model of a cultural nationalism as the primary source for the illiberalism and eventual downfall of Arab nationalist-socialism.

Alongside secular nationalist-socialist discourse and amidst attempts to reform Arab states along more democratic lines one finds an increase in rhetoric aimed at distinguishing Islamic political forms from those in the West in general and from "democracy" in particular. A number of Islamist reformist thinkers envisioned a state where the Qur'an forms the constitution, the ruler implements the *shari'a*, to which he is also bound, and the ruler engages in *shura*. As Sayyid Qutb (Egypt, 1906–1966) writes, "political theory in Islam rests on the basis of justice on the part of the rulers, obedience on the part of the ruled, and collaboration between ruler and ruled" (Kotb 1980, 93). In this ideologically charged context, some of the most fully articulated arguments resisting equations of *shura* with democracy emerge. Islamists during this period leveled two arguments against democratic governance, both based on the notion of *tawhid* (the oneness or unity of God). First, they denounce democracy as *shirk bi-allah* (attributing partners to God). According to this argument democracy is said to assert itself as a new "religion" that deifies humans by awarding them the right to legislate without being bound by a superior Divine authority, and thus contradicts the Qur'anic decree: "The command is for none but God. He has commanded that you worship none but Him" (12:40).

The second point of criticism of democracy as a form of government is articulated through the notion of *hakimiyya*, the absolute sovereignty of God over the universe. According to Abu-l-'Ala Mawdudi, "no person, class or group, not even the entire population of the state as a whole, can lay claim to sovereignty. God alone is the real sovereign; all others are merely His subjects" (1982, 271). Whereas in democracy the legislator is the people, according to the *tawhid* of Islam, sovereignty *(hakimiyya)* is the sole prerogative of God and any usurpation of the legislative author-ity from God undermines that *tawhid*. Democracy that is based on the idea of popular sovereignty, not the sovereignty of God, is considered a *jahiliyya* (ignorant) form of government. According to Qutb, those Mus-lims who argue for human sovereignty in politics confuse the exercise of power with its source. In his view, the people do not possess, and thus cannot delegate, sovereignty. Rather, they must implement what God, the sovereign, has legislated. Since Islamic law provides a complete legal and moral system, no further legislation is either possible or necessary. Both points of critique are articulated by Mawdudi: "Islam, speaking from the view-point of political philosophy, is the very antithesis of sec-ular Western democracy. . . . [Islam] altogether repudiates the philoso-phy of popular sovereignty and rears its polity on the foundations of the sovereignty of God and the vicegerency *(khilafah)* of man" (1982, 254).

Yet even here, democratic values are not completely rejected. For ex-ample, while Mawdudi is specific that "Islam is not democracy," he does champion a form of Islamic governance founded on *tawhid,* which he calls a "theo-democracy" or "divine democratic government." In such a government "the entire Muslim population runs the state in accordance with the Book of God and the practice of His Prophet . . . The executive under this system of government is constituted by the general will of the Muslims who have also the right to depose it" (Mawdudi 1982, 254). Thus Mawdudi conceptualizes a form of government in which the peo-ple rule through some unspecified procedure for determining the gen-eral will, but short of a full popular sovereignty in at least one sense: even the consensus of the Islamic community cannot alter or oppose any as-pect of Islamic law.

Shura is further democratized in the writings of Hasan al-Banna (Egypt, 1906–1949), the founder of the Muslim Brotherhood in Egypt, through his distinction between divine *hakimiyya* and human *hakimiyya.* "The first, Banna argues, can never be properly represented. . . . However, the legitimacy of representing human *hakimiyya* must be sought in fulfilling and adhering to Qur'anic instructions (or, in Banna's words, 'the Islamic constitution') on the proper conditions for carrying out *shura*" (Moussalli 1999, 126; 2001, 68). Among these principles are the injunctions to the *umma* to enjoin good and forbid evil *(al-amr bil-ma'ruf wa al-nahy 'an al-munkar)* in keeping watch over government.

According to Ahmad Moussalli, many Islamists interpret *hakimiyya* "not [as] political rule or a system of government but [as] a doctrine used to empower people through divine texts to counter the naked force, despotism, and totalitarianism of rulers" (Moussalli 2001, 19). Thus, although reformers such as Banna and Mawdudi spoke directly to the Muslim masses in their call to account for defending Islam, applying it to their daily life, and becoming conscious and self-reliant in their faith, in their call for moral change, nowhere do they suggest the believers at large should directly hold power in the regimes. Banna rejected Egyptian parliamentary politics and suggested the *umma* must be directly represented through the government's implementation and adherence to Islam (Moussalli 1999, 127–28). Moussalli further notes that "whenever *hakimiyya* is mentioned nowadays, it means [a] kind of rule based on scriptural Qur'anic precepts extracted from their social, economic, political, and historical contexts. This is the reason all fundamentalists, radical or not, advocate the fulfillment of God's *hakimiyya* by at least replacing existing governments with Islamic ones" (2001, 129). In general, the writings of these Islamists do not speak to the form of rule directly at all, but instead suggest the need for the founding of an Islamic regime, without reference to structure or procedures for implementing or carrying out that regime, in order to fight the destructive ills of Western society. Even thinkers, such as Qutb, who call for replacing errant rulers who have failed to abide by Islamic law and to provide for the material and spiritual well-being of fellow Muslims, neglect questions of how one might provide for good decision-making and rules of succession once the goal of authentic Islamic government has been achieved.

Dimuqratiyya and *Shura*: Divergence or Convergence?

The desire to "build bridges" has persisted among many Islamist reformists (for example, Turabi 1987; Huwaydi 1992, 1993). Fahmi Huwaydi (Egypt, b. 1937) argues that democracy is so crucial to the development of the Islamic world that if it had not already been sanctioned in Islam (in the form of *shura*) "we ought to 'invent' it by any means possible" (Yvonne Haddad 1995, 18). Nonetheless, among the more recent generations of Salafiyyun, the rejection of the use of "foreign" words and the total insistence upon the use of terms with a wholly Arab-Islamic pedigree reflects a desire to create a fissure between European thought and the Arab-Islamic tradition (for example, Nabhani 1961; 1965). According to Jabiri, such thinkers refuse use of the word *dimuqratiyya,* insisting that the word *shura* better captures the "intended meaning" of the concept (Jabiri 1994, 41).[3] This gesture was intended both to reject the use of foreign words and to legitimize a distinctly Islamic democracy by creating a distinction from the European Enlightenment tradition. The counterpart to the formulation "Islam is the solution" *(al-islam huwa al-hal)* is the critique of "imported solutions" *(al-hulul al-mustawrada).* In the book of the Islamist ideologue Yusuf al-Qaradawi (Egypt/Qatar, b. 1926), which bears the latter title, democracy tops the list of imported solutions to be rejected (Qaradawi 1977). More recently, the author of a small book entitled *Islam's Judgment on Democracy and Party Pluralism* asserts that the equivalent term in Arabic for *democracy* is *ibahiyya* (laxity, permissiveness), which involves the removal of all limits on the freedom to do that which God forbids, from drinking, homosexuality, and adultery to apostasy (Halima 1993, 40).

On the other hand, most proponents of distinctly secular conceptions of good governance prefer to use the term *dimuqratiyya,* a direct transliteration of *democracy* that signals a commitment to Western, liberal forms of democracy. The tension within both strains of *shura* advocates and the *dimuqratiyya* advocates has only become more apparent with the growth of the Islamist movement in the Arab region, and the rejectionist attitude is not a characteristic of the *shura* advocates alone. This tension became apparent when, in 1985, Khalid Muhammad

---

3. Just how undemocratic *shura* can be in practice is apparent in the Saudi *majlis al-shura* (consultative council), established in the early 1930s when 'Abd al-'Aziz Al Sa'ud assumed the title of King of Saudi Arabia. In this context, the concept is tied to the notion of a monarch "in consultation" with a very select group of advisors. The Saudi political system, along with a few of the other Gulf emirates and shaykhdoms, are the only Arab states that do not even claim to be democratic.

Khalid (Egypt, 1920–1998)—a former secularist who in the last years of his life grew increasingly concerned with anchoring his political ideas in the *shari'a* (Islamic law)— was asked what kind of state he would like to see established. He declared that the *shari'a* necessarily entails an Islamic legislature that takes the form of *shura,* which he defined as involving "parliamentary opposition, a multiparty system and a free press" (Flores 1997, 89). Although some liberals hailed Khalid's statement for its support of democratic institutions, others ridiculed the characterization of his desired state as Islamic. The liberal Egyptian philosopher Fu'ad Zakariyya asked, with no small measure of sarcasm:

> Would he have been able to define the *shura* [in the way he did] . . . had he not been influenced by the thoughts of some weak mortals like John Locke, Montesquieu, Rousseau, and Thomas Jefferson, and had the experiences of the modern states that preceded us in the field of democracy not come to support the thoughts of those philosophers by way of practice? Would Khalid Muhammad Khalid have been able to explain the *shura* in this way if he were not himself a man who acquired democratic leanings though his readings, his culture, and his acquaintance with the experiences of the modern peoples? And if it were said that he was able to arrive at such a definition by the study of the heritage alone, how was it that these principles were never discovered, nor applied, throughout the history of that heritage? (quoted in Flores 1997, 89–90)

Thus, rather than being lauded for his liberalism, Khalid was taken to task for dressing his liberal notion of democracy in what many view as dangerous Islamic garb.

If anything, the lines between the advocates of democracy and democracy's opponents seem to have become more polarized. Yet few today reject democracy outright without offering their own, more authentic understanding of popular rule. Ayatullah Baqir al-Sadr (1936–1980), a Shi'i thinker executed by the Iraqi government, articulates a sentiment that seems to be shared by many Sunni thinkers as well. He maintains that although "the theory that the influential persons could represent the general public was operative in Islamic society in a particular period of history," "representative government" constitutes a new and important development in Islamic history: "in view of the changed circumstances and in consideration of the principles of consultation and juristic supervision, it is essential that this theory should give place to the formation of an assembly whose members are the real representatives of the people" (al-Sadr 1982, 82). While one still finds Islamist rhetoric that equates democracy with blasphemy, as in earlier times, often the rejection of democracy is more a rejection of the West and what are seen as Western values than a rejection of a notion of the rule of the people. One must look beyond a mere rejection or affirmation of democracy—and, so too, one must certainly look beyond the common advocacy of *shura* to the way in which either of these terms is conceptualized. In addition, the polarization between advocates of democracy and advocates of *shura* belies an underlying consensus about the value of democracy in general that seems to have firmly taken root. The breadth and complexity of this consensus both is apparent in and seems to grow amidst the debates throughout the last two decades over civil society.

Civil Society: Western Ambiguities and Eastern Opportunities

The question that opens our discussion of democracy also must open our discussion of civil society: where to begin? While the first engagements with democracy seem to easily trace back to Athens in the case of both Western and Eastern thought, the path of the history of the concept of (as opposed to the term) democracy is a labyrinth. The concept of civil society presents a different case: while the search for a term in Arabic to signal "civil society" is clearly recent, the origins of the contemporary concept of civil society in both Arabic and Western languages are not so easily identified. Certainly civil society designates a form of association that exists somewhere between the state and the individual, but beyond that rather vague baseline definition one is hard pressed to find agreement on the function, activities, and organizations that constitute this sphere. The challenges of discussing this concept's history in Arabic are in many ways a point of contrast with the challenges of discussing democracy in Arab political thought. The origins of democracy are clear in Western political thought, while its origin in Arab political thought is unclear to the point that some argue the idea still has not fully taken root there. Most Arab intellectuals agree upon the origin of the civil society idea in Arabic (although disagree in both Arab and Western scholarship about when the empirical existence of such a sphere emerges), yet there seems to be considerable variation in the recent and growing literature that seeks civil society's origins in Western contexts. For example, Marvin B. Becker focuses his discussion of civil society's "emergence" during "a privileged moment" in eighteenth-century England, Scotland, and France (1994). Jean L. Cohen and Andrew Arato begin their work *Civil Society and Political Theory* with Hegel because, "while Hegel's *conception* of civil society may not be the first modern one, [they] do believe that his is the first modern *theory* of civil society"; and they find him to be "the most important theoretical forerunner of several later approaches that have preserved their potential to provide more global, intellectual orientation even in our own time" (1992, 91). In *The Idea of Civil Society,* Adam B. Seligman maintains that "it is nevertheless with John Locke that we must begin our understanding of the modern concept of civil society," because he represents "a transitional figure, building on the tradition of individual rights (so important to the civil society tradition) . . . but . . . rooting these rights in a religious vision" (1992, 21–22).

One problem with each of these works is that neither offers a comprehensive account of the history of the concept of civil society.[4] Becker's work (1988, 1994) remains focused on the "genesis" of civil society, and does not attempt to analyze the concept's history after the eighteenth century. Similarly, Seligman's work opens with a chapter that traces the roots of the modern concept of civil society to the natural law tradition and shows how early modern thinkers, such as Locke and various Scottish Enlightenment philosophers, used the concept in theorizing about the state in light of various dilemmas of modern society (predominantly the tension between individual autonomy and morality). Seligman's dis-

---

4. A recent work that does offer the scope that Seligman and Cohen and Arato lack is Ehrenberg (1999). However, this work falls into the opposite trap I discuss below: it includes too much under the rubric of "civil society," so that the expression loses conceptual coherence.

cussion of the civil society concept in European political thought is paltry at best. In fact, Seligman identifies "two antithetical lines" of the civil society concept in the mid-eighteenth to the mid-nineteenth century: one that he calls the "post-Hegelian or Marxist tradition" and a second that he terms "Anglo-American" (1992, 10). As a result, Tocqueville is largely overlooked.[5] In addition, in the few pages he does devote to Hegel and Marx, Seligman characterizes these thinkers (along with Hume, who seems to have crossed the "antithetical" divide between the two traditions) as "signposts on the way toward the increasing loss of coherence in the civil society idea" (1992, 59). Much of the rest of Seligman's book is devoted to discussing how the dilemmas he identifies throughout the history of the concept play out in various contemporary settings.

Seligman locates the "theoretical dissolution" of the concept precisely where Cohen and Arato argue that this theory begins: with Hegel. In the first part of Cohen and Arato's three-part work, they analyze the central role civil society played in the theories of thinkers such as Hegel, Tocqueville, and Parsons. In the second part, they examine various critiques of civil society in the works of other thinkers such as Arendt, Foucault, and the early Habermas. In part 3, Cohen and Arato develop what they term a "post-Marxist" conception of civil society that takes into account the history of the concept,[6] the criticisms of the concept, and contemporary political reality, particularly in Eastern Europe. Nonetheless, despite the great breadth of this vast work, pre-Hegelian notions of civil society in general and British notions in particular are sorely neglected.

Both Becker's history and the first chapter of Seligman's book complement Cohen and Arato's more European-centered analysis. However,

5. The neglect of Tocqueville is surprising in light of the fact that his work animates so many of the contemporary debates over civil society, and all the more so since Seligman identifies the issues of "maintaining solidarity," the "loss of a shared public sphere," and "social trust" as the defining problems for contemporary discussions of civil society in the final two chapters and conclusion.

6. Cohen and Arato characterize post-Marxism as involving "a revision of Marx's identification of civil and bourgeois civil society as well as his various political projects aiming at the reunification of state and society" (1992, 71). It is in this latter sense that post-Marxism is said to be a "self-limiting" project.

all three of these works neglect the more recent and very influential American scholarship on civic society and civic engagement, such as that found in *The Essential Civil Society Reader* (Eberly 2000). The tradition of civil society found there traces its origins to Montesquieu and Tocqueville. Integrating these traditions is important for understanding the full range of ideas that Arab scholars have drawn from, as well as for providing a fuller understanding of "Western" political thought—its historical legacy and its inherent possibilities.

A second and equally important problem with much of the contemporary work on civil society is a failure to recognize the important historical shifts of meaning of the idea and its relationship to the state.[7] Rather than providing a history of the transformation of the concept of civil society, a number of works provide a history of the *term* (Colas 1997; Eberly 2000; Riedel 1975). Such works tend to unproblematically equate civil society, understood as political society, with civil society in its modern conception: civil society as distinguished from the state. For example, Dominique Colas (1997) argues that the English term *civil society* and the French term *société civile* comprised vernacular translations of the Latin term *societas civilis,* which was itself a translation of the Greek term *koinonia politikè.*[8] Colas's reading of Latin, French, Italian, and German translations of Aristotle's *Politics* and *Nicomachean Ethics* reveals that the term *societas civilis* was used to translate the Greek as early as the fifteenth century: "Although the Latin term had been used in a commentary on Aristotle by the medieval theologian Giles of Rome, the decisive lexical choice was made by the great Florentine humanist Leonardo Bruni. . . . [I]t was Bruni's Latin translation of Aristotle's *Politics* (together with the original Greek) that was used by [Philipp] Melanchthon, close friend and fellow combatant of Martin Luther, as the basis for a Latin commentary on that text in the course of which

7. Examples of writings that neglect shifts in the state-civil society distinction include Cohen (1982), Frankel (1983), and Urry (1981).

8. James Schmidt argues that it was the Florentine humanist Leonardo Bruni who rendered Aristotle's *koinonia politike* as *civilis societas* and established the pattern followed by subsequent translators (1986, 295–319).

Melanchthon made *societas civilis* his own. From there by way of transla-tion, and at a moment when printing was revolutionizing the circula-tion of signifiers, the term passed into the vernacular languages" (Colas 1997, xvii).[9] Colas's book aims at demonstrating that "civil society" has been consistently presented as conjoined with and in opposition to the notion of "fanaticism" in Western political thought since Melanchthon's work.

In fact, *civil society* has passed through numerous dualistic opposi-tions (in addition to fanaticism/civil society) that have served to define the expression: family/civil society, church/civil society, state of na-ture/civil society, state/civil society. Whatever the defining opposition of this term, until at least sometime in the eighteenth century, as Colas ac-knowledges, *civil society* was considered a synonym for *political society* or *political order*: "even the least gifted etymology hound can immediately see that 'civil' is the Latin equivalent of the Greek 'political' " (1997, 32).[10] *Societas civilis* is one of the possible translations of *koinonia politikè*, but the latter could also be translated into French as *cité* or *état*; into English as *polity, commonwealth,* or *state* (Colas 1997, 23); or into German as *Staat* or *Stadt*.[11] In medieval political philosophy, civil society had a fluc-tuating presence in contradistinction with ecclesiastical institutions. For theorists of the seventeenth century, civil society was contrasted with the state of nature, as a condition in which men lived under government. With the notable exception of Rousseau—who, incidentally, considered giving the title *De la société civile* to the first version of *Du contrat so-*

9. Similarly, Riedel shows that the phrase *koinonia politike* (political union or asso-ciation), which Aristotle first used, was afterwards normally translated as *societas civilis* and became, together with its synonyms *civitas* and *res publica,* a general term for inde-pendent political entity or the state (1972, 672–724).

10. Manfred Riedel (1972) demonstrates that Thomas Aquinas, Jean Bodin, Thomas Hobbes, Benedictus de Spinoza, John Locke, and Immanuel Kant used "politi-cal" and "civil" as synonymous.

11. Despite the etymological focus of his work, Colas attempts to distinguish the *bürgerliche Gesellschaft* tradition from that of civil society because the former does not fit well with Colas's civil society/fanaticism philosopheme. However, the common etymo-logical and philosophical roots are affirmed in Riedel (1975).

cial[12]—most seventeenth-century political theorists valued civil/political society for the increased strength and safety it provided individuals.

The difference between the modern concept of civil society and the phrase that draws its etymology from *koinonia politikè* or *societas civilis* is apparent in Locke's writings. Locke calls the state "civil society," but the concept he has of the pre-political phase of humanity—a state of nature characterized by a predominance of social relations that are regulated by natural laws—anticipates more Hegel's *bürgerliche Gesellschaft* than it continues Hobbes's state of nature. Thus we return to our original question: where do we begin a history of the *concept* of civil society?

Despite the many examples of usage of the expression throughout the long history of political thought, civil society did not develop into a distinct concept until at least the early modern period, shortly after which it became associated with the phrase that most commonly marks its presence today. Colas's work focuses on mapping the distinction between the political and the civil, at times obscuring the fact that this distinction presupposes another: one between state and society. In its original meaning, the word *society* (*koinonia* in Greek, *societas* or *communitas* in Latin, and *Gesellschaft* in German) means nothing more than "association" or "union." In the eighteenth century, one could speak of enjoying a person's "society"—that is, enjoying their company—but it was also common to use *society* to refer to "a mode of life adopted by a body of individuals for the purpose of harmonious co-existence or for mutual benefit, defense, etc." (Murray 1933, 913–14). To this extent, state and society were tied together by a single concept in early modern Anglo-European political thought.

In perhaps the best account in English on the genesis of the modern civil society idea, the historian Marvin Becker shows that it was not until at least the late seventeenth century that an awareness of a disjunction between the state and society intensified and not until eighteenth-

---

12. We know this from the first version or "Geneva Manuscript" of *The Social Contract*. Rousseau frequently used the phrase "civil society" in the earlier draft (Derathé 1950, 380–86).

century England and Scotland that the idea began to take form (1988). Civil society became increasingly delineated by reference to such things as property rights, intermediate institutions, the market, and the interaction of interests protected from state intervention. As a result, classical definitions of civil society as being coterminous with the state were now rivaled by political theory arguing for independent forms of associative life to be legitimated by state power. Furthermore, the sphere of economic relations (what physiocrats of the eighteenth century termed *société naturelle*) was contrasted with political society *(société politique),* and the term *civil society* began to assume the meaning of *"civilized* society." According to Becker, in the eighteenth century the old expression *civil society* began to take on its specifically modern form until, by the nineteenth century, for example, in Hegel's *Philosophy of Right,* the term *civil society (bürgerliche Gesellschaft)* refers not to the whole of an organized society but to a sphere in which men might satisfy their needs through work and, in Marx's writings, the "political development" of society is said to correspond with a progressive differentiation of society from the state (Becker 1994).

Charles Taylor (1995) has identified two "streams" in the history of Western political thought that come together to form our modern concept of civil society. He traces the first to Locke's conception of a society defined independently of its political constitution. Taylor locates a second "stream" in the works of Montesquieu. According to Taylor, "the central feature of the L[ocke]-stream is the elaboration of a richer view of society as an *extrapolitical* reality," whereas the "M[ontesquieu]-stream" focuses on independent associations that "form the basis for the fragmentation and diversity of power *within* the political system" (1995, 215, 222). Montesquieu, Taylor argues, identifies free society with a particular form of political constitution that fragments and diversifies power among a layer of intermediate bodies [*corps intermédiaires*]. In *The Spirit of the Laws,* Montesquieu maintains that the traditional privileges of the nobles and the clergy, by virtue of their relative independence, serve as a bulwark against the despotism of European monarchies. In a despotism, he argues, there is an empty space between the ruler and the people because the intermediate institutions that can deflect the central power have been destroyed or tamed: "Despotism is of itself sufficient; round it there is an absolute vacuum" (Montesquieu 1977, 154).

Although the problem of political despotism—how to break its grip or prevent its emergence—is a central and recurring theme in political theory, Montesquieu's influential account marks the first time that despotism was linked to an absence of intermediary organizations, and his account played a decisive part in the modernization of the classical concept of civil society (Richter 1973, 1). Yet the societal implications of Montesquieu's *corps intermédiaires* were not drawn until the extrapolitical character of society as such was further elaborated in the "L-stream." There is much to Taylor's claim that these two streams come together in many contemporary conceptions of civil society. However, the course is not one of a single or decisive convergence, but one of muddy waters that threaten but fail to merge at various bends.

What is interesting in returning to the history of this concept is that, unlike contemporary conceptions, civil society was not originally thought of as a solution to political problems so much as it was considered part of the problem itself, nor was it viewed as a particularly progressive force for democracy. Rather than the unequivocally good thing that civil society has come to represent in recent years, earlier "civil societies" were conceptualized as as much a threat to as a promoter of civil freedom. Nor was civil society originally tied to democracy. Becker notes precisely this point: "That civil society had its modern beginnings in eighteenth-century England and Scotland itself underscores a crucial, if perhaps obvious point: this was a world far distanced from that of liberal democracy. In so many respects it was . . . a privileged society existing at a privileged historical moment. This seems a heartening message for exponents of civil society in our own times. Numerous models of civil society can and do exist and flourish under a variety of regimes distinct from liberal democracy" (Becker 1994, xix). As we will see, these lessons are not lost on a number of Arab thinkers.

The ambiguity that surrounds the origin and history of the concept of civil society in Western discourse is at least part of the explanation for the vast space the debate over the term has created in Arab political thought, such that in a very short period of time (since no earlier than the 1980s) a vast number of intellectuals from diverse ideological traditions have found themselves engaged in a shared project of debating that history and its relevance to Arab politics. In contrast to Western political thought, the "when" of civil society's emergence as a subject of contention in Arab political discourse is fairly clear. It is to the questions of why and how Arab intellectuals turn to this concept when they do—the issues and interests that form the general horizon of contemporary actors' particular attempts to engage the notion of civil society (analyzed in chapters 4, 5, 6, and 7)—that we turn in chapter 3.

3

The Politics of Translating
Civil Society into Arabic

With firm and careful calligraphy he added these two lines to the manu-
script: "Aristu (Aristotle) gives the name of tragedy to panegyrics and
that of comedy to satires and anathemas. Admirable tragedies and
comedies abound in the pages of the Koran and in the *mohalacas* of the
sanctuary."

—Borges, "Averroes' Search"

A short essay written by the Argentinean author Jorge Luis Borges presents a fictionalized account of the great Muslim philosopher Averroes'
(Ibn Rushd) failed attempt at translation—a view at odds with the transcultural approach presented here. Averroes is in his library, grappling
with a problem that has brought his work to a standstill. At the beginning
of Aristotle's *Poetics,* on which he is writing a commentary, Averroes has
stumbled over two words: *tragedy* and *comedy.* "No one in the world of
Islam could conjecture what they meant" (Borges 1988, 149). He con-
sults the authoritative translations of the Nestorians Hunayn Ibn Ishaq
(808–873) and Abu Bishr Matta Ibn Yunus (870–940), but to no avail.
"These two arcane words," Borges writes, "pullulated throughout the text
of the *Poetics*; it was impossible to elude them."

In the course of the story, Borges twice places before Averroes' eyes
intimations to the answers he seeks. The first occasion occurs when
Averroes is distracted from his work "by a kind of melody." He looks
down from his balcony where "below, in the narrow earthen patio, some
half-naked children were playing. One, standing on another's shoulders,
was obviously playing the part of a muezzin; with his eyes tightly closed,

he chanted 'There is no god but God.' The one who held him motion-lessly played the part of the minaret; another, abject in the dust and on his knees, the part of the faithful worshipers. The game did not last long; all wanted to be the muezzin" (Borges 1988, 149).

The second occasion occurs later that evening, when a traveler re-counts a strange scene he had witnessed in a foreign land. In a "house, which was rather a single room, with rows of cabinets or balconies on top of each other," he describes "some fifteen or twenty" persons with crimson-colored masks "who were praying, singing and conversing" (Borges 1988, 152). These masked individuals "suffered prison, but no one could see the jail; they traveled on horse-back, but no one could see the horse; they fought, but the swords were of reed; they died and then stood up again." The traveler refutes the suggestion that the inhabitants of this foreign land were mad, insisting instead that they were actually representing a story to an audience. "In that case," one of the other inter-locutors suggests, "twenty persons are unnecessary. One single speaker can tell anything, no matter how complicated it might be" (Borges 1988, 153).

The objects of Averroes' search—the Greek concepts of tragedy and comedy—presuppose knowledge of the theater. Given that the theater was an art form unknown to Arab culture in Averroes' day, another cul-tural category—that of the storyteller—must take its place. Thus, after returning to his library, Averroes adds the following lines to his manu-script: "Aristu (Aristotle) gives the name of tragedy to panegyrics and that of comedy to satires and anathemas. Admirable tragedies and come-dies abound in the pages of the Koran and in the *mohalacas* of the sanc-tuary" (Borges 1988, 155).

Many Arab thinkers look to Ibn Rushd for inspiration in their at-tempt to engage in cross-cultural dialogue. In an article entitled " 'Clash of Civilizations': The Relations of the Future?" articulating a "Rushdian dialogue" as an alternative to Huntington's conflictual view, Jabiri notes that in 1996 "the governments of Morocco and Spain decided to create the 'Ibn Rushd (Averroes) Commission' with the purpose of improving mutual understanding" (al-Jabri 1999b, 75–76). In 1998, a number of Arab intellectuals established the Ibn Rushd Fund for Freedom of

Thought in Berlin to recognize those who challenge the parameters of contemporary Arab political thought.[1] Borges' story quite beautifully illustrates a rather different view of Ibn Rushd, one that suggests pessimism regarding the possibility—or, rather, the virtual impossibility—of translating concepts across cultures, a view that finds its counterpart in contemporary studies that argue that civil society and democracy are not only materially absent from the Arab region, but also conceptually absent, categorically "foreign"—that is, the idea that Arab political thought does not possess the linguistic, intellectual, or material context necessary to sustain such concepts. This is the extreme statement of this position. Usually variants of this view take a subtler or less explicit form, though the extreme position does find expression in the writings of scholars such as Samuel P. Huntington (1996) and Ernest Gellner (1994; 1995), among others. One striking example is provided by John Hall's claim that "the logical clarity enshrined in Islam . . . [precluded] . . . any equivalent to occidental 'liberties': possession of the truth was so complete that the culture was radically contractualist rather than corporatist. In addition, its social institutions did not allow for the autonomy of cities, that is, the shell within which many of the practices of civility have been born" (1995, 14). It is this dichotomous view of cross-cultural engagement that I wish to contest here.

It is true that the phrase *civil society* was neither a coin of political discourse nor did it indicate a significant conceptual category in discussions of democracy or democratization until at least the late 1980s. For example, as recently as 1984, the Center for Arab Unity Studies held a conference on "The Crisis of Democracy in the Arab World," which brought together more than seventy Arab scholars from around the world. In the nearly one thousand pages of the published proceedings, the expression *civil society (al-mujtama' al-madani)* was used only once, in a footnote referring to Antonio Gramsci's notion of hegemony ('Adil

1. According to the website of the Ibn Rushd Fund for Freedom of Thought, the name "was selected in recognition of the philosopher's intellectual achievements, his independent interpretation of Islamic ideas, his tolerance of convictions and cultures differing from his own" (http://www.ibn-rushd.org).

Husayn 1984, 205). One of the earliest uses of the concept as such is found at a conference organized by the Arab Thought Forum in Amman, Jordan, in March 1989. The conference organizer, Saad Eddin Ibrahim (Egypt, b. 1938)—who, incidentally, claims to have been the person who introduced the phrase to the region (Ibrahim 1998)—gave one of the sections of the published proceedings the title of "Civil Society and Democratic Transformation."[2] However, this title, as well as Ibrahim's introduction (which uses the phrase once), was conceived subsequent to the conference. Only one of the papers presented refers to *al-mujtama' al-madani*, and the phrase does not appear at all in the recorded discussion that accompanies the presentations. In this single usage, the author of the paper, 'Ali al-Din Hilal (a political scientist and Egypt's former minister of youth) refers to the idea in a preliminary way, stressing the importance of further studying civil society, which he defines as the "organization of citizen activities" (1989, 339). In addition, Ibrahim's use of quotation marks around the phrase in its single appearance in his introduction suggests that he was quite aware of the expression's novelty. The expression did occasionally appear prior to this time in various translations of Western writings, including Locke, Hobbes, and Gramsci, as well as, less often, in discussions of the works of such thinkers, but was seldom employed as a term of political discourse in original works in Arabic until recently.

This is not to suggest that Arabs did not posses a concept *similar* to Western notions of civil society prior to the late 1980s. In fact, the contrary is more likely true: Arabs have a number of concepts from which to draw to designate the realm of self-generated associative life outside of

2. Although one might question whether Ibrahim can decisively claim this distinction, it is quite apparent that he has done more than any other single individual to propagate the term in the past decade through the various activities of the Ibn Khaldun Center for Development Studies (est. 1988) project on "Civil Society in the Middle East," including the publication of various country studies, a "Civil Society" newsletter in English and Arabic, an annual update of the status of civil society in Arab countries, and even the production of a weeklong television series on the topic that aired in Egypt in 1998.

the state. The Arabic word for society, *mujtama'*, is a noun of place derived from the root *jama'* (to join together, assemble), from which the words for group *(jama'a)*, club *(jam'iyya)*, university *(jami'a)*, and assembly *(ijtima')* are also derived. This root has more of a connotation of unity and totality than the English *society*. For example, other derivations of *jama'* have the meaning of "total" *(jami')*, "whole" *(ajma')*, "collective" *(jama'i)* (as opposed to "individual" [*fardi*]), and "agreement" or "unanimity" *(ijma')* (Lane and Lane-Poole 1968). As a noun of place, *mujtama'* literally means "a gathering place" or "a place of assembly." The concepts of community or nation *(umma)* and solidarity *('asabiyya)* also hold an important place in Arab political and religious thought. However, the concern with specifying the particularly *civil* sphere of society vis-à-vis the state is a new phenomenon, one precipitated largely by the international interest in civil society.

By the early 1990s the phrase could not be avoided in discussions of democracy, pluralism, human rights, political reform, or revolution, and had itself become a topic of rather heated debate. It could be found not only in academic writings and conferences, but also in the print and broadcast media and in the speeches of the political elite throughout most of the world. A number of Arab scholars who were engaged in discussions outside of the Arab region or who write for a foreign-language audience began to discuss civil society or *société civile* considerably earlier (Laroui 1977; Hermassi 1983; Zghal 1985; Bin Sa'id 1985). Yet, as one Arab intellectual noted, writing and speaking about civil society in the context of Arabic led to new questions and problematized the idea in new ways (Messarra 1998). So too, the introduction of the concept into Arabic has left an indelible mark on Arab political thought. 'Abd al-Ilah Bilqaziz of Morocco has gone so far as to claim that the reason that "Arab thought has not produced a science of politics (in the precise academic sense)" lies in the fact that "thinking about our problem of power was not begun from its actual starting point—civil society—but, rather, from the starting point that dominates our consciousness: the state" (1992, 10). Thus, he argues, "thinking about the state, power [*sulta*] and social change from the starting point of civil society essentially overturns previous political conceptions adhered to in Arab rhetoric" (Bilqaziz 1992, 117).

In this chapter, I examine the politics of words and concepts involved in the translation of civil society into Arabic, and map the transportation of the concept into the Arab political discourse, attempting to offer an explanation of why and how this transcultural conceptual translation has taken place. In the section that follows, I look at the intellectual climate in which Arab intellectuals operate, focusing in particular on three broad sets of issues involved in appropriating this "foreign" political concept into Arabic, those issues that problematize the idea in Arabic in the way intimated by Messarra. In the chapter's final sections, I focus on some of the competing political discourses—or ideologies—that have attempted to adapt and adopt the concept of civil society in some form, comparing the travail of civil society's travels to that of an earlier pioneer and current companion: democracy. While the conceptual horizon of the appropriation is distinct to each ideological tradition, the appropriation in all cases has contributed to a restructuring of those very discourses—a phenomenon that will be explored at greater depth in the book's remaining chapters.

The Intellectual and Linguistic Context
of Contemporary Arab Political Thought

Political philosophy has a long history in Arab countries. The Arabic word for philosophy, *falsafa,* dates back to the eighth century when the works of Plato and Aristotle were studied and translated into Arabic. However, whereas Western political philosophy has become decisively secular in the modern period, much of Arab philosophy continues to exist within the periphery of the study of religion. As a result, the perception on the part of some Western scholars is that philosophy in Arab countries has not "matured." At the same time, and not surprisingly in light of the history of colonialism in the region, many Arab intellectuals have been educated in foreign countries. A large number of scholars, especially from the North African countries as well as Lebanon and Syria, have studied in French universities or have been significantly influenced by French schools of thought. During the cold war, numerous Arab students, particularly from Syria, Iraq, and Egypt, attended universities in the Soviet Union or Eastern European countries. Thus the issue of the influence and domination of modern Arab philosophy by foreign schools of thought—the intellectual onslaught *(al-ghazw al-fikri)*, as it has become known—has remained a particularly acute one, especially since independence, as intellectuals continue to work out the implications of their "colonialist legacy." As a result, whereas the West views "maturation" as a matter of liberation from religion because of its own history, the issue of liberation from colonialism and the Western "cultural and intellectual assault," as well as mitigation of the unequal power relation that exists between East and West, is the concern at the center of much Arab political philosophy.

The Moroccan philosopher Sa'id Bin Sa'id (b. 1946) argues that one of the main tasks of political philosophy is to "authenticate" various modern concepts that he acknowledges as having entered contemporary Arab discourse from modern Western thought. He maintains that "the appearance of new concepts at a certain point in time and in a particular scientific field constitutes an original event, usually foreshadowing the rise of a new scientific theory. This is true not only of the history of exact sciences, but also, to a considerable degree, of the history of political thought since the seventeenth century. The latter owes its modernity to the appearance of a set of concepts that were totally new, such as 'people' and 'citizen,' 'social contract' and 'civil society,' 'nation' and 'fatherland' " (Bin Sa'id 1987, 149).

Many of these terms, he argues, are "new notions and the terms which express them are not familiar in classical Arabic rhetoric. Here one senses the influence of new ideas which have been introduced through student missions, and through Western colonialism" (Bin Sa'id 1987, 153; also Bin Sa'id 1985). Western concepts, such as civil society, have had to be reconciled with different notions of publicness and the family, as well as different understandings of the relationships between the individual and the community, state and society, religion and politics, that one finds in the Arab context. However, just as the advancement of political philosophy is viewed as much a matter of its liberation from domination by foreign schools of thought as of its extrication from religion, the fruitful appropriation of foreign concepts does not involve abandoning previously held concepts any more than it requires the wholesale adoption of the worldview from which that concept hails.

The challenges posed by this intellectual context must be kept in mind throughout our examination of the various issues that have come to the fore as Arab intellectuals have sought to "translate" the very political concept of civil society. Not all of the issues of the day have grown directly out of the particular context of the Arab political and intellectual milieu, but many are the result of events largely external and beyond the control of Arab intellectuals. This fact gives rise to an important question: where does the impetus for the Arab interest in civil society come from? Are internal or external factors more responsible for this interest? Certainly, the extent to which any particular issue influences both the initial interest in the civil society idea and the way in which it is appropriated differs from case to case, as we will see in the chapters that follow. However, I think it is possible to characterize the onset of the interest in civil society on the part of the Arab intellectuals and activists discussed here in the following general terms. The contemporary interest in the civil society idea began outside of the Arab region, largely in Europe and the United States. As a result of their shared and individual experiences, Arab thinkers were compelled to search for a way of addressing the problems they faced within their immediate context. The debate over civil society, which was going on in other languages, began to be employed as a weapon in debates that were taking place at home.

One might say that the questions posed by Arab intellectuals are more their own than their answers—although the answers are made their own as they adopt and adapt the concept. However, this act of appropriation is fraught with numerous problems and questions, as acutely attested by one Arab scholar's attempt to find a workable conception of civil society for studying the Middle East:

> Whatever definition of civil society is adopted, it continues to present a problem once exported to Islamic societies (and no doubt in its countries of origin too). If, following Hegel, we view civil society as prima-

rily a factor in the process of state formation, how do we adjust that definition to situations where the state has indeed been 'imported' . . . and when in any case that state has seen its bureaucratic apparatus set up even before civil society in its Hegelian sense has come into being? Should we then follow certain Hegelian and islamicist sociologists in distinguishing two civil societies, the traditional one which did in fact give rise to innumerable traditional states, and the modern one, dependent, westernized, brought into being by the modern state and born with the original sin of its colonial parentage? Can we really speak of the co-existence, even the superimposition, of the rivalry or the conflict of two societies, one 'authentic,' the other artificially created?" (Salamé 1994, 12)

Ghassan Salamé's series of questions identify at least two types of issues—which I categorize as "external" and "internal," for lack of better words—that Arabs seeking to enter into the contemporary discourse of civil society face: those arising from the original context of the concept—that is, from Western political thought—and those already inherent in the Arab context. The latter provides the real impetus for the Arab interest in Western political thought; the former plays an important part in turning that interest toward a discussion of civil society, but also renders it problematic.

External Considerations

The first set of issues Arab "translators" face are those that arise from the tradition of Western political thought, the place of civil society within that tradition, and the relationship of that history to the Arab region. Arab scholars and intellectuals are very aware of civil society's foreign pedigree, as well as of the plurality of meanings it has held for different Western thinkers throughout history. As the last chapter illustrated, the concept has a somewhat ambiguous and definitely variegated history. As a result of the various shades of meaning given to this concept, as well as the sometimes very different uses to which the civil society idea has been put, Arab thinkers have had a wide range of possibilities from which to pick and choose their weapons for debate in the equally "live" political-conceptual arena of their own contexts. At the same time, the content of discussions of civil society in the West is such that Arab thinkers have not been able to appropriate without problems, hesitations, or questions. For example, Arab thinkers are aware that many of even the most liberal of liberal thinkers (such as Jeremy Bentham, James Mill, and John Stuart Mill) were among the most ardent enthusiasts of British imperialism, to which a considerable part of the Arab region was subjected.[3] In a similarly aggressive fashion, Karl Marx claimed that "England has to fulfill a double mission in India: one destructive, the other regenerating—the annihilation of old Asiatic society, and the laying of the material foundation of Western society in Asia"; and Friedrich Engels wrote that "the conquest of Algeria is an important and fortunate fact for the progress of civilization" (Avineri 1969, 43, 132).

However, one of the most important aspects of the Anglo-European tradition that Arabs who write on civil society face is the fact that an "East" has long provided a common framework against which thinkers have conceived of civil society in the "West," as well as "civilization" and "progress" (as Marx's and Engels' quotes above attest). As demonstrated in Edward Said's classic study of "Orientalism," "the Orient has helped to define Europe (or the West) as its contrasting image, idea, personality, experience" (1979, 1–3). This is true in classical political thought, with its notions of "Oriental despotism" and "Asiatic modes of production," as well as in discussions of the absence of civil society in the "East." According to Bryan Turner, "the debate about oriental despotism took place in the context of uncertainty about enlightened despotism and monarchy in Europe. The orientalist discourse on the absence of civil society in Islam was a reflection of basic political anxieties about the state of political freedom in the West. In this sense, the problem of orientalism was not the Orient but the Occident. These problems and anxieties were consequently transferred onto the Orient which became, not a representation of the East, but a caricature of the West. Oriental despotism was simply Western monarchy writ large" (Turner 1994, 34). Similarly, Richter argues that "the concept of despotism began (in the seventeenth

---

3. For a study of the relationship between liberalism and empire, see Uday Singh Mehta (1999).

and eighteenth centuries) as a distinctively European perception of Asian governments and practices: Europeans as such were considered to be free by nature, in contrast to the servile nature of Orientals. Concepts of despotism have frequently been linked to justifications, explanations, and colonial or imperial domination" (1973, 1). This argument corresponds to Said's assessment that "Orientalism is—and does not simply represent—a considerable dimension of modern political-intellectual culture, and as such has less to do with the Orient than it does with 'our' world" (1979, 12). The Orient, as the "other" of the West, becomes the perspective from which Western people reflect upon their world.

Patricia Springborg argues that "the East/West dichotomy drew upon important distinctions made by Greek thinkers in the Ancient period, particularly Aristotle, between Greeks and barbarians, freemen and slaves, types of entitlement to property and other rights" (1992, 1). She points to particular historical circumstances—most important, the advance of the Ottoman Empire into the heartland of Europe—as the source of the early modern juxtaposition of Oriental despotism and Western republicanism. With the rise of the early modern state, the East became a constant reference point for the West as the definitively different and characteristically despotic "other." This is seen most starkly in Western sociology, which attempted to account for the apparent absence of capitalism in Islamic society by conceptualizing that society as a series of social and historical gaps. According to Turner, "the orientalist view of Asiatic society can be encapsulated in the notion that the social structure of the oriental world was characterized by the absence of a civil society, that is, by the absence of a network of institutions mediating between the individual and the state. It was this social absence which created the conditions for oriental despotism in which the individual was permanently exposed to the arbitrary rule of the despot" (1994, 23). In fact, the theme of an absence of civil society in the East—that is, the notion of Oriental despotism—cuts across political and intellectual divisions in the West, providing a common framework for thinkers as different as Montesquieu, Mill, Marx, Weber, and Gramsci.

The classical Orientalist view posits a strong state and a weak society in a broad category of the "East." A few examples of this intellectual tradition must suffice here. Montesquieu's *Persian Letters* (1973) uses the Orient (specifically Persia) as a foil for discussing European despotism, which he identifies by the absence of intermediary organizations and social differentiation. Adam Ferguson suggests that the reason "there is scarcely a people in the vast continent of Asia who deserves the name of a nation" lies in the transitory nature of the associations they form (1995, 117). In *The History of British India,* James Mill observed that "among the Hindus, according to the Asiatic model, the government was monarchical and, with the usual exception of religion and its ministers, absolute. No idea of any system of rule, different from the will of a single person, appears to have entered the minds of them, or their legislators" (1975, 212). Gramsci distinguishes between the "West," in which there is a widespread consensus based on civil society, and the "East," where the state had to rely on coercion instead of consensus (1997, 238).

What explanation was given for the weaknesses of Eastern society? Although the notion of the absence of civil society was formulated in reference to the East as a whole, it played a particularly prominent role in the analysis of Islamic societies where the religion is identified as the source of society's weakness, as well as the source of the region's other peculiarities. Islam, according to this argument, consists of not only a religion, but also a way of life—ironically, the slogan of the contemporary Islamist movement, "Islam is a religion and a state" *(islam din wa dawla),* echoes the Orientalist view. This perspective on Islam is especially apparent in Max Weber's writings. In *The Sociology of Religion,* Weber (1993) suggests that the effect of Islamic expansion has been to convert that religion into a "national Arabic warrior religion," and thus he claims that the Islamic ethos "is inherently contemptuous of bourgeois-commercial utilitarianism and considers it as sordid greediness and as the life force specifically hostile to it." Weber (1958) believed that Islam was incompatible with the "spirit of capitalism"—that the patrimonial nature of Muslim political institutions precluded the emergence of preconditions of capitalism, such as rational law, a free labor market, antonymous cities, and a bourgeois class.[4] This view of "Oriental" difference was common among the classical economists and utilitarian philosophers of the nineteenth century. For example, Adam Smith (1976), James Mill (1975), and John Stuart Mill (1994) all thought that there exists a strong contrast between European feudalism and Oriental despotism, and that the political form of the latter gives rise to stagnant economic conditions that militate against the sort of capitalist development that one finds in the former. In addition to Islam as the cause for Oriental despotism, one finds Karl August Wittfogel's "hydraulic despotism" thesis (1957), which attributed the state's power over society to its organization of essential irrigation works.

The classical view of Orientalism continues to be found in contemporary scholarship. For example, Bernard Lewis argues that Islam discourages the formation of groups that might resist despotism since "Islamic law knows no corporate legal persons; Islamic history shows no councils or communes, no synods or parliaments, nor any other kind of elective or representative assembly" (1964, 48). Elie Kedourie describes Arab society as "accustomed to . . . autocracy and passive obedience," and thus incapable of sustaining the democratic culture necessary for civil society (1992, 103). This view of Arab-Islamic society has proved enduring, but the shock of the Iranian Revolution of 1979 and the growth of radical Islamic movements that have been challenging a number of Arab states since the 1980s have led a few analysts to reexamine the received wisdom. In the case of Iran, one could argue that the clergy, supporters of the clergy among the traditional bourgeois of the bazaar, and the new urban middle classes looked quite like an example of "civil society against the state"—one capable not only of challenging, but of toppling the state. As a result of these changes, the findings of recent political science research have begun to offer yet another view of "Eastern" state-society relations. According to Yahya Sadowski, the 1987 Social Science Research Council (SSRC) project to fund research on "Retreating States and Expanding Societies" in the Middle East grew out of a conviction that the growing weakness of states in the Middle East could provide new

---

4. For an excellent analysis of Weber's understanding of Islam, see Turner (1974).

opportunities for civil society to expand, develop, and assert its independence there (1997, 37). A number of recent works emphasize the strength of Arab society vis-à-vis the state (Sadowski 1997, 34).[5]

Sadowski finds a counterpart to the SSRC's rather optimistic view in the skepticism on the part of those scholars he designates as the "new Orientalists." Sadowski argues that "in the 1980s a new generation of Orientalists inverted some of the old assumptions and employed a new vocabulary which allowed them to link their work to a wider, international debate about the relationship between 'civil society' and democratization." In Sadowski's view, "these updated arguments sought to prove not only—as neo-Orientalist Daniel Pipes put it—that 'Muslim countries have the most terrorists and the fewest democracies in the world,' but that they always would" (1997, 34). In direct contrast to the earlier Orientalist works, the new Orientalists argue that the Arab-Islamic region is characterized by a history of a strong society that has consistently withheld its support from a weak political authority. Among the many examples of such scholarship that Sadowski points to is John Hall, who argues that the strength of society in Islamic civilizations has not only made the state unstable, but also hindered the development of civil society and democracy (1988, 29–31). According to Hall, Europe alone possessed an "organic state, a *stronger state,* in place over long periods of time, and forced to provide infrastructural services for society, because of both the preexistence of a civil society and the need to raise revenue to compete in war with other similarly stable states. In Islam such stable states did not exist. The fear of tribesmen meant that urban strata could not rule themselves, and a premium was accordingly placed upon military power. The states that resulted were transient and predatory" (1985, 102).

Gellner similarly maintains that the development of democracy

5. See, for example, Sivan's article (1990) that came out of the SSRC project, Migdal (1988), and Zoubir (1999). Goldberg, Kasaba, and Migdal argue that "in recent years there has been a variety of social movements and organizations that are trying to expand the spheres of social, political and civil rights, and to constrain the power of the states in many countries in the Middle East" (1993, 4).

(and capitalism) ultimately depends upon cooperation between state and society. Gellner (1979; 1981) modifies Weber's Protestant ethic to explain the origins of the modern state: rather than the rise of the modern economy, he claims that civil society, understood as a "civilized" assemblage of groups that expand production without threatening state power (as opposed to a raucous band of solidarities that check the state's tendency toward despotism), provides a necessary element in the development of the state. Thus, here too, the "East" is shown to be lacking— whether of a particular strength of state or a particular character of society—vis-à-vis the West.

In light of the fact that the history of Western political thought has conceived the Arab-Islamic state in connection with the theories of "oriental despotism" (Montesquieu), the "sultanic state" (Weber), the "Asian modes of production" (Marx), or, alternatively, has identified the Arab-Islamic state as weak and transient and its society as "raucous," it is not surprising that much of Arab democratic thought has been written in response to this history of "Orientalist" political theory, and Gellner's works, as well as the writings of a number of the other thinkers mentioned above, provide much fodder for the current discussions of Arab civil society. Such works problematize the debate over civil society in Arabic—not because of some problem they identify as inherent in the Arab region, but because they render Arab society as antithetical to, or unsuitable for, a political discourse Arab intellectuals seek to appropriate.

Internal Issues

While "civil society" signals a political concept that hearkens from Western political thought—with its colonialist and Orientalist history intact—both the tools for addressing the issues involved in translating it and the impetus for doing so arise out of considerations inherent to the Arab context itself.[6] So too, the Arab context presents its own limitations that bear on the appropriation.

6. The few works in English that deal comprehensively with the context of contemporary Arab thought include Laroui (1976), Arkoun (1988), Salvatore (1995), and Abu-Rabi' (1996). An excellent article by Ismail (1995) places Arab democratic discourse

The most common word one hears Arabs use in characterizing their contemporary context is *azma* (crisis).[7] A symposium held in Kuwait discussed "The Crisis of Civilizational Development in the Arab World" (Sahkir Mustafa 1974); the Moroccan historian Abdallah Laroui (b. 1933) wrote of *The Crisis of the Arab Intellectual* (1976); and the Center for Arab Unity Studies held a conference in Beirut on "The Crisis of Democracy in the Arab World" (Ibrahim 1984a). In fact, one of the earliest sustained discussions of civil society in Arabic places the concept in the context of the "crisis of freedom" and the "crisis of creativity [of thought]" (Karru 1992). Thus, in Arab political thought the crisis has been explored as a cultural, intellectual, and political phenomenon. The Moroccan philosopher Muhammad 'Abid al-Jabiri characterizes this sense of crisis in a way that captures the commonality underlying the various manifestations of crisis. Armando Salvatore (1995) characterizes this sense of crisis in the writings of Jabiri and other Arab intellectuals as a situation of profound uneasiness emerging from a feeling of disjuncture reached when one's fundamental framework of reference (the Arab-Islamic heritage, *al-turath*) is no longer capable of sustaining the claims of distinctions normally allowed by the framework or the demands of one's historical situation. The crisis, Jabiri (1989; 1999a) argues, is something that is experienced at the level of consciousness, as a form of cultural disorder in which the individual becomes increasingly unable to relate social and political ideas and values to his or her life situation. He maintains that the crisis is also apparent at the level of the current political, social, and economic reality in which societal institutions and structures are increasingly experienced as fetters denying the individual the opportunity to grow and to realize his or her potential. Many Arab thinkers, including Jabiri, diagnose the problem particularly as a "crisis of democracy" *(azmat al-dimuqratiyya)* whose symptoms are exhibited

---

against the backdrop of the notions of crisis, renewal, and authenticity, and I follow her here in my discussion of the discourse of civil society.

7. The Moroccan scholar Muhammad Guessous has said that "there is so much talk in the Arab world of crisis, al-azma, that I now refer to it as 'azmatology' " (Dwyer 1991, 15).

in the apathy, alienation, and passivity on the part of the masses, as well as in the limited participation and the repressive practices at the level of the state (Khalid al-Nasr 1983; Ismail 1995).

Many Arabs trace the onset of the "crisis" to the 1967 defeat of Egypt, Jordan, and Syria in what is known as the Six Day War against Israel. Despite efforts by the nationalist regimes to minimize the impact of this loss, it is considered by many to be a turning point in the history of the Arab people. The great Arab historian Albert Hourani observes that the event was experienced not only as a military defeat, but also as a kind of moral judgment: "If the Arabs had been defeated so quickly, completely, and publicly, might it not be a sign there was something rotten in their societies and in the moral system which they expressed" (1989, 422). Jabiri traces the sense of crisis to the failure of the Nahda project, which attempted to address the "backwardness" of the Arab and Islamic world when viewed in contradistinction to the modern West. Jabiri asks, "Why did the Muslims fall behind while the others—the West in particular—advanced?";[8] which immediately prompts the further inquiry "How do we catch up?" (1985, 35). Jabiri maintains that this is precisely the question that drove the Arab Nahda and calls for a renewal *(tajdid)* of this project based on new principles appropriate for the currently existing reality. While Jabiri employs ideas of both *nahda* and *tajdid,* in most contemporary literature, the former term tends to be more common among Arab modernists and liberals to mark a rebirth or awakening along modern lines, liberated from the shackles of the past (Jabiri 1989; 'Alim 1997). More orthodox Islamists, on the other hand, tend to prefer to speak of *tajdid* or *islah* (reform), to stress the need for the revival and revision of Islamic tradition in a modern setting ('Imara 1980; Hanafi 1981; Turabi 1993). Seyyed Hossein Nasr claims that "a renaissance in its Islamic sense would correspond to *tajdid* or renewal, which in its traditional context is identified with the function of a renewer or *mujaddid*"

8. The same question was posed by the Muslim modernist and Arab Nahda thinker Emir Shakib Arslan (1965), whose book title asked, *Why Did the Muslims Fall Behind While the Others Advanced? (limadha ta'akhkhara al-muslimun wa limadha taqaddama ghayruhum).*

(1979, 39). One important exception to this is the Islamist movement in Tunisia, led by Rachid al-Ghannouchi (Tunisia, b. 1941), which has given itself the name of al-Nahda.

The understanding of crisis articulated in Arab political thought corresponds to that found in Reinhart Koselleck's work on the European Enlightenment (1988), which presents modernity as a problematic, crisis-ridden condition and points to "critique" as a necessary accompanying manifestation of crisis. According to Koselleck, crises mark particular points in the unfolding of modernity and he nicknamed the period of change accompanying such crises *"Sattelzeit"* (saddle-period). Commenting on Koselleck's *Sattelzeit,* Keith Tribe writes that "before this transition period, there lies a conceptual field whose topography is no longer immediately comprehensive for us without exegesis and interpretation; after it, there exists a conceptual world in which we, more or less with justification, feel at home" (1989, 181). The attitude of needing to "catch up" suggests that the problematic is constructed on the basis of an understanding of the encounter as one between "unequal forces," with the weaker or lesser side—the Arabs—attempting to address the charge of inferiority vis-à-vis some greater or more advanced force (Ismail 1995, 94). There is a sense from the theorists of the Arab crisis that the onus lies on them to prove that Arab-Islamic political thought is compatible with such things as "progress," "advancement," and "civilization," or at least that the differences that do exist are not evidence of some fundamental absence or lack. According to Ismail, "proof" of this compatibility is often sought by establishing "conceptual equivalences" or alternatives for such things as democracy (which becomes *shura*), the social contract (which is said to be established through *ijma'* [consensus] and *bay'a* [an oath of allegiance]) and, most recently, civil society (1995, 94).

The sense of crisis is experienced by all aspects of Arab society, but intellectuals who wish to counter this trend of crisis commonly must also face the issues of *mu'asara* (contemporaneity) and *asala* (authenticity)—that is, the basic problem of how to catch up or rebuild Arab thought while still maintaining an "authentic" connection between self, community, and tradition. In fact, crisis, contemporaneity, and authenticity are concepts that commonly occur together in academic discourse. A conference held in Cairo, entitled "The Heritage and the Challenges of the Age: Authenticity and Contemporaneity," drew together all of these concepts in an attempt to delineate a common Arab-Islamic framework for facing the modern age (Yasin 1985).[9] "Authenticity" is understood as the opposite of "imitation," with different thinkers placing various emphases on whether the texts, ideas, and practices threatening authenticity are those containing foreign or native cultural elements.[10] For example, while some Islamist thinkers might suggest that the tension is between traditional, authentic values and modern, inauthentic (Western) values, many Arab liberal thinkers use the term *al-mu'asara* instead of *al-hadatha*, which is the term used for "modernity," in order to assert that the more important tension is not between authenticity and modernity (identified with the West) but between authenticity and the requirements of the contemporary age. As the review of Orientalism in the last section revealed, the "East" is commonly conceived as the counterpart to "Western" modernity. Roxanne Euben points out that "designations of

9. 'Ali al-Din Hillal (Dessouki)'s 1981 assessment of political science in the Arab world relates this concern directly to his field. He argues that "Arab political science faces two crises, a crisis of orientation and a crisis of authenticity. The first is methodological and the latter is substantive. The crisis of reorientation is related to the question of what paradigm should the discipline adopt? What are the questions that must be asked? And how do they reflect the state of the discipline? The crisis of authenticity is likened to the issue of specificity, the question of what makes Arab political science really 'Arab'. . . . A genuine social science, and in particular political science, reflects the needs and problems of its society" (1981, 14–15).

10. Issa Boullata recounts the tension within the notion of authenticity itself that is analyzed in a 1971 paper by Shukri Ayyad (Egypt, 1921–1999). Ayyad argues that the term *"asala"* was seldom used in Arabic literatures until the 1950s, when it came to signify, on the one hand, "individuality, invention and liberation from tradition," and, on the other hand, "the continuous preservation of original ancestral elements in one's culture." The two aspects are united in a notion of "personality" that suggests that individual innovation can only be understood through the collective personality in which that individual is incorporated (1990, 14–15). A nice discussion of the contemporaneity-authenticity tension in Islamic thought and its comparison to similar tensions in Western political thought is found in Lee (1997) and Salvatore (1997).

premodern, antimodern and postmodern have taken shape against the backdrop of western experiences and evaluations of modernity," which involved a "commitment" to such things as science, secularism, and the rational-bureaucratic state (1997b, 430). When viewed from this modernist perspective it is possible to argue that there is a sense in which modernity has "passed by" Arab-Islamic civilization. At the same time, most Arab scholars reject—wholly or in part—both the description of their society as "premodern" and the claim that they must adopt a Western framework of rationality, secularism, and politics to advance their civilization and meet contemporary challenges. The choice for these intellectuals should not be stated as one between "Mecca or mechanization" (Lerner 1958, 40).

Implicit in Jabiri's question of "how should we deal with the heritage?" is a question of how to remain authentic in a way that addresses both the Arab-Islamic heritage and contemporary reality. Salvatore argues that "from an Arab-Islamic point of view modernity entails the double dimension of a subject which is transculturally embedded in a Western-centered age, i.e., contemporary to it *(al-mu'asara)*, but also involved in a potentially universal, although still Western-based, process of qualitative search for the new *(al-hadatha)*" (1997, 226). Arab modernity can consist of neither an unproblematic adoption of Western modernity nor a wholesale opposition to it. Jabiri often uses the two terms together *(al-hadatha wa al-mu'asara)* to designate "modernity" as such, drawing attention to the fact that addressing both Western modernity and Arab contemporaneity—that is, addressing both Western hegemony and the pressing questions of their time—is a necessary facet of an Arab project of modernity. There is also an interesting body of literature that views the Islamic resurgence as a postmodern project (Akbar Ahmed 1992; Tibi 1995). However, my concern is not in finding the appropriate label for what is occurring in the Arab region, but in drawing the contours of contemporary Arab discussions of the appropriation of the modern Western concept of civil society.

Other projects, such as that undertaken by the Egyptian "leftist Islamist" thinker Hasan Hanafi (1991), attempt to construct a science of Occidentalism through which social scientists from the Orient could explore Western civilization with the aim of rising from being an object of Orientalism to devising it as a subject of their own. The contents and structures of European consciousness must be "relativized," he argues, in order to curtail their influence, while emphasizing the content and structures of one's own heritage. Hanafi believes this will serve to restore European thought's historical dimension—that is, it will refute its claim to universality and dominance, and thus returns Europe and its culture to what he terms its "natural size" (1981, 152–53). Hanafi argues that European modernity should not be considered as the only route to civilization, but as merely one of a number of parallel periods and paths in history, including Egypt, China, and other civilizations of the ancient Orient. Like Jabiri's project, Hanafi's method of Occidentalism seeks to draw from both the Arab-Islamic heritage and the experiences of Europe, but in a way that mediates the authority the latter has claimed throughout history, while still managing to address the modern age, and must be seen in the context of a reaction to the Nahda's appropriation of foreign concepts and ideologies that became increasingly problematic in societies confronting, first, colonialist aggression and, later, the shortcomings of postindependence states. This concern with formulating a critical-constructive method for studying both Western and Arab-Islamic political thought—which, in the hands of Hanafi, is elevated to an Islamic liberation theology—permeates all attempts to formulate a notion of Arab civil society.[11]

In addition to these ongoing intellectual projects, there is one recent political development in the Arab world—which is itself a response to the crisis—that has colored all attempts to mediate between the demands of the modern age and the heritage: the "Islamic awakening." The power of the Islamic movement in the Arab region has underscored the issue of authenticity, but in a way that puts those wishing to counter this crisis by appropriating from the Western tradition of political thought on a more defensive footing. For example, Arab thinkers of both Marxist and liberal persuasions have had to rebut charges that their ideas lack au-

---

11. A number of works have noted a high level of concern for methodology in Arab political thought (Butalib 1987; Ismail 1995).

thenticity and hence legitimacy. They have come to realize that grounding their ideas in authenticity has become increasingly important for their validation. One strategy employed by many to address this concern has been to disarm their critics from the outset by tracing the roots of Marxism and liberalism to the Arab-Islamic tradition. In regard to the civil society ideal, this concern for authenticity has led some thinkers to argue that the concept has roots in older, more "authentic" notions, as we will see in the next chapter. In general, the renewed interest in the question of authenticity has increased the pressure placed on all Arab intellectuals schooled in Western political thought to locate their ideas firmly within the historical framework of Arab-Islamic thought. Aziz al-Azmeh articulates the various forms this "authentication" can take: "[P]arliamentary democracy is presented as a simple revalorization of the *shura*, a process of consulting clan chiefs in early Islamic times, and rationality becomes the reclamation of the work of Averroes and of Ibn Khaldun, while freedom becomes a repetition of Mu'tazilite theological theses on free will, and socialism is made to stand in direct continuity with peasant rebellions of the tenth and eleventh centuries" (1996, 56). Nonetheless, at the root of this sometimes overly political and simplistic approach lies a genuine problematic that the most serious reformers and revolutionaries feel a need to address.

In addition to this larger phenomenon, there is, of course, the more particular context in which each of the thinkers discussed here is situated, with its immediate political problems that the particular writing is meant to address and its political actions that civil society is meant to contribute to. In discussing each translation of civil society, I delineate those issues specific to the context in which an author writes, as well as the individual's status in that milieu as they have attempted to negotiate among concerns regarding authenticity, modernity, and (Western) forms of domination that color the process of appropriating from a "foreign" intellectual tradition.

The Politics of Translation

In addition to these two sets of factors—external and internal—that influence discussions of civil society in Arab political thought, there is also a third issue, which is really the very first issue that Arabs face in translating this political phrase: What do you call it? Civil society is not *civil society* in Arabic. Any words used to express this concept in Arabic already carry with them their own set of "conceptual baggage." The ambiguity of the phrase most commonly associated with the idea of a self-ordered sphere of associational life—*civil society*—has to do at least in part with the conjunction of *civil* and *society*. One must ask not only "what is society?" and "what is civil?" but also at least two other questions: "which 'society,' or what aspect of society, is civil?" and "what are the societal aspects of civility?" The problem, as noted earlier, is not that the Arabs lack notions of civility or society, or even a concept like civil society. Rather, as discussed in the previous chapter, they have a number of related concepts and relevant works from which to choose as they attempt to enter into a debate that is already taking place outside of their language context. The Arab intellectual debates analyzed in the remaining chapters (4, 5, 6, and 7) demonstrate that the concepts one seeks to associate with civil society, as well as the phrase one chooses to signal the notion, are significant, both politically and theoretically.

According to Quentin Skinner, "if we wish to grasp how someone sees the world—what distinctions he draws, what classifications he accepts—what we need to know is not what words he uses but rather what concepts he possesses" (1989, 7). Skinner points out that one can possess a concept without having applied the corresponding term, just as one can correctly apply a term without possessing a concept that agrees to it. While Skinner rightly cautions against the making of inferences between the use of words and the understanding of concepts, the term chosen (or rejected) for designating a concept can be very telling in studies of conceptual change, especially change that occurs across cultures or languages. Skinner acknowledges the "systematic relation" between words and concepts: "the possession of a concept will at least *standardly* be signaled by the employment of a corresponding term." He maintains that "the surest sign that a group or society has entered into the self-conscious possession of a new concept is that a corresponding vocabulary will be developed, a vocabulary which can then be used to pick out and discuss the concept with consistency" (1989, 8). However, in translation the connection between words and concepts holds particular significance. As the translation of civil society into Arabic demonstrates, in the act of translating itself one can "possess a concept" and "self-consciously" play with words in order to contest a given formulation of that concept.

The introduction of a concept of political or social discourse into a new (foreign language) context constitutes an event that may precipitate politically significant conceptual change. One initial issue of debate is how to translate the concept's corresponding term into a similar term in the language of its new context. Often we attempt to avoid such translations and draw attention to the concept's original context by leaving the word that corresponds to the concept in the foreign context "as is," or, if necessary, transliterating it. We see this quite often in academic discourse where one speaks of *Weltanschauung, coup d'état,* and *virtù,* words for which we might find a corresponding term in English—even a word with the same root—but only at the price of distorting the sense and meaning of the concept.

Arabic has traditionally been averse to borrowing from foreign languages, both because of its conceived sanctity, which some argue is free from the "corruption" of lexical intruders, and because of its special homogenous morphology, which makes loanwords look awkward and unaesthetic. The guardians of the language, hoping to preserve its pristine character, prefer to meet new needs through such means as deriving neologisms from existing roots (for example, *radio* in Arabic is *ida'a,* from *da'a,* "to spread") or occasionally creating cognates that more closely correspond to classical Arabic form (for example, *television* in Arabic is *tilfaz* and *to televise* is *talfaza*).[12] On the other hand, Arabic's root-based system makes the creation of new words possible. Arabic language academies were established in most countries in the region during the latter part of the Arab Nahda in order to facilitate the introduction of new con-

12. It is worth noting however, that in common spoken discourse, one almost always hears "television" and "radio" preferred to the Arabic neologisms.

cepts into Arabic (Khalil 1985). However, many Arab thinkers, especially those who see themselves as carrying on the Nahda tradition, express concern about Arabic's failure to "keep up" (Laroui 1977, 156).

One sees the political significance of the relation between words and concepts in contemporary Arab political discourse about the concepts of democracy and civil society. As indicated in the last chapter, *democracy* and questions surrounding its translation have long provided a source of contestation in Arab political thought, and the more recent translation of *civil society* has both added fuel to that debate and changed it in fundamental ways. However, one difference between these two cases of political translations is that whereas the debate over *democracy* provides an opportunity for drawing conceptual equivalences—as well as creates a disjuncture between those said to champion *dimuqratiyya* and those who advocate *shura*—the debate over *civil society* has been more contingent on the translation itself and the (political) opportunity that translation has provided those engaged in longer-standing debates.

The international pressure toward democratization at least since the fall of the communist states in Eastern Europe has further electrified this more recent debate within Arab political discourse over democracy— what it means in general and its significance for the Arab region in particular. However, the introduction of *civil society (al-mujtama' al-madani)* into the debate has altered the constellation, as well as meaning and sense, of the available concepts. Not since the *democracy/shura* debate has a term and the question of its translation evoked such controversy. The interest in civil society cuts across religious, political, and social lines. The civil society idea has generated fewer rejectionist responses than the idea of democracy. Yet the two ideas most often occur together, according to the Lebanese sociologist Dalal al-Bizri: "little by little democracy has become inseparable from 'civil society' such that they have become two eyes searching as one for what can be done to deliver them from the great Arab plagues" (1994, 5). Some exceptions to this democracy-civil society coupling are noted in the chapters on Islamism (chapter 5) and Arab socialism (chapter 6). On the other hand, its controversy has not been as short-lived as, for example, the debate over corporatism, multiculturalism, or pluralism, though one hears now of *civic pluralism.* It is unclear why this is the case. Perhaps it is because the Arab region has such a strong tradition of nonstate associations. Perhaps it is because those corners of society that are most likely to reject "foreign" ideas are those most embedded in these sorts of associations—namely, religious groupings. Perhaps this is owing to the trailblazing accomplished by the debate over democracy since at least the Arab Renaissance that has been renewed in the past three decades.

There are also a number of historical and material conditions that seem to offer at least a partial explanation of why certain ideas are taken up or ignored, put to use or discarded at various times. In comparing the greater problems raised by the idea of democracy relative to the idea of nationalism in the Nahda period, even as wide sectors of Arab society were politically engaged, "It is fairly simple to shelve or play down the theoretical and doctrinal issues which are likely to divide a nation when it faces a foreign aggressor or usurper. It is far more difficult, especially in times of sober stock-taking and decision-making, to agree on a set of principles and mechanisms to ensure equal possibilities of self-expression and access to the levers of power for the citizens of a state which needs strong, centralized leadership in the solution of its urgent problems" (Enayat 1982, 125–26). Thus, despite the inherent tensions between nationalism and Islam's universalism, nationalism better served the interests of Arab societies in throwing off the yoke of colonialism. Lamenting the failure of democracy in the postindependence Middle East as early as 1956, Charles Issawi notes two tendencies in the region: to rely upon "government for the necessary guidance and initiative" in bringing about reform and to "seek a short cut by way of a military dictatorship" (1956, 41). As those states created in the name of nationalism (and, in most cases, secularism) are increasingly seen as part of the problem rather than the solution—as they have been by many since at least 1967—people seek alternatives. So it is no surprise that both transnational movements (such as Islamism) and substate forms of organization (such as civil society) have emerged in recent years as powerful currents of opposition and reform. Again the particular challenges of democracy "as a set of principles and mechanisms" are being debated.

What is clear is that the transportation or translation of this new concept/word, civil society, has both revitalized the long-standing debate over democracy and opened it up to further possibilities, a different constellation of conceptual weapons to wield on a more confused (and hence more fluid) battleground. Much of the debate again centers on the issue of the choice of the appropriate term for this concept, in order to signal the appropriate tradition being drawn from. Not surprisingly, the question of how to translate civil society was one of the most fervently debated topics in the first gathering of Arab intellectuals from throughout the region organized around the concept (Bin Sa'id 1992b). But the fact remains that individuals from all ideological traditions in the region are engaged in its translation.

Neither East nor West: Civil Society and Contemporary Arab Political Ideologies

According to Saad Eddin Ibrahim (1998), at the very outset there were "questions and suspicions about the term ['civil society'] coming from three quarters." First, the military in general and the Egyptian leadership with a military background in particular thought *civil society* suggested a counterpart to the military—for example, civilian society. Second, the Islamists viewed *civil society* as a code word for secularism, for example, secular society. Third, Arab Marxists saw *civil society* as a bourgeois liberal term, not surprisingly because in the Marxist tradition before Gramsci, *bourgeois society* and *civil society* (both rendered *bürgerliche Gesellschaft* in German) were often used interchangeably. In addition, most Arab intellectuals were sensitive to the issues they faced in appropriating a concept that had been used to contrast Western societies with their own. Nonetheless, with very few exceptions, each of these groups has come to adopt a discourse that includes a conception of civil society.

In the chapters that follow, I discuss the substance of the concept of civil society advanced by members of three broad ideological tendencies in the Arab world—liberalism, Islamism, and socialism—before embarking on an analysis of writings on civil society by Arab feminists from a range of ideological backgrounds. In their classic textbook on the topic, Terence Ball and Richard Dagger define ideology as "a fairly coherent and comprehensive set of ideas that explains and evaluates social conditions, helps people understand their place in society, and provides a program for social and political action" (2004, 4). For example, Islamists may offer an explanation of social disintegration based upon the failure of the community to adhere to religious principles, and thus call for the re-Islamicization of society. Arab socialists might explain social crisis as an outgrowth of a struggle between economic classes and requiring the intervention of either the state or a highly disciplined vanguard party, or the creation of a counterhegemony aimed at promoting equality in political and economic spheres. Arab liberals might understand social conflicts as evidence of the lack of freedom that can only be ameliorated by increased tolerance of difference and a democratic ethos. Ball and Dagger's definition outlines what ideologies do; Michael Freeden outlines more precisely what ideologies are: "distinctive configurations of political concepts" that "acquire meaning not only through accumulative traditions of discourse and not only through diverse cultural contexts, but also by means of their particular structural position within a configuration of other political concepts" (1996, 4). Thus we can identify and analyze ideologies at the level of concepts in relation to other concepts, traditions of discourse, and the historical, social, and political contexts that they intersect, draw from, and engage. But this understanding also suggests that ideologies are not the clear and well-demarcated "camps" they are often presumed to be, but rather it makes more sense to speak of ideological "families" or "groupings" that display a high degree of fluidity and are capable of diverse forms.

As discussed in the last chapter, one is able to characterize political conflicts in the Arab region beginning in the 1920s as having an increasingly ideological character. Salem identifies four ideological currents that competed in Arab societies during the period between the late 1920s and the early 1970s: Arab nationalism, Islamic fundamentalism, Marxism, and regional nationalisms (primarily Egyptian, Lebanese, and Syrian)—as well as accounts for the significant overlap and interaction among the groupings. Salem's account gives priority to nationalism, because the political imperatives of overthrowing colonialism, combating imperialism, and modernization led political actors in the region to look to macrostructures for reform. However, nationalism in this context—as elsewhere—takes many different forms and is entwined with many different ideologies. Since the Second World War nationalism has formed an important part of Arab socialism (al-ishtirakiyya al-'arabiyya), and Arab nationalism has long espoused a distinct form of socialism. So too, Islamism has shared the concerns of nationalists for unity and independence from foreign domination. Liberalism, conspicuous by its absence in Salem's typology but not absent in the Arab region, forms a central component of many of the regional nationalist trends he discusses. For example, Salem analyzes how Ahmad Lufti al-Sayyid (1872–1963) "promoted the idea of an independent Egyptian nation, organized according to the principles of liberalism, governed democratically, and linked educationally and culturally to Europe" (1994, 213). Sayyid, a self-declared disciple of John Stuart Mill and other nineteenth-century liberal thinkers in the West, provides the classic statement of early Arab liberalism: "A constitution is the nation's right, just as freedom is the right of the individual, and since every individual is born free, it must follow that the nation was also freely established since man is by nature a social animal. This right means the nation's right to govern itself in the way it sees fit, and this is a right which no one may infringe upon" (1963, 73–74). Contemporary liberals differ from nineteenth-century and early twentieth-century Arab liberals in some respects. For example, whereas early liberals prioritized the rule of law, contemporary Arab liberals tend to emphasize the necessity of instituting processes aimed at fostering increased tolerance of difference and a democratic ethos, and, further, one can detect a move from less statist approaches to ones that designate a nonstate realm as the locus of political reform.

Arab nationalism, or pan-Arabism, lacked a political program beyond independence until fused with liberal and socialist ideas (Hourani 1983, 357). The two most influential socialist trends in the Arab region, Ba'thism and Nasirism, each espoused a socialist ideology that gave priority to Arab nationalism. The Syrian intellectual George Tarabishi reflects back on how Arab socialists "embarked on the road of a nationalistically interpreted socialism": "When asked about the content of our socialism, we replied: our socialism is an Arab, nationalist one, not internationalist. And when we were asked about the differences between our socialism and communism, we answered: our socialism acknowledges mind and matter. We understood spiritualism as an idealistic value for which we adolescents strove and we understood our socialism as one which devoted itself to the whole people and not just the proletariat" (in Tibi 1986, 23). More recently—since at least 1967—nationalist ideologies have receded in importance, while other ideological groupings have become more prominent. Because of this fact, and because of the priority of nationalist aspirations in all of the ideologies during even the "age of ideology," I follow the lead of Ball and Dagger (2004) and other studies of ideologies that deem it better not to treat nationalism as a distinct ideology. I depart from Ball and Dagger in treating Arab feminists as joined not by a feminist ideology, but by a common feminist struggle against women's marginalization and subordination. Liberalism, socialism, and Islamism each emerged in response to the debates of the 1920s and has been apparent up until the present time. Yet secular nationalism remained the dominant ideology of the independence movements in the Middle East and it was the founding ideology of many of the states set up after independence. Further, by the 1950s Arab political and social thought was clearly dominated by Arab nationalist-socialism. However, beginning after the 1967 war and the "self-criticism after the defeat" (as Sadiq Jalal al-'Azm [Syria, b. 1934] so aptly puts it in the title to his famous book [1968]), the secular states are called into question by Islamic forces with growing vociferousness, and with the Iranian revolution of 1978–79 it became increasingly common to see Islamists as the primary oppositional force in Arab politics. A renewed Arab liberalism, both secular and in forms more accommodating to the rise of political Islam, reemerges at the same time in a less nationalist form. If the period from the 1920s to the 1970s emerges as the "age of ideology," one witnesses a period after the 1967 war until the present that warrants characterization as the "age of ideological reformulation."

These three ideological traditions—liberalism, Islamism, and socialism—are broad and fluid and the conceptual overlap between them is significant. Each deals with various "cluster concepts" in related but significantly different ways. For example, whereas Arab liberals have traditionally focused on nationalism *(qawmiyya)* as a unifying theme in the attainment of national independence *(istiqlal)* and saw modernization (often conceived as Westernization) as a means to that aim, Arab socialists focused on unity *(wahda)* and nationalism *(qawmiyya)* through a combination of Arabism *('uruba)* and populism *(sha'bi)*, and Islamists saw Islamicization and a return to the fundamentals *(usul)* as the basis of the only true unity *(tawhid,* the oneness or unity of God). Despite the family resemblances among the concepts that surround the orientative aspects of these ideologies, there exist wider divergences once we analyze the practical-programmatic aspects of each ideology. Each ideology characterizes both the external and the internal obstacles, as well as the means to overcome those obstacles, quite differently. Where Arab liberals lament the arbitrary rule of existing states and the backwardness of their societies, Arab socialists speak of imperialism *(isti'mar)* and reaction *(raj'iyya)*, and Islamists take aim at ignorance of Islam *(jahiliyya)* and disbelief *(takfir)*. Where Arab liberals seek political reform in order to establish constitutionalism, parliamentarianism, and the rule of law, Arab socialists seek a revolution *(thawra)* to establish a more just socioeconomic order, and Islamists engage in holy struggle *(jihad)* to renew *(tajdid)* and restore a balance *(tawazun)* and justice *('adala)* to the Islamic community *(umma)*.

Salem argues that the level of ideology in the Arab region "can be linked generally to the high level of strain and stress experienced at the individual level" (1994, 271). The parallels between the importance of crisis in engendering conceptual change and of increased strain and stress in increasing the spread or strength of ideology suggest that ideology can play an important role in conceptual change. Certainly, during periods of strain and stress ideology might become more visibly available as a resource for reevaluating concepts or putting them to different use by different groups. Yet it also seems possible that during moments of crisis, ideologies, like concepts, are more likely to be challenged. The research presented here suggests that one of the results of the current "crisis" in the Arab world is that these ideological groupings have become looser or less well defined at the same time that the importance of ideology both as a weapon used by one group against another and as a dynamic that conditions how individuals and groups view the world, independent of their interest, is being accentuated.

In the chapters that follow, I examine recent changes in the discourse of each of these ideological groupings, focusing on the arguments about, around, and with the concept of civil society, and the attempts to articulate an understanding of civil society both to explain sociopolitical changes and to steer it in a desired direction in practice. I also extend the discussion to analyze the ways in which their conceptual strategies have shaped and been shaped both by their ideological orientation and by their political practice. Specifically, in exploring the history of the idea of civil society in Arab political thought, I am interested in the question posed by the Tunisian sociologist Abdelkader Zghal, at a conference in Cairo that forms one of the subjects of chapter 6. Zghal asks, "what are the political and theoretical stakes of this concept?" (1992b, 41). In the best writings there exists a symbiosis between theoretical analysis and strategy. Ideology, to borrow Marx's observation about philosophy, seeks not only to explain the world, but also to change it. The writings discussed here are written in a specific context and broach, to varying extent, questions of tactics and strategy like Lenin's "What is to be done?" I attempt to define what the elements of strategy were in particular cases, and to highlight those available catchwords and especially categories of political discourse atypical in Western political discourse.

The thinkers dealt with here—consisting primarily of college professors, journalists, *ulama* (religious leaders), and activists—have a discernible impact on their society that exceeds their role as (elite) intellectuals. Those considered part of the "opposition" address not only the state, but also society itself, and the civil society debate has highlighted the importance of aiming one's message toward the latter sphere, as well as the significance of intellectual discourse for that sphere. The Moroccan author Fatima Mernissi (b. 1940) summarizes the importance of Arab intellectuals in categorical terms: "contemporary philosophers and ideologues like Muhammad 'Amara, Husayn Muruwwa [1910–1987] (who was killed a few years ago in Beirut), and Muhammad 'Abid al-Jabiri (one of today's most important thinkers) have become more well known in the Arab world today than hit singers and often more popular than the heads of state who try to repress them. The Moroccan Jabiri is probably the philosopher most read by Arab youths, if I can judge by the remarks of students in conference debates and informal discussions" (1992, 38).[13] This assessment seemed overstated to me until I witnessed firsthand Professor Jabiri, with 'Abd al-Kabir al-Khatibi (b. 1938), another Moroccan philosopher of note, pack a very large lecture hall at Muhammad V University in November 1995. Jabiri, who spoke for only about twenty minutes, was interrupted twice by applause. Transcripts of his and Khatibi's speeches were published less than two weeks later in at least one Moroccan journal and one newspaper. A similar scene occurred at the 1992 Cairo International Book Fair when prominent Islamists (Shaykh Muhammad al-Ghazali [1917–1996], Ma'mun Hudaybi [b. 1921], and Muhammad 'Imara) debated secular thinkers (Farag Fouda [1945–1992] and Muhammad Khalaf Allah [b. 1916]) on the issue of the role of religion in government before a crowd that reportedly drew an audience of tens of thousands.

While I do tend to focus on some of the best-known Arab intellectuals and on three of the most significant ideological traditions in the region, my aim in the chapters that follow is not so much to articulate the most "representative" view of these ideologies, nor to generalize about Arab liberals, Islamists, or socialists. It is beyond the scope of this study, as well, to determine the extent to which the intellectuals discussed reflect a broader public sentiment or are attempting to shape public opinion, whether they are responding to society's demand for more democratic political thought and practice or working against an existent undemocratic ethos. In some cases, in fact, the thinkers exist somewhat uneasily within the ideological traditions they draw from and engage in their interventions on civil society. For example, Muhammad 'Abid al-Jabiri's extensive body of philosophical works shows influences from Arab nationalist socialism as well as liberalism. So too, Hasan Hanafi sees

13. Mernissi (1992) speculates that the lack of Western interest in Jabiri and others like him results from the fact that he does not convey the exoticism the Western media looks for in order to depict a frightening, rejectionist Islam.

himself as part of the "Islamic left" (his own nomenclature), but one finds socialist as well as liberal concepts within his corpus. Yet Jabiri's most recent political writings draw most distinctly from liberal traditions in Arab and Western political thought and Hanafi defines his approach as first and foremost Islamic in source and content (2002b), and asserts his perspective as an alternative to less progressive Islamist projects. In the final analysis, my choice and placement of texts and thinkers has been determined by what I have found most theoretically interesting or innovative vis-à-vis the discussion of the concept of civil society, in order to fulfill the purpose of this study: demonstrating translation as an opportunity for conceptual and political contestation. Under these ideological groupings, particular aspects of civil society's travels and travails in Western political thought are emphasized or deemphasized according to the needs and interests of individual thinkers working in particular contexts and existing within particular political relationships with the state and with the other social-ideological groupings in society. We will see that, for Arab liberals, civil society is most importantly tolerant and democratic. For Islamists, it is most important that society be Islamic and that an "Islamic civil society" be independent from the existing uncivil (secular) state. Arab socialists seek to construct a civil society that provides a progressive force able to contribute toward the creation of a socialist counterhegemony. Finally, Arab feminists challenge aspects of each of these ideological traditions—and often directly the intellectuals and interlocutors—involved in perpetuating exclusive and patriarchal notions of civil society and democracy. What is striking about this current period of ideological reformulation is that all three traditions are engaged in a shared debate, not always in a civil manner, but increasingly drawing upon a common store of concepts.

4

Civil Societies and Arab Liberalisms

> Is it possible to establish democracy in a society that is not "civil," and is
> it possible to establish a civil society in a non-democratic form?
> —Muhammad 'Abid al-Jabiri,
>   *The Dilemmas of Democracy and Civil Society in the Arab Nation*

The Ibn Khaldun Center: Civil Society Untranslated?

Civil society in the Middle East has often been associated with initiatives
like that of the Ibn Khaldun Center for Developmental Studies in Egypt,
which in January 1992 began an important research program with this
title, as well as a monthly newsletter (in English and Arabic), *Civil Soci-
ety/al-Mujtama' al-Madani.* The Center's director, Saad Eddin Ibrahim,
defined civil society as consisting of voluntary, nongovernmental associations such as trade unions, professional syndicates, voluntary societies
and clubs, pressure groups, and political parties, which are said to act as
conduits for the peaceful expression and organization of members'
rights and demands vis-à-vis the state. Ibrahim is an American-educated
sociologist who seeks to present a view of civil society that is indistinguishable from that of mainstream liberal American political science's
version of civil society, since any deviation from that view would result,
he believes, in a watering down of the analytical value of the concept. An
essay by Ibrahim (1995) outlining this understanding of civil society and
its applicability to the Arab context, as well as an overview of the socioeconomic, state, nonstate, and external variables that suggest the region is
moving in a similar direction as other democratizing areas, has appeared
in English as part of a project funded by the Ford Foundation (Norton
1995) and in Arabic as the introduction to every country study the Ibn

Khaldun Center has published (for example, 'Abd Allah 1995; Abu 'Amr 1995; 'Ali 1996; Birah 1995; Fakhru 1995; Messarra 1995).[1]

Despite the importance of the Ibn Khaldun Center for Arab—and especially Arab liberal—discussions of civil society owing to its singular focus on the idea, the expanse of its projects, and its consistently liberal stance, the nature of its research precludes its discussion at length in a work on intercultural conceptual change and political theory. The concept of civil society, for Ibrahim, is understood and then applied to assess its absence or existence in the Arab context in a manner virtually indistinguishable from that of Western social scientists, except perhaps for the vast knowledge of the region he brings to the topic.[2]

This chapter focuses on the work of scholars who have taken a rather different approach. For these thinkers, civil society had to be interpreted in order to be applied to the Arab context. They viewed the "translation" of the concept into an appropriate Arabic terminology as part of that process of interpretation. The translation required to talk about this concept in Arabic is an opportunity for a different (from both Western social science and status quo politics) understanding—that is, for political and conceptual contestation among Arab political thinkers. As noted

1. Interestingly, the unity suggested by Ibrahim's introduction belies differences among the various scholars who write the country studies for the Ibn Khaldun Center. Compare Abu 'Amr (1995) and Fakhru (1995) on the role of Islamist organizations in civil society. This same lack of conceptual unity is apparent in the Norton volumes (1995; 1996). Compare, for example, Moussalli (1995) and Hinnebusch (1995) on the question of whether the most important aspect of civil society is its independence from, or connection with, the state.

2. This orientation suggests at least part of the explanation for why work of the center has been regarded with suspicion by some Arab intellectuals and activists in the region. Among those few Arab intellectuals who have discussed Ibrahim's work, it is often dismissed for tailoring its language to foreign funders and criticized for upholding the status quo, though his persecution in Egypt calls into question the latter point of critique ('Alim 1998; 'Azm 1998b; Traboulsi 1998). See also Sana' al-Masri's (1998) critique of the relationship between NGOs and foreign funding. She suggests that Ibrahim's work toward "normalizing" relations with Israel is motivated by his relationships with Western funding institutions. Both the left's critique of Ibrahim and his persecution by Egyptian authorities are discussed further in chapter 6 of the present work.

in the first two chapters, the "transition phase" of conceptual contestation amidst loosely formulated, partially translated understandings of a concept can prove more productive—and perhaps even necessary—for conceptual transformation than either the hasty appropriation (as in Ibn Rushd's claim that Cordoba after 1107 was "completely democratic") or rigid rejection of foreign terms (as in the claim of 'Ali Belhaj of Algeria's Islamic Salvation Front [FIS] that democracy is an alien concept). So too, the process of translating the concept reveals many of the constraints placed on Arab liberals as they attempt to adapt it to the needs and aims of their political context.

Arab Liberalisms

Unlike the Arab Islamists and socialists I discuss in the next two chapters, a number of the individuals mentioned here often do not refer to themselves under the category I place them. Following Leonard Binder (1988) and Charles Kurzman (1998), I use the "liberal" appellation as a "heuristic device." But unlike Binder and Kurzman, I do not see fit to use the term "Islamic liberals" in all such cases since, although most (but not all) are Muslim and write within a predominantly Islamic context, they are distinct as a group, not by virtue of this, but for their commitment to some form of democratic governance as a bulwark against tyranny (whether from state or society); their emphasis on personal liberties, especially freedom of conscience, speech, and expression; and their call for a more democratic, tolerant ethos. They also seldom, if ever, base their arguments directly on the authority of either traditional Islamic sources (such as the Qur'an and *sunna*) or the reinterpretation of traditional Islamic concepts (such as *shura* [consultation], *ijma'* [consensus], and *maslaha* [exigency], each of which have been asserted as components of an Islamic form of democracy), though some do occasionally address or draw from such sources in their work. Thus I refer to "Arab liberalism" as one would speak of French, German, or British liberalisms.[3]

Because of the features that they share with Western liberalism, as well as their untraditional forms of debate, Arab liberals are commonly

---

3. For a discussion of liberalisms in other national contexts, see Bellamy (1992).

grouped together—albeit wrongly so in the view of many of these liberals—under the appellation of "secularists" by Islamists. Certainly there are those among Arab liberals who define themselves chiefly by their secularism, such as the Syrian Christian thinker Farah Antun (1874–1922) and the Muslim Egyptian writer Farag Fouda. But most have a more complex or ambiguous relationship to secularism, as will be apparent in the discussion below, and are better grouped by the other aspects of liberalism to which they more consistently and vigorously appeal. Perhaps the most consistent element that defines Arab liberalism is an emphasis on toleration, especially religious toleration, for which they are criticized by both Islamists and Arab socialists: by the former because this means that they advocate a form of state that forgoes questions of the highest good (the realm of religion), by the latter because they insist that this does not involve a formal separation between the political and the religious.

The debate on Islam and secularism is one of the most sensitive issues facing liberal Arab intellectuals. A number of Christian writers, many of whom were Syrians who had immigrated to British-occupied Egypt in the middle and late nineteenth century to escape Ottoman rule, were the first to champion the concept of secularism. Shaykh 'Ali 'Abd al-Raziq, whose famous book *Islam and the Fundamentals of Governance* (1972) was published in 1925, is considered by many to have been the first Muslim scholar in the Arab region to uphold the concept of the separation of religion and state. The recent resurgence of Islamic fundamentalism has only served to further complicate this intense debate.

According to the Arabic Language Academy in Cairo, the Arabic term for secularism, *'almaniyya,* "is derived from *'alam* (world), and not from *'ilm* (science [or knowledge]), as some think, thus giving the wrong impression that science is opposed to religion" (Fauzi M. Najjar 1996, 2)—though both *'alam* and *'ilm* share the same root *('lm).* This nomenclature is preferred by most Islamists, as well as by Arab liberals who wish to avoid the Islam-secularism dichotomy altogether or to subject Islam to "scientific" modes of interpretation. In contrast, one Islamist Shaykh argues both for the use of the term *'ilmaniyya* (here meaning rationalism) and for its application to Islam in presenting an antisecularist perspective. Islam, he maintains, is a religion and a state as well as *'ilmaniyya* since it is a truly rational religion applicable to all realms of life (Shams al-Din 1994, 11). In order to avoid confusion, some writers have suggested an Arabic neologism, *'alamaniyya,* which draws attention to *'alam* as its source, whereas others prefer to render it *dunyawiyya,* meaning "that which is worldly, mundane, or temporal," in contrast to *dini,* meaning "that which is religious" (Najjar 1996, 2). Nonetheless, as Fauzi M. Najjar notes, "nowadays, Islamists have succeeded in equating [secularism] with atheism in the mind of the public, using it as a slogan to intimidate their political adversaries" (Najjar 1996, 2–3). For example, the well-known Egyptian Islamist Muhammad 'Imara argues that secularists are of two types: "the extremists, a minority, who reject religion altogether; and the moderates, the majority, who believe in God, may even observe religious rites and duties, but they advocate separation between religion and the state." The latter, he says, "are believers in God as Creator of the universe, and non-believers in Him as an administrator and ruler of worldly affairs. They are not absolute infidels, neither are they full believers; they believe in parts of the Book and disbelieve in others" (Najjar 1996, 6). Thus it is not surprising that so many Arab liberals adamantly insist that their perspective is not wedded to secularism.

There is also a more empirical or historical reason that Arab liberals find themselves in an ambiguous relationship with secularism. In the Middle East, secularism is associated with the state, first the various colonial regimes erected in the region, but more recently and perhaps more importantly from the perspective of contemporary Arab liberals, with the postcolonial Arab states as well. Secularism was intended to support state development projects and, in many cases, "did not seek to separate religion from politics" so much as it sought "to subjugate religion" and other social forces to political control (Vali Nasr 2003, 68). Many Arab liberals do their best to dissociate themselves and their ideology from this tradition, in some cases merely because secularism remains a "dirty word" in popular discourse (associated with atheism and military regimes), in others out of a desire to tolerate (or accommodate) the Muslim faith of the masses, and sometimes because they fear that secularism will act as a distraction from other, more pressing concerns.

Many also do not wish to repeat or buttress existing states' undemocratic policies aimed at controlling religious forces in the region. Yet, as the debate over civil society reveals, the more fervently Arab liberals assert that secularism *is not* the issue, the more markedly they prove the contrary.

Three Questions for an Arab Understanding of Civil Society

In January 1992, the Center for Arab Unity Studies (CAUS) in Beirut brought together intellectuals from throughout the Arab region in the first conference organized around the theme of "Civil Society in the Arab World and Its Role in the Realization of Democracy." As indicated by its name, the sponsoring organization was established in 1975 by intellectuals sympathetic to the Pan-Arab movement. According to the organization's pamphlet "the identity of contributors to the Center's activities is subject to no preconditions apart from the requirement that they believe firmly in Arab unity, whatever other beliefs and opinions they may hold. The Center represents a forum for free dialogue in which there is room for a full range of opinions."[4] Although the Arab nationalist ideology that formed the Center's founding principles tends to be associated with a socialist orientation, in the context of this organization, that ideological coupling has become much looser over time. As the CAUS has attempted to bring a wider range of perspectives into its conferences—not least of which includes a (liberal) Islamic perspective[5]—it has increasingly become a meeting place and conduit for the expression of what I am calling "Arab liberalism."

In his introduction to the proceedings of the conference, the Moroccan scholar Sa'id Bin Sa'id noted that disagreement, as well as "ambiguity and vagueness," surrounds discussions of civil society in the Arab region (1992a, 11). As noted in the last chapter, Bin Sa'id holds the view that one of the main tasks of political philosophy is to "authenticate" var-

---

4. This statement can also be found at <http://www.caus.org.lb/guiding.asp>.

5. See the various conferences organized around the theme of a nationalist-religious/Islamic dialogue (Bishri 1989; Center for Arab Unity Studies, 1995; 1999; 2004a; 2004b). This dialogue is discussed at greater length in chapter 6.

ious modern concepts that he acknowledges as having entered contemporary Arab discourse from modern Western thought. In the spirit of his mandate to "authenticate" as part of the translation of concepts, Bin Sa'id opened the CAUS conference with the suggestion that Arab intellectuals must address three questions to help disperse the confusion that clouds Arab discourse on civil society. The first question he identifies as a "theoretical" one regarding the concept itself: what is civil society—what organizations comprise it and what are the boundaries between "civil" and "political" society? This first question, perhaps better characterized as "definitional," seeks to delineate civil society as it is understood in the West.

Bin Sa'id then poses what he describes as a "theoretical-epistemological question" with "methodological" implications. Since the concept of civil society emerged from the particular historical experience of modern Western societies (an "outcome of the birth of the state" in its modern form and "the development of industrial society taking into account the historical development of each culture, society and country") in which it had a "particular philosophical and intellectual quality," Bin Sa'id argues, it remains necessary to inquire into "the forms of organizations Arab society has known in relation to the state in its particular historical experience—the experience of Arab civilization." He asks, "Is not the [Arab] scholar in a position to say whether [these forms of organization] have a form and conception other than those of [Western] civil society?" (1992a, 12). Bin Sa'id's second question calls for the identification of an authentic or indigenous Arab equivalent to Western civil society. However, by pointing out the methodological implications of this line of questioning, Bin Sa'id also intimates the stakes involved in prioritizing one tradition or one theoretical-epistemological position vis-à-vis the concept of civil society over another in discussing this "Western" concept in the Arab context.

Bin Sa'id's third question is one he sees as directly addressing some of the "practical and theoretical-epistemological" implications for the "social analyst": he inquires whether "civil society in its construction and basic structure is one society in the Arab nation—despite the fact that its various countries are many and diverse—or does it vary according to the different social forms and political structures in those countries?" (1992a, 12). He argues that this is both a practical and a theoretical-epistemological question in that it seeks to account simultaneously for "the arrival of modes of modernity in contemporary Arab society," "the struggle between the forces of closedness and the forces of openness," and "the nature and meaning of the public and the private" within each of the various Arab states and societies.

I will discuss four related attempts by liberal Arab intellectuals to address Bin Saʿid's three questions. Each focuses most attention on the second question ("What are the forms of social organization that Arab history has known?") as a way of approaching both a comparison of Western notions of civil society and an assessment of the prospects for Arab civil society. They each employ a particular discursive or definitional strategy and provide a historical narrative for delineating the nature, locale, boundaries, and strengths or weaknesses of Arab civil society. Although the debate among the liberal intellectuals is conducted in a manner that seeks to avoid the question of the relationship between religion and civil society, secularism proves to be a sort of red herring in the discussion—and democracy is thrown up as the red flag. These liberal accounts of civil society have been subjected to criticism by other more decidedly secular intellectuals, including other liberals, but perhaps more consistently by socialist intellectuals. Although leftist debates will be discussed at greater length in chapter 6, the work of one socialist intellectual, Sadiq Jalal al-ʿAzm, will be presented here, because it directly challenges nonsecular notions of civil society, as well as the liberal tradition, for what he deems an avoidance of the most important issues for democratic transformation.

Competing Translations of Civil Society

Authentic Civil Society: Kawtharani's Ahli Society

Among the papers presented at the same conference Bin Saʿid addressed, one that drew perhaps the most attention was written by the Lebanese scholar of Islamic history Wajih Kawtharani (1992). While in the past Kawtharani has been affiliated with the Arab nationalist ideology, today he considers himself to be a "liberal Muslim" (1998). It is worth noting that although he does identify himself by his religious as well as his political sentiment, and he may very well be considered closer to the Islamists than almost all of the other participants at the CAUS conference (which was attended primarily by liberal, socialist, and especially Arab nationalist intellectuals), Kawtharani is not considered (nor does he consider himself) a part of the Islamist trend (discussed in chapter 5). Importantly, he does not use traditional Islamic methods or sources of analysis. Rather, all of his academic training has been in modern schools of historical study, including advanced degrees in history from universities in Brussels and Paris.

Kawtharani begins his discussion by arguing that the translation of the term *civil society* invokes a conceptual ambiguity in the Arabic language. Kawtharani points out that in European languages there is a measure of conformity in both the linguistic and the conceptual etymologies among the terms *civic, civil, city,* and *citizen.* In fact, Kawtharani draws his linguistic examples from the French terms *société civile, civique, civil, cité,* and *citoyen,* but the fact that the etymology works just as well in English only underscores his point. Yet, in the Arabic language, one finds *madina* (city) and *madani* (civil), while the expressions *muwatiniyya* and *muwatin* that have been commonly used to translate *citizenship* and *citizen* are not derived from *madina* and *madani* but from *watan* (homeland or nation) (1992, 119–20). In the European context *citizenship* and *citizen* are two terms connected with the spread of the nation-state and with groups within the state that emerged in the modern period. However, the terms expressing the historical social and political relations in the Arab and Islamic heritage are *akh* (brother), *akhawiyya* (brotherhood), *ikhwan* (brethren), and *ahl* (kin), each of which is an expression indicating and growing out of a form of association that has as its basic characteristic the loyalty to the community or the group and an adherence to Islam.

The latter term, *ahl,* can also be translated as family, inhabitants, and natives and may even be used as a translation of citizen: it designates members of a group that are tied by close association and a shared space. *Ahl* (and its adjectival form, *ahli*) marks one of those concepts that are not easily expressed in English. On the one hand, *ahli* designates a sort of substate realm of communal life. On the other hand, *ahl* should not be equated with *private,* as in *private property,* which would be identified by the Arab word *khas* or *khususi.* Arabic maintains a distinction between *ahli, khas* (private), and *hukumi* (governmental). An example of this is seen in the distinction popularly made between two types of mosques in Egypt: those that are "government" *(hukumi)* and those that are "private" or "popular" *(ahli).* The first are those subsidized by the government and staffed by imams who are civil functionaries, while the second—described as *ahli,* not *khas*—are built and supported by local initiatives, and their imams are chosen by the community (Gaffney 1997, 260–61). In the same sense, two leftists parties, the Egyptian Tagammuʿ Party and the Jordanian People's Democratic Party, each publish a newspaper called *al-Ahali* (the plural of *ahli*), which is best translated as "of the masses." So too, Arabic distinguishes between what is *ahli* and what is *ʿamm,* the latter of which is generally translated as "public," but is better understood as "for the public," such that we speak of public welfare *(maslaha ʿamma)* in contrast to private interest *(maslaha khassa).*

Kawtharani suggests the use of the term *al-mujtamaʿ al-ahli* (from *ahl*) for civil society, because, in his view, it better captures the form of the historical relationship between traditional Arab societies and the state: the former comprising the historical space for the generation of social life, culture, commodities, and relations of exchange, and the latter representing the ruling force, organization, and policing of those interactions (1992, 120). This is not a new argument for Kawtharani. Much of his earlier work focuses on this realm of socioeconomic networks that emerged in order to manage public services independent of the Ottoman state. In the thesis he submitted in 1985 for his doctorate *dawla* (the highest degree in Lebanon), he juxtaposed *al-mujtamaʿ al-ahli* with the military sector of the Ottoman state (1988, 55–56). Nonetheless, the conference represents the first time that Kawtharani had discussed *al-mujtamaʿ al-ahli* normatively and had placed it in the context of contemporary discussions of democracy and civil society.

In Kawtharani's view, *al-mujtamaʿ al-ahli* in Arab-Islamic social-political history is what best corresponds to the modern concept of civil society as the symbol of the independence of society from the state through autonomous—or at least quasi-autonomous—associations and organizations. He traces this formulation to the works of Ibn Khaldun. In the *Muqaddima,* Ibn Khaldun argues that tribal society was egalitarian and nomadic, and held together by an intense sense of social solidarity *('asabiyya),* a form of cohesion that functioned outside of and in spite of the state structure (1992, 120). Ibn Khaldun identifies various solidarity groupings *(ahl al-'asabiyya)*—guilds, tribes, brotherhoods, and sects—that formed the institutions of social interactions, the means of production and exchange, the modes of cultural and intellectual and legal struggles, and the expressions of political and cooperative action, and which enjoyed relative autonomy from the centers of power in the Arab region during the period of the Ottoman Empire in the nineteenth century. Using a similar concept, although preferring the locution *al-mujtama' al-madani,* a Yemeni intellectual attending the conference argued that tribes, with their customs, traditional electoral arrangements, and division of labor practices, comprise the oldest institutions of civil society in Yemen (Mutawakkil 1992, 588).

Kawtharani offers this historical account of Arab civil society as a counterpoint to Western notions of "oriental despotism" (Montesquieu), the "sultanic state" (Weber), and the "Asian modes of production" (Marx), more recently resurrected by Huntington (1996), which argue that the Arab-Islamic state firmly held the reins of society with a powerful grip. At the same time, Kawtharani affirms in part Gellner's well-known description of traditional Islamic social formations, while disagreeing with Gellner's (1994; 1981) negative assessment of them. According to Kawtharani, traditional Arab civil formations existed within a public space shared by merchants, guilds, and Sufi (mystical) orders and sects, and within traditional rural group formations made up of peasants, tribes, and families (1992, 123–28). He also points to traditional Arab-Islamic formations that resemble the notables that make up Montesquieu's *corps intermédiaires,* in what the Arabs call "those who loosen and bind" *(ahl al-hal wa al-'aqd),* the elders and other notables who played an important role in mediating intercommunal affairs and as advisors to those who rule. The most important of these are the ʻulama (men of religion).

Kawtharani points out that these various social solidarities, which existed primarily along religious, occupational, and ethnic lines, were historically quite autonomous from the central authority, whose function remained limited to the collection of taxes or tribute, the administration of shariʻa (Islamic law), and the maintenance of public order and defense.[6] The "state" was not considered responsible for social services and had no direct economic function; these affairs were left mostly to the local communities. According to Kawtharani's account, society under the Arab-Islamic state was furnished with a considerable degree of independence from the state despite the fact that the state itself was one of power and coercion. These groups formed diverse centers of power outside of the state and possessed a sufficient level of internal organization and assertiveness to resist arbitrary exercises of state power if necessary. In other words, Kawtharani identifies various social groupings in Arab history that performed the function of at least one conception of modern civil society organizations vis-à-vis the state.

In the context of the CAUS conference, Kawtharani claims that his "correction" and his comparison between these two terms are "not intended to substitute, nor even state a preference," between al-mujtamaʻ al-madani organizations and al-mujtamaʻ al-ahli associations. Neither is this retrieval of the historical manifestations of al-mujtamaʻ al-ahli aimed at providing a historical model for modern civil society (1992, 129). Rather, Kawtharani argues that his work is intended as a critical history that best shows what traditional Arab civil society (al-mujtamaʻ al-madani) is and is not. It was not what took place in Europe: interest groups using their power to advance their claims through the state machinery and to acquire legal rights and official recognition of their status. But neither was its independence negated and its dynamism destroyed by a "sultanic state" that oppressed society and extended into its farthest

---

6. Similar accounts of the history of state-society relations in the Arab region are presented by Ibn Batuta (1969), Lapidus (1984), and Zubaida (1989).

crooks and crannies, as the theory of Oriental despotism contends. Rather, both the state and civil society derived their boundaries and functions from the primary principles of religious law *(shari'a)*, which was said to transcend the interests both of the state and of civil society. In other words, Kawtharani's historical narrative assumes and responds to two different "counter-discourses": one that has taken place in the West (in the works of Montesquieu, Hegel, Marx, Weber, Gellner, and others) about the East and a second that has taken place in the Arab region about the experiences of Europe that it asserts as a model. The second foil remains unidentified, but would seem to be both those early Arab modernists who viewed the state as vehicle for the modernization of society and those contemporary modernists who continue to look to the state as the last bastion of rationality against the popular strength of political Islam.

Yet, despite Kawtharani's declaration of political innocence in this debate, he has separated these two civil societies and provides no way of reconciling the two, thus forcing the very political choice of prioritizing one civil society over the other. In fact, as the other conference participants begin to discuss his paper, lines begin to form between two camps: those who accept the idea that traditional (predominantly religious) associations could contribute toward democratization and those who do not.[7] Kawtharani's expressed desire as a historian to set the record straight through this "academic exercise" is undermined during the ensuing discussion, where he suggests that the formulation that presents a more "authentic" and thus more "possible" form of a modern civil society is the one that has its basis in *al-mujtama' al-ahli,* the informal network of relations based in the more primordial associations of kinship, tribe, village, and religious communities.[8] Kawtharani moves the discus-

---

7. Compare the favorable comments by Khalid Ziyada, Ahmad Sidqi al-Dajani, and Majdi Hammad to those of Mustafa Kamil al-Sayyid, Hasan Tawfiq Ibrahim, and Riyadh Qasim who reject *ahli* society as the basis for democratization (Bin Sa'id 1992b).

8. Recent research by various liberal democratic Lebanese political scientists is confirming Kawtharani's characterization of civil society in that country. For example, Ziad Majed maintains that "virtually all of the non-governmental organizations established

sion of civil society into the debate about authenticity and, ultimately, into questions of Islamic legitimacy. In the process, he shows that Islamic history provides for a dynamic interaction between two distinct spheres, neither of which claims a monopoly over political or religious authority.

Kawtharani's claim to be merely setting the record straight at the CAUS conference is further belied by his more recent book, entitled *The Project for an Arab Resurgence, Or the Crisis of Transformation from a Sultanic Praxis to a National Praxis.* Kawtharani reprints his conference contribution in this later work with only one change: the omission of the two paragraphs qualifying his intentions regarding *al-mujtama' al-ahli* (1995, 85–102). While agreeing that the Ottoman legacy left a "sultanic" state in the Arab region, Kawtharani argues that this system of rule maintained a balance between state and society through its ability to integrate local mediators of authority *(wasa'it al-sulta).* He points in particular to the presence of a relatively independent court system that allowed the limits of political power to be defined largely by local urbanites (1995, 88–91). In the later work, Kawtharani assumes continuity between traditional and modern social forces in calling specifically for the reinvigoration of informal civil associations (Islamic and non-Islamic) as a means of forging a social contract within Arab societies (1995, 100).

A few scholars have adopted the appellation of *al-mujtama' al-ahli* as a way of discussing this realm of voluntary social activity in a broader sense than that suggested by *al-mujtama' al-madani* (Kandil and Ibn Nafisa 1995; Ashraf Husayn 1996), and some have even adopted a conception of *ahli* society that closely resembles Kawtharani's (Shukr 1997; Zahran 1997). One of the most interesting uses is found in an article published in a journal Kawtharani edits, *Minbar al-hiwar,* where the head of the Supreme Islamic Shi'a Council in Lebanon, Shaykh Muhammad Mahdi Shams al-Din, uses the two phrases *(al-mujtama' al-madani* and *al-mujtama' al-ahli)* interchangeably (1994, 24). Conversely, Farid Zahran, a leftist Egyptian thinker and Tagammu Party member, adopts

---

during the war in Lebanon, as well as a number of prewar citizen groups, were rooted in extended family groups, neighborhoods, or religious organizations" (1998, 39).

the language of *al-mujtama' al-ahli* to articulate a critical understanding of Egyptian group activity throughout history, which he claims is characterized by the worship of the personality of the leader, president, or director, and thus a negative force throughout Egypt's history that must itself be fundamentally reformed. However, the most common phrase used to designate civil society in Arabic is *al-mujtama' al-madani*, which derives from *madina* (city) and *madani* (civil). In fact, this was the wording used in the title of the conference in which Kawtharani spoke and was left as the title of the published proceedings of the conference, despite Kawtharani's arguments. Further, Kawtharani's very political translation did not go uncontested, either at the CAUS conference or in writings subsequent to the conference.

Modern Civil Society: Jabiri's Society of the City

In contrast, to Kawtharani's *ahli* society, the Moroccan scholar Muhammad 'Abid al-Jabiri claims that it is a "basic and self-evident fact . . . that civil society is, first and foremost, the society of cities [*mujtama' al-mudun*]; its foundations are those that people (voluntarily) establish among themselves in the city in order to regulate their social, economic, political and cultural life" (1994, 116). Jabiri draws upon the meaning of *madani* as city-dwelling or urban. According to Jabiri, civil society is the "antithesis of the foundations of the village (Bedouin, tribal) society which is distinguished by its 'natural' basis; [in the latter] the individual is born a member of it and is firmly embedded in it." As such, civil society represents the antithesis of Khaldunic forms of solidarity, because it is based on legally inscribed patterns of association that are voluntary (Jabiri 1994, 117).

Jabiri also draws connections between civility, civilization, and civil society. *Madani* also contains the same root as the verb *madan*, meaning to civilize or refine. Thus, *al-mujtama' al-madani*—civilized society—is used to refer to a particular kind of modern, nonviolent, rational political order. This modern civilized society is contrasted in Jabiri's writings with both *al-mujtama' al-badawi*, referring to Bedouin society, the society of the nomadic Arab tribes to whom Ibn Khaldun attributed great civility, and to *mujtama' al-sahara*, the society of the desert, with its connotation of an unrefined, even savage, life. In another article, Jabiri specifies that by civil society he means "the society which organizes the relations between individuals on the basis of democracy . . . that practices rule on the basis of a political party majority and respects the political, social, economic and cultural rights of the citizens—in other words, a society in which there exists established modern institutions such as a parliament, individual issues, parties, elites, publics, etc." (1989, 6). Civil society, for Jabiri, represents the realm of voluntary associations that foster individual autonomy and provide experience in exercising social and political rights and responsibilities.

Jabiri, like many Arab intellectuals of his generation, uses a Marxist-inspired historicism in his arguments, while reaching conclusions that resemble most closely those of Western development models.[9] Jabiri draws from both liberal and socialist discourses, as is apparent in the conclusion of his critique of "fundamentalist," "Marxist," and "liberal" contributions to political thought: "I believe that we ought really to set the problematics as follows: how can contemporary Arab thought regain and reinvest the rationalist and the 'liberal' gains from its own tradition—in a similar perspective to that within which they were invested the first time: the struggle against feudalism, gnosticism, fatalism, and the will to found a city of reason and justice, to build the free, democratic and socialist Arab city?" (al-Jabiri 1999a, 129). However, as is apparent in his writings on civil society and democracy, Jabiri's most recent political interventions are best situated in a liberal discourse.

The historical narrative that Jabiri offers is one based on "the rapid succession of elites, with each new elite taking the form of an antithesis emanating from within the last" (1994, 119). Jabiri recounts that the colonialists' modernization project gave rise to an elite class from the core of the traditional urban aristocracy. This elite class eventually led the nationalist movement, but continued the modernization project after independence. Before long, their policies gave rise to its own antithesis/opposition. Leading this subsequent opposition were elements

9. For a discussion of this form of theorizing in the works of Jabiri, as well in his fellow Moroccan Laroui, see Binder (1988).

associated with the circle of the traditional urban aristocracy, but the majority of the opposition was made up of individuals who inhabit the cities as a result of immigration from the countryside. Jabiri has in mind here the Free Officers' Movement, whose members toppled numerous regimes in the Arab region, and a general phenomenon where an army creates both its state and its party in its image, which he contrasts with the Soviet model of creating a state and an army in the image of the party (1994, 121). However, soon another "new 'opposition' came into existence in the form of a new elite, springing to the surface, as if at its appointed historical juncture with the failure of the adherents of the 'revolutionary state.' The ruling elite did not find anything with which to meet the popular demands except excess of 'tyranny'. . . . [And, in turn,] voices grow in demanding democracy, in most cases resounding from the old ranks of elites. However, the voices of most extensive duration and most powerful reverberation in the present time are those which raise the banner of 'Islam is the solution' " (1994, 122). This latest "opposition" is found in the rise of political Islam, which emerges from the same process of development as the last, that is, urbanization, increased education, economic competition, and secularization. Jabiri's concern is with breaking the cycle so that the next political transformation does not lead to yet another undesirable alternative.

Jabiri's historical narrative attributes the cycle of undemocratic states to the weakness of Arab civil society and the general vulnerability of the Arab (and Islamic) *civis* in the face of the strangleholds presented by both rural society and the state. In his view, both the state and society's primordial associations represent spheres of authority and coercion that hinder the development and exercise of individual autonomy. Thus, rather than challenging the authority of arbitrary rule, Jabiri argues that traditional groupings in Arab society more commonly provide vehicles of supplication and collaboration, especially when the groups' atomized chiefs struggle to secure the sponsorship of elite patrons. In addition, they contribute to the personalist and inefficient nature of supposedly modern organizations. As a result, Jabiri argues that the problem that distinguishes the Arab world is that rural society *(al-mujtama' al-badawi),* with its institutions, values, customs, and demographic predominance, has been and remains the "hegemon," and that this is so not only in the countryside, but also in the city itself, where the rural inhabitants have emigrated. In other words, Jabiri presents traditional social formations as the "problem" to which civil society *(al-mujtama' al-madani)* provides a solution. Jabiri poses the dilemma for contemporary Arab discourse on civil society in the form of a question that captures the dichotomy: "Is it possible to establish democracy in a society that is not 'civil,' " and is it possible to establish a civil society that is not democratic?" (1993, 4). The history he outlines provides evidence of the lack of society's "civility" and the dearth of "democratic practice."

Yet if, as Jabiri suggests, civil society (and democracy) cannot be expected to emerge from either a "state experiment" or from (traditional) social activities exerting power to limit the state, where does he hope to see it emerge? Jabiri is somewhat vague on this point. The problem of "moving from non-democratic circumstances . . . to true democratic circumstances" requires a solution that, he maintains, is necessarily different from the " 'natural' historical transition" he identifies with modern Europe. Framed as such, Jabiri seems to suggest the possibility of an "artificial" (as opposed to "natural") solution to the problem, that is, a solution that does not seem to get completely beyond the statist approach to political reform so common among liberal intellectuals, even those of a liberal stripe—one which Jabiri himself seems to criticize with his recounting of the region's history of revolutionary transformation from one form of undemocratic rule to another (1993, 5). At the same time, Jabiri seems to hold out hope that the exercise of such things as an urban ethos, or civility, and competition in economic and social spheres might form a precursor to the expansion of a democratic and civic ethos—which suggests a form of sociohistorical acculturation. Based on Jabiri's earlier writings (1984), this acculturation would most likely involve some form of renewal of "Arab reason," the development of a critical rational faculty that strikes a balance between the Arab-Islamic heritage *(turath)* and Western modernity in meeting the needs of the contemporary age.

In the works of Kawtharani and Jabiri we are presented with notions of civil society that exist in tension or competition with competing visions of society: *al-mujtama' al-madani* juxtaposed with *al-mujtama' al-ahli,* or modern or Western civil society juxtaposed with traditional or authentic civil society, in the work of Kawtharani; and the society of the city juxtaposed with the society of the village, or civil society with rural society, in the writings of Jabiri. Kawtharani's archaeology demonstrates that "the roots of civil society lie deep in the historical depths of the Arab consciousness and [that] this consciousness of history is the precondition for continuity and renewal, as well as critique or overcoming of the past" (1992, 129). It is important to note that Kawtharani too wants to do more than just affirm traditional socioreligious formations, though he certainly sees them as the most likely starting point. In contrast, Jabiri places these two renditions of civil society in a direct dialectical relationship through a historical narrative that remains critical of Arab political culture at the level of both the state and society as he searches for a way to bring about the replacement of rural, traditional formations by modern social and economic formations in the city to contribute toward the simultaneous emergence of both civil society and democracy in Arab politics.

Hybrid Civil Society: Ghalyun Joins the Madani to the Ahli

In his contribution to the civil society conference in Beirut, the Syrian political scientist Burhan Ghalyun (b. 1945) takes a critical view toward attempts to contrast *madani* society with *ahli* society—that is, to limit the former with modern organizations and structures such as parties, trade unions, and human rights associations and equate the latter with "carriers of traditional values" that are said to be religious, tribal, or regional in nature. He views this distinction as an attempt by champions of civil society to revive the doctrine of modernity, which has suffered as a result of the failure of the socialist-nationalist projects in the Arab region. Ghalyun charges that this revival, clothed in democratic rhetoric, is sought through a new alliance between modern elites who fear social demotion and a monopolistic state that claims to be the only guarantor of modernity and rationality (1992, 733–35). Calling more statist perspectives (such as that of Jabiri) to account, Ghalyun presents a view of civil society as a sort of "unofficial society" that encompasses all economic, cultural, and religious institutions falling outside the purview of ruling authorities and thus able to act under conditions that permit them to expand their activities and compete with each other (1992, 738).

At the same time, Ghalyun questions the view of civil society itself as the reservoir of democratic practice and freedoms. Rather, he argues, civil society is characterized by a diversity of groups and individuals, partial and imperfect solidarities, and various forms of competition and contradictions. According to Ghalyun, Arab society is in this sense a hybrid society *(mujtama' hajin)*, and thus civil society must be viewed as encompassing both communal and familial formations in Kawtharani's conception and Jabiri's more "modern" and "urban" civil associations. Distinguishing between the *madani* and the *ahli* to the detriment of the latter, as Jabiri does, in Ghalyun's view runs the risk of truncating society's strength and depriving it of much of its natural and creative capabilities (1992, 736–39).

Ghalyun locates this same destructive approach in the modern bureaucratic state, which rather than addressing and surpassing the diversity emanating from its society has attempted to eliminate its expression: "The socially alienated state fears its own society and views every move or whisper coming from civil society as political opposition, a rejection of state authority and a direct threat to the existence of the community, the nation and the revolution. As a result, the state has turned inward, toward its own coercive forces, which are developed at great expense, not to provide for the needs of society, but to better crush it" (1992, 744–45). Rather than organically developing out of the expression of this hybrid society, the modern Arab state has sought to artificially "develop" social consensus by extending its bureaucratic reach and interpolating the state for civil society (Ayubi 1995).

Ghalyun admits that his assertion of a broader notion of civil society is in large part strategic (1992, 751–54). He maintains that the only way to circumvent the state's reach is to support civil society structures that have been revived by largely Islamist social forces, such as the mosques, *zawiyyas*, brotherhoods, and other religious orders that provide a dynamism lost in the more modern civil associations, which remain dominated by nationalist and socialist elites still struggling with their relationship with the modernizing state (1992, 750). To exclude these populist forces would amount to yet another attempt by the dominant elite to relegitimize its own authoritarianism in the name of protecting the integrity of society and the unity of the state. In this respect, he shares a common starting point with Kawtharani.

According to Ghalyun, the problem of contemporary Arab politics derives from an absence of normal political discussion in the aftermath of the "sacralization" of politics by the military regimes in power since the 1950s, an absence that has given rise to the further "sacralization" of politics in the response of the contemporary Islamist movement (1991, 59–60). He argues that only democracy provides a model for the development of a majority consensus regarding the principles of state-society interaction and for regulating the state. Democracy "desacralizes" politics by presenting the state as the procedural basis of politics, but not itself the source of authority and legitimacy. State institutions provide the procedural framework for generating the expression of and correspondence between the values and goals of official politics, on the one hand, and of the unofficial politics of civil society, on the other (1991, 441). What Ghalyun deems more rightly termed "politics" consists in the collective activity that draws from the hybridity of "civilizational" *(hadariyya)* spheres that support and are supported by the state that grows out of them. Further, since politics must draw from the values of society and religion provides a source of values, religion has a role to play in politics (1991, 415).

Civil Society in Light of the Ruralization of the Cities: Falih's Return to the Ahli

In a book-length study of what he terms "the ruralization of cities" *(tarayyuf al-mudun)* in the Arab region, the political scientist Matruk ibn Hayis al-Falih (Saudi Arabia, b. 1953) returns to what he describes as Kawtharani's "attempt to replace *al-mujtama' al-madani* with *al-mujtama' al-ahli*," in order to affirm that the former "is connected with the western experience of development," while the latter refers to "civil formations in the framework of Islamic cities" (2002, 30).[10] In one respect, Falih's argument echoes that of Jabiri in that he attributes the ineffectiveness and weakness of civil society in regard to its ability to bring about democratic transformations to the influx of rural values and populations into Arab cities. Yet, unlike Jabiri, he faults intellectual discourse with popularizing the term *al-mujtama' al-madani* and thus excluding that which has origins outside the city—that is, in the countryside—as well as that which is traditional or religious (Falih 2002, 172). Falih aims to "popularize the idea of *al-mujtama' al-ahli*," which he argues provides a preferential frame for the work of state and society," because it includes forces described by "the city" *(al-madina)* and "the countryside" *(al-rif)* as well as the traditional and the religious. Like Ghalyun, then, Falih seeks hybrid forms of social forces or, as he puts it, "those points of intersections between the Arab countryside and city" to push for political reform (2002, 34).

While Falih provides considerable evidence to support his argument that Arab cities are being "ruralized," he provides no evidence that these *ahli* social formations that have resulted from ruralization of the cities are proving or will prove any more effective and significant a force than the weak and "nearly nonexistent" Western-style civil society of the cities, in bringing about the democratic transformations he seeks. One gets the sense that Falih believes that it is the sheer quantity of *ahli* social formations and the numerical superiority of those who subscribe to traditional ideas that provide the force of the idea. He asks, "What is the relationship between the idea of 'civil society' [*al-mujtama' al-madani*] and the inhabitants of the tombs [City of the Dead in east Cairo] in the mentality of its dwellers?" (2002, 169). He suggests there is really little relation when that civil society is associated with modern, Western, urban values and structures that are foreign to these people. In Falih's view, it is

10. In March 2004, Falih was arrested, along with a dozen others, for circulating a petition calling for the peaceful transition from a monarchy toward a constitutional democracy in Saudi Arabia. Sentenced to six years for sowing dissent and sedition, Falih remains in a Saudi prison at the time of writing.

necessary that "elements associated with these rural and popular formations be incorporated into the actions of civil societies" and that "other
liberals and agents of domination and the state" cease to "limit, reject, or
hinder" these marginalized groups. Appealing to these groups requires
that liberal intellectuals heed the examples of "Arab democratic experiences in Lebanon, Yemen, and even in the political reforms in Oman, and
to some extent Qatar (and perhaps Bahrain in the near future)," which
"despite their incomplete nature and the existence of forces, such as fac-
tionalism, tribalism and forces connected with religion or fundamentalism," proved change approaching democracy in Arab cities does not
require the "dissolution of traditional forces" (2002, 169). It further requires that Arab liberals appeal to these groups in the language of *al-
mujtama' al-ahli*.

Opposing Phrases, Common Projects

What are we to make of these competing translations? The authors whose
works are discussed here present a central concept, civil society, rendered
subtly but importantly different by each through the use of different
phrases (*al-mujtama' al-ahli, al-mujtama' al-madani,* and *al-mujtama'
al-hajin*), all expressions that carry their own conceptual baggage. While
each of these thinkers views himself as engaged in a contestation over a
core idea of a self-generated realm of associative life existing between the
individual and the state, each conceptualizes that concept slightly differently and offers different assessments of the various types of social formations existing throughout Arab history. In light of the varied history
the concept of civil society has had in Western contexts, one should ex-
pect no less disagreement within non-Western contexts.

On the one hand, each of these liberal accounts of civil society draws
upon a similar understanding of traditional social formations that account for much associational life in the Arab region, though with different emphases and prescriptions. Jabiri identifies them with a
nondemocratic, rural, hegemonic force and puts them in tension with
urban, civil formations seeking a venue for articulating their interests
(democracy). Despite joining traditional and modern civil society according to their similar function vis-à-vis the state, Kawtharani even

more decisively separates traditional *(ahli)* society from modern *(madani)* society by definitional fiat; and, in the process, he provides no way to rejoin or reconcile the two: Arab civil society must be formed out of the former and not the latter to be authentic, a perspective further developed in Falih's work, which attempts to popularize Kawtharani's expression. Jabiri believes the contrary to be true: a civilized society and civilizing associations must replace primordial groupings in society, as a precondition to democratic reform. Ghalyun puts the two notions back together through his strategy of supporting all of the dynamic elements in a "hybrid" civil society as a way of limiting state power and fostering pluralism in the public realm.

On the other hand, despite the fact that each of the discussions among the Arab liberals turns upon an examination of traditional, predominantly religious associations, one pairing is conspicuous by its absence: that between religious society and civil society. In fact, Kawtharani and Falih locate a distinct history of civil formations in traditional groupings, most if not all of which are religious in some sense, but all of which also have a measure of autonomy from state institutions. Ibn Khaldun, to whom both Kawtharani and Falih make reference, speaks of social solidarity *('asabiyya)* as drawing its greatest strength from a commitment to religious values. Ghalyun specifically draws religious groups within the purview of civil society as well. Jabiri makes no reference to religion at all in his account, not even in his critique of Khaldunic forms of solidarity. Rather, his point of reference (and critique) is "premodern," largely tribal social forces, regardless of whether or not they have a religious basis. None of these liberals aims to exclude religion (nor secularism either, it is worth noting) from the forces that could potentially contribute toward democratization.

Secularism proves a "nonissue" in this debate over civil society. This is an argument one finds throughout Jabiri's works. He views efforts to position one's self and one's opponents under the banner of "secularism" or "Islamism" as a way of avoiding other, more pressing concerns.[11] Ac-

---

11. Salwa Ismail discerns an attempt to refocus the secular-religious issue in both Ghalyun's and Jabiri's works. In regard to the latter, she points out that "he contends that

cording to Jabiri, "the question of secularism in the Arab world is a false question *(masala muzayyafa),* insofar as it expresses real needs by reference to categories which do not correspond to them: the need for independence within a single national identity, the need for a democracy which protects the rights of minorities, and the need for the rational practice of political action. All of these are objective—even reasonable and necessary—needs in the Arab world. However, they lose their justification and necessity when expressed through the use of dubious slogans like 'secularism' " (1996, 113). Similarly, Ghalyun maintains that where "modernists make a drastic mistake of thinking that mass resistance [to the process of Arab rationalism] is intertwined with or derived from Islamic resurgence," Islamists "make the same mistake when they assume that the mass refusal of modernity is a collective plea for the establishment of a religious state" (1990, 300). Yet, in his view, the "secularist ideology" also proves incompatible with the plurality of beliefs required for the democratic regulation of the state because of its lack of acceptance of religious perspectives. Ghalyun points to the Soviet Union and its passing as illustrative of this point (1991, 406). In this sense, the "false problematic" of secularism has been "transcended" by the more "real" issue of the lack of democratic social and political institutions. This attempt to suspend the secularism issue stands in stark contrast to Western studies of Arab civil society, where Islam is most often put forth as precisely *the* issue.

Secular Responses to Hybrid Forms of Civil Society

However, not all Arab thinkers are willing to bypass the issue of secularism in the search for a modern or democratic civil society, nor perhaps so

---

the *ulama* (religious scholars), fearing exclusion from modern systems of government, have clung to a vision of government they termed Islamic and that allowed them continued participation. On the other hand, thinkers and activists originating from minority groups, who were and are apprehensive about the majority rule that characterizes a democratic system, have sought guarantees of their rights in the secular state. This, in Jabiri's opinion, was nothing more than formulating the concept of democracy in mistaken and artificial terms" (1995, 101).

hesitant in proclaiming the necessity of fundamentally transforming—
rather than evading or reforming—existing undemocratic states. At the
1992 Center for Arab Unity Studies conference on civil society, two
Egyptians, Mustafa Kamal al-Sayyid and al-Sayyid Yasin, drew the clear-
est connections between civil society and secularism. In general, the
more sustained and consistent defenses of secularism and critiques of
hybrid forms of civil society have come not from Arab liberals but from
Arab socialists. In a book-length study of the concepts, *al-'Almaniyya wa
al-mujtama' al-madani* (Secularism and Civil Society), the Syrian
philosopher Sadiq Jalal al-'Azm argues that "secularism, requires and is
required by civil society" (1998a, 16). 'Azm, a professor of philosophy at
Damascus University, identifies himself as a Marxist. His understanding
of civil society is dealt with here, rather than in chapter 6, because his
book on the topic is directly intended as a critical response to the
thinkers and ideas expressed by Arab liberals, rather than as a contribution to the issues discussed in chapter 6. Like Kawtharani, Jabiri, and
Ghalyun, 'Azm's argument relies upon a distinction between modern
civil society (as *al-mujtama' al-madani*) and traditional, religious civil
society (which he, following Kawtharani, terms *al-mujtama' al-ahli*).
But the latter, in 'Azm's view, is not civil society at all.

'Azm defines "the concrete relationships" of *al-mujtama' al-ahli* as
those of "kinship, family, affection, doctrine, sect, clan, village, etc.,"
which he characterized as "natural, organic, group-based, coercive and
hierarchical" (1998a, 12–13). *Al-mujtama' al-ahli* relies upon "four great
social divisions" that 'Azm argues date back to the Roman Empire: those
of "free and slave, man and woman, Muslim and non-Muslim [or
Roman and non-Roman], and public and private" (1998a, 13). Various
rights, privileges, ranks, and responsibilities flow from the position of an
individual within these four divisions in *al-mujtama' al-ahli*. In contrast,
'Azm argues, the concrete relations of civil society (as *al-mujtama'
al-madani*) "center around and in the relationships of citizenship" and
are characterized by a "flexibility" because "they are civil, voluntary, contractual, rights-based, horizontal and equal." Thus "this model of civil
society nullifies the four great divisions of the model of *al-mujtama'
al-ahli* since it does not associate the rights, duties, responsibilities and

tasks of any individual by his position [within that division] . . . but rather associates these according to the central and concrete category of civil society, that is the category of citizenship and the [individual's] association with it" (1998a, 14). According to 'Azm, the move from *al-mujtama' al-ahli* to a modern civil society of the type found in Western liberal societies is one from "the consensus of the community" to "the general will"; from primary identities such as those of religion, doctrine, or tribe to the identity of citizenship; and from a system that places the rights of the master in opposition to the slave or the rights of the nobility in opposition to the generality of the people, to ideas of human rights and the rights of citizens. The concept of civil society also "crystallizes notions like 'the people,' 'the people's will,' and 'citizen rule,' just as it gives an expression like 'the community' [*umma*] its modern national meaning, like our expression today of the Arab *umma* for example, that takes the place of the community with its old, religious, kinship [*ahli*] meaning" (1998a, 14–15).

Unlike Jabiri, Kawtharani, and Ghalyun, in 'Azm's view civil society is always secular by definition, because civil society, like secularism, is a product of modernity. Here, as in other of 'Azm's works, he argues against those who are concerned with notions of "authenticity" and cultural particularity. 'Azm claims that Arab and Muslim authors "orientalize themselves" when they claim a frame of reference different from those of the rest of humanity and assert that Arab civil society and Arab liberalism are exempt from the historical process of secularization experienced by others. 'Azm characterizes this epistemological move as "orientalism in reverse" (1981). In addition, while in the view of Kawtharani and Jabiri, the values of traditional society *(al-mujtama' al-ahli)* still predominate in Arab politics and culture, 'Azm maintains that, at least in Syria and Egypt, which have been subject to a period of secularization on the part of a modernizing state, there has been a considerable move from *al-mujtama' al-ahli* to something that looks like civil society over the past forty years, a shift he has characterized as a "move from *Gemeinschaft* to *Gesellschaft*"—a move from communities of "natural" internal solidarities to (economic) interest-type groupings—thus emphasizing the economic aspect of this shift, as well as revealing his historicist approach. "The backbone of *al-mujtama' al-madani* movement," 'Azm explains, "is the merchants who deal with others on basis of an open market, rather than based on feelings of kinship or religious solidarity" (1998b).

As evidence of this move toward secularism, 'Azm points to the work of Muhammad Shahrur, a Syrian civil engineer whose writings, including his important study entitled *The Book and the Qur'an: A Contemporary Reading* (1990), are widely read, especially by the business-orientated middle class.[12] "[I]f Islam is sound for all times and places," Shahrur maintains, Muslims must reinterpret the sacred texts and apply them to contemporary questions as if "the Prophet just . . . informed us of this Book." In his own reinterpretation, Shahrur comes up with fairly progressive ideas about everything from the status of women to democratic political procedures, to the necessity of a pluralism of perspectives. Dale F. Eickelman (1998) has compared Shahrur's book to Martin Luther's 95 Theses.[13] 'Azm offers a similar account of Shahrur's impact and status as the harbinger of the "Islamic Reformation." According to 'Azm (1998b), Shahrur is popular among the middle class in particular because "he reinterprets Islam in a way that makes it easy to be a modern businessman at the office and good Muslim in one's heart." 'Azm has himself contributed to the offensive against intolerant certitudes of conventional religious wisdom. In May 1997, a debate between 'Azm and a conservative religious scholar and preacher, Shaykh Yusuf al-Qaradawi, was seen on al-Jazeera Satellite Television (based in Qatar, but broadcast throughout the Arab region), and "for the first time in the memory of many viewers, the religious conservative position came across as the weaker and more defensive one voice," while the representative of secularism appeared eminently reasonable (Eickelman 1998).

12. Shahrur's expensive eight-hundred-page work had sold more than thirty thousand copies by 1993 despite being banned in several countries. It has since been reprinted several times. He has since published three additional works further explicating the method and substance of his "contemporary reading."

13. For a review of the uses of the Reformation analogy in analyzing transformations in Islamic thought, see Kurzman and Browers (2004).

'Azm points to these debates as evidence that Arab society has already moved away from being *ahli* (based on primordial or organic relationships). Further, in contrast to Jabiri, 'Azm sees the cities as digesting the values of the countryside, of *al-mujtama' al-ahli,* not the other way around. Both traditional civil society and modern civil society are distinct from the state, in 'Azm's view, and most commonly (and certainly in his own context of Syria) there is a "mishmash of the two together" (1998a, 12). However, it is only the latter—modern civil society—that 'Azm views as having a "dialectical relationship with the modern and modernizing state that to a great extent creates it in cities and attempts to re-form the surrounding *al-mujtama' al-ahli* in an image of civil society that was formed in the cities and to spread over the remainder of the country from the center" (1998a, 15).

However, 'Azm suggests that the region is faced with an additional problem: it is developing a bourgeois civil society, a form of liberalism, not a system of democracy. In this sense, 'Azm offers a socialist critique of what I have characterized here as a liberal discourse on civil society. He argues that those thinkers discussed above are using "civil society" in a way that reflects more an interest in its promotion of the liberal than the democratic component of democracy; negative rather than positive freedoms; and a more strictly political than socioeconomic conception of democracy. 'Azm further suggests that significant sections of society that may contribute toward democratization are not encompassed by this liberal, bourgeois notion of civil society. A similar assessment of contemporary debates over democracy and civil society has been made by Sami Zubaida. According to Zubaida, "Middle Eastern intellectuals seem to focus on associations, because they regard them as expressions of democratic practice. . . . In doing so they tend to neglect the sphere of socio-economic processes, not in themselves 'democratic,' but which may engender resources of power and autonomy outside the state" (2001, 248–49).

In 'Azm's view, the result of the move from traditional to modern civil society is that the modern and modernizing state has stepped in to perform the task of preserving the unity of society and deterring the disintegration and collapse that threatens it owing to the socioeconomic contradictions, pressures, and tensions arising from this modernization. Drawing upon Hegel, 'Azm notes how the German thinker "did not sanctify the state . . . but rather saw in it the only power capable in his time of creating German society from the fragments . . . and avoiding disintegration under the pressure of the processes of its accelerated movement from traditional civil associations to a modern bourgeois civil society" (1998a, 16). Yet, he continues, "in the present stage, civil society has begun to grow with the withdrawal of the state that launched and guarded it." Thus one begins to detect in 'Azm's book a move from a discussion of the state's role in fostering the development of a modern civil society, to an argument about the changing role for both the state and civil society in history—a move that takes him from Hegel to Marx.

In rather cryptic prose, 'Azm concludes his discussion of these two forms of civil associations by noting that "whenever the notion of civil society matures and becomes powerful, whenever its demands on the state are strengthened and [the state's] pressures in meeting the demands are intensified, it is necessary that we not forget on this occasion the symbolic saying of Freud: 'A person is not truly matured until he kills his father' " (1998a, 17). Does 'Azm mean the death of the traditional and religious society that spawned the modern civil society? Or of the state that expands its power to force the unity of society? Or of something even more subversive (the leader of Syria, President Hafiz al-Asad, as that "father" to be overthrown)?

The custom of naming individuals after their oldest son is prevalent throughout the Arab region. In the 1990s there were efforts in Syria to "humanize" the distant President Asad (d. 2000) by utilizing the image of a father. Lisa Wedeen's research uncovers the extensive use of father images in the perpetuation of what she refers to as Asad's 'ambiguous domination' " (1999). Wedeen points out how, for example, President Asad was referred to as 'Abu [Father of] Basil [his oldest son] until his son's death in 1994. Most interpreted this as an attempt to designate his son as his successor (Ziser 2001, 158). In addition, political leaders often have an "Abu" nom de guerre. Thus Asad also went by the name of "Abu Sulayman," presumably after his grandfather but containing an explicit reference to Sulayman the Magnificent, the ruler of the Ottoman Empire at the height of its power and prestige.

Understandably, 'Azm does not clarify his use of Freud. However it is apparent that, at the very least, 'Azm's move from Hegel to Marx is one from an understanding of the necessity of the modern state to an understanding of the necessity of its overthrow, and of the necessity of the move from a liberal to a more radical, revolutionary project.

'Azm's account of civil society and critique of nonsecular conceptualizations is interesting, not only because of the bold implications of his argument, but also for what his critique reveals about the shortcomings of the Arab liberal perspective. On the other hand, if he is correct that a dynamic and critical (and secular) consciousness is already brewing in Arab civil societies, this suggests that Arab liberals' "faith" in formal democratic procedures and the democratic potential of the Arab public at large is not as naïve or misplaced as some Western liberals might have us believe. This "faith" is questioned most starkly by Elie Kedourie, who argues that "those who say that democracy is the only remedy for the Arab world disregard a long experience which clearly shows that democracy has been tried in many countries and uniformly failed" (1994, 105).

Despite critiques from more decidedly secular thinkers, among many Arab liberals there seems to be an acknowledgment both of an Islamic ethos that permeates society and of the strength of the Islamic movement, such that they view efforts to exclude Islam and Islamic groups from political or civil society as having undemocratic consequences. At the same time, a religious state would be unacceptable as a political form for each of these thinkers. For Jabiri, an Islamic state would only be the latest formulation in his historical narrative (the last in the line following the colonialist state, the postindependence state, the revolutionary-military state, and the pseudodemocratic state) and, as such, another example of an undemocratic *civis*. Although he argues that the secularist ideology of demarcating between religion and the state should be discarded, he suggests that another division be seriously considered: "we Muslims," Jabiri asserts, should neither "practice politics within religion," nor "use our religion for political purposes" (1990).

Kawtharani denies both the historical precedence for (or authenticity of) and the desirability of an Islamic state in the strict sense, but no less emphasizes the undesirability and impossibility of a nonreligious, modern civil society. Ghalyun claims with satisfaction that the religious state is a relic of past ages.[14] Each of these perspectives relies upon a distinction between religious authority (which none of these thinkers wishes to see institutionalized in the state) and religious reasoning (which all of these thinkers view as impossible or undesirable to separate from politics). Secularism, or the separation of the religious and the political, appears here (or, we might say, does not appear here) to be a displacement of the real issue, which is, for all of the liberal thinkers discussed here, democracy.

In fact, unlike the formulations of civil society and democracy we find in the history of Western political thought and more recently in the conceptualizations that came out of Eastern Europe, Jabiri and Ghalyun, as well as Kawtharani (though he seems at times more concerned with an "authentic" civil society), prioritize democracy above civil society. So too, each of these thinkers articulates an awareness that democracy in its fullest sense must achieve procedural and substantive aspects. Ghalyun views democracy as the best political form for achieving a correspondence between the values of society (of which religion forms perhaps the most important source) and state policies (1991, 441).[15] Kawtharani views an undemocratic state as the enemy of traditional civil formations he discusses. He also argues that "democracy, and its basic introduction in the alternation of rule through elections and parliaments . . . are preconditions for the establishment of modern civil society in the countries of the Arab world" (1992, 130–31). Kawtharani rejects the means but not the goals of Jabiri's democratic project. Jabiri focuses his concern on both the lack of democratic institutions in Arab politics and the absence of democratic norms in Arab society's existing civil formations. All of

14. Falih's perspective is less clear on this matter. He has pushed for democratic reforms—elections, rule of law, human rights protections—but I am not aware of any statement he has made in regard to the theocratic character of the Saudi state.

15. This aspect of Ghalyun's thought is discussed in Ismail (1995, 103–6).

these views are critical of the state, which they characterize as stifling, corrupt, and detrimental to human freedom. Each sees *more* civil society—albeit differently understood—as a means to further their political interests. Kawtharani, Jabiri, and Ghalyun share with contemporary Western political science an understanding of civil society and democracy as existing within an important relationship with each other. Yet, whereas many Western liberals tend to prioritize civil society as a precondition for a vibrant democracy,[16] Arab liberals prioritize democracy without reluctance.

At the end of his introduction to the 1992 conference, Bin Saʻid asks, "if we are permitted to borrow from western history and from its modern and contemporary civilizational experience, particularly a social concept [that of civil society], are we dependent upon that definition . . . or have we in the act of borrowing taken steps in adapting it to our particular civilizational identity?" (1992a, 12). This question strikes at the heart of the politics of translation: the transportation or appropriation of political concepts presents a political event, in which the weapons for this conceptual contestation are forged from the context both from which and to which it is translated. As the distinct and competing views expressed thus far reveal, the outcome of this translation is open to multiple possibilities.

---

16. Much, though not all, of the contemporary literature in English on the relationship between civil society and democracy prioritizes the former. For example, James Turner Johnson claims a causal link: "in short, democracy begins from the bottom up, with the creation of a civil society consisting in a complex web of interrelationships and mutual responsibilities formed by the free choice of individuals and by the natural relationships amongst them" (1992, 45–46). See also O'Donnell and Schmitter (1986). Similarly, as noted previously, the weakness or absence of a civil society is used to explain the lack of democracy in Arab countries. In contrast, Michael Walzer argues that both elements are equally necessary: "only a democratic state can create a democratic civil society, only a democratic civil society can sustain a democratic state" (1991, 302).

5

Civil Society in Contemporary Islamist Discourse

There is not merely a fight, but a debate.
—Abdou Filali-Ansary, "The Challenge of Secularization"

"Spectacle" at the 1992 Cairo International Book Fair

In February 1992 the sponsors of Cairo's annual International Book Fair held an open debate on the question of "Egypt Between a Religious and Civil State" *(Misr bayn al-dawla al-diniyya wa al-madaniyya)*, which pitted Farag Fouda, a controversial secularist thinker, and Muhammad Khalaf Allah,[1] a leader of the Leftist Tagammu' (Progressive) Party, against three prominent Islamists: a popular member of the Azhar *'ulama*, Shaykh Muhammad al-Ghazali; Muslim Brotherhood spokesperson Ma'mun Hudaybi; and the self-proclaimed neofundamentalist Muhammad 'Imara.[2] The debate drew an estimated 20,000 specta-

---

1. Khalaf Allah first came to the attention of Islamists when he presented his doctoral dissertation in 1947, in which he argued that the Qur'anic narratives on the life of prophets and other historical events should be understood figuratively, as stories aimed at moving the believers, rather than as precise factual accounts. Khalaf Allah resigned his university position as a result of the furor over this work, which was eventually revised and published as *al-Fann al-qisasi fi al-qur'an al-karim* (The Art of Narrative in the Qur'an) (1950).

2. The term "Islamist" is used here to indicate those who emphasize the conscious choice of an Islamic doctrine as a guide for political thought and action. As such, Islamism is an ideology and a political phenomenon that has developed and spread in the Muslim world only fairly recently, in the middle of the past century, and is not to be con-

tors, most of whom were Islamists and who were reportedly responding to their leaders' calls to attend.[3] Different spectators give vastly different recollections of the manner in which the debate was conducted and the response of those in attendance. Some described a generally dignified encounter, in which the speakers expressed themselves courteously and the audience listened respectfully (Viorst 1998, 25). Fouda, a man known to refer to "Islamic groups" *(jama'at islamiyya)* as "gloomy or dark groups" *(jama'at izlamiyya)* (Darwish 1992, 14), is said to have softened his usual sarcasm. But others, perhaps more familiar with Fouda's views, detected a distinct sarcasm in his addressing Shaykh Ghazali as "our venerable master and eminent shaykh" *(ustadhuna al-jalil wa shaykhuna al-fadil)* and in such questions as "Which of the contemporary Islamic states, Iran or the Sudan, would you wish us to take as a model?" (Sarhan 1992).[4] Some claim that Fouda's challenge to the Islamists to present a coherent political program and his exposition of the flaws and contradictions in their conception of an Islamic state provided a poignant critique (Alrawi 1992, 19). One commentator noted that although Fouda faced "an angry, often abusive" audience, his "rational and in-depth knowledge of the Muslim faith made a laughingstock of his opponents" (Darwish 1992, 14). And many Islamists recalled Fouda as hateful, offensive, and even heretical in his remarks and demeanor.

The picture that emerges from the published versions of the debate

---

fused either with "Islam," which is a much broader concept referring to the Islamic religion and civilization as a whole, nor with "Muslims," who may or may not subscribe to the Islamist ideology.

3. The published account of the conference included photographs that showed an audience populated by a disproportionate number of bearded men and veiled women, and a large section in which the men had been seated separately from the women (all signs of strict adherence to Islam). The large number of people standing around the seating areas suggests that the debate drew many more spectators than expected (Sarhan 1992).

4. Fouda's sarcasm was quite rightly noted by Najjar (1996, 5). Fouda's respectful addressing of Shaykh Ghazali would be out of character if taken at face value, and his aversion to the Islamist regimes in power in Iran and the Sudan had been clearly voiced in the weekly column he writes in *Uktuber*.

confirms that most of these different views contain at least some measure of truth. Fouda's sarcasm was apparent but, for the most part, remained subtle. In addition to referring to Shaykh Ghazali as "the honorable," he addresses Hudaybi as a "dear person" *(insan 'aziz)* and feigns enthusiasm for particular points made by the latter (Sarhan 1992, 81). At the same time there is some indication that the written form of the debate reflects an Islamist sympathy—and even a hostility toward the representatives of more secular ideas—on the part of its publishers. The book opens with a passage from the Qur'an on "unbelievers," [5] and the dedication refers to Egypt as an "Islamic country" (Sarhan 1992, 9). This sympathy is not apparent so much from the speech transcriptions (although one page of Fouda's speech was mysteriously deleted and then tacked on at the end as a "correction," noted without apology). The style and substance of all the speeches as printed are consistent with the speakers' other works. Rather, it is the way in which the debate is framed, especially the parenthetical remarks, which give the impression that Khalaf Allah and especially Fouda were expressing views radically out of step with an existent Islamic consensus. For example, after each speaker is introduced, applause is recorded. Whereas the Islamists are said to have received "applause" or "much applause," Fouda and Khalaf Allah only occasionally are said to get "a little applause." Although no questions or comments from the audience were allowed, the text indicates points where the Islamist speakers are interrupted with an affirming *"allahu akbar!"* (God is great!), as well as where Fouda is said to have been interrupted by unfavorable laughter or by a hostile spectator, such as one who asks, "how much do they pay you?" (Sarhan 1992, 39).

Nonetheless, even from this transcript one can see the academic rigor in Khalaf Allah's presentation of numerous Qur'anic passages to support the argument that "Muhammad was a prophet, not a ruler" and in Fouda's critical examination of undesirable Islamic states, which he

5. "If God wills to guide a man, He opens his bosom to Islam. But if He pleases to confound him, He makes his bosom small and narrow as though he were climbing up to the sky. Thus shall God lay the scourge on the unbelievers" (Surat al-An'am 6:125) (Dawood 1994).

too supports with evidence from Islamic sources. The Islamists' responses remain defensive. All three speakers counter Khalaf Allah by asking, in essence: why, if Muslims want to conduct their life according to Islamic principles, would they not want to be governed by Islamic principles? The response to Fouda's critique also takes the form of a question. When one of the Islamist speakers asks, "does the fault [of the unjust Muslim governments] lie with Islam or with the people?" the transcript tells us the crowd replies "in unison": "the people" (Sarhan 1992, 51).

Thus, regardless of whether the appearance of an Islamist consensus among the spectators is created by the way in which the publishers have framed the debate, or reflects the overwhelming number of Islamists in attendance, or truly represents the sentiment of the public, the defensive tone of the Islamists in their speeches indicates the existence of a significant counter-discourse to which they feel a need to respond.[6] This defensive tone is most apparent in the opening remarks by Ghazali and Hudaybi where they question the choice of the title for the debate and discuss the "Islamic state" in negative terms. That is, they spend most of their effort in the debate in clarifying what the Islamic state is *not*, despite the direct challenge Fouda puts to them to present a coherent political program for such a state.

In reference to the title of the debate, "Egypt Between a Religious and Civil State," Shaykh Ghazali clarifies that Egyptians do not want a religious state, in the sense that they could have a Christian, Hindi, or Jewish state (Sarhan 1992, 15). Rather, he argues, 95 percent of Egyptians are Muslim;[7] and, if one wishes to live one's life according to the principles of

6. Fouda's critiques of Islamists have been consistently scathing. He has scolded them for naively believing that the implementation of the *shari'a* will immediately result in a good society with all its problems solved (Fouda 1988, 12; also 1987). He has faulted them with not knowing their own history, which, he argues, shows that the ideal Islamic state they seek to (re)establish has never been achieved in the past. In his recounting of early Islamic history (the sacred utopia of the Islamist), he informs his readers that three of the first four "rightly guided Caliphs" (the companions of the Prophet) were assassinated (1988, 15–32).

7. Most analysts agree that Copts (Christians) account for at least 10 percent and perhaps as much as 15 percent of Egypt's population.

Islam, why would one not wish to be ruled by Islam as well? Thus, the Islamists seek not a *religious* state, but an *Islamic* state, that is, one based upon Islamic principles of good governance, which in the view of the Islamists at the Cairo Book Fair involves a system of *shura* (consultation/democracy) and reflects Islam's principle of *tawhid* (literally "oneness"), which Islamists use to indicate that Islam is a comprehensive doctrine that unifies the political, moral, and social aspects of human life. The principle of *tawhid* is summed up as a political ideal in the Islamist slogan "Islam is a religion and a state" *(din wa dawla)*.

Building upon this argument, Hudaybi argues that the opposite of an Islamic state is an "un-Islamic" state. On the other hand, "what is civil government?" he asks. "Is it not [a] military [state]?" (Sarhan 1992, 17). Since the Islamists do not wish for that, he argues that a better title for the debate is "Egypt between the Islamic state and the un-Islamic state." Much of the remainder of the Islamists' speeches are intent on proving that their two secular opponents want precisely that—an un-Islamic state—and expressing shock and disbelief that any Muslim could want such a thing. "Are you not a Muslim?" they inquire of Fouda and Khalaf Allah at several points.

Four months after the debate at the 1992 Cairo Book Fair, Fouda was assassinated while leaving the office of a political society called "Enlightenment," which he founded in 1989 in order to promote the right of Egyptians to dissent from conventional Islamic beliefs and particularly to challenge the dogmas of Islamic fundamentalism. His two assassins were members of the Islamic Jihad group, which is considered responsible for the assassination of President Anwar Sadat in 1981. One of the shooters, captured after the attack, is reported to have said, "We had to kill him, because he attacked our beliefs." When Shaykh Ghazali testified at the murder trial, he argued that when an apostate *(kafir)* represents a danger to Islamic society, it is the duty of the government to put him to death, adding that, should the government fail to do so, Muslim groups or individuals are permitted to carry out the sentence (Najjar 1996, 5). The Muslim Brotherhood spokesperson, Ma'mun al-Hudaybi, similarly blamed the government for the attack, claiming that it was their fault for supporting "people who use their pens to stab Islam in the back" (MEED 1992, 9–11).

Getting Back in the Debate:
Refuting the Civil-Religious Dichotomy

The intolerant note upon which the Cairo International Book Fair debate was conducted, and the violent act that brought its final conclusion for Fouda, call into question the civility of Islamist discourse and practice at the same time that the existence of the event itself and a number of the ideas expressed there reveal a desire on the part of the Islamists to enter into a debate about such issues as civil government, democracy, and state-society relations. Commenting on the Cairo Book Fair debate in a book published the following year, entitled *Islam and Democracy,* the prominent Egyptian writer and Islamist Fahmi Huwaydi again took up the issue of the choice of title for what he characterizes as the "spectacle" of the Cairo International Book Fair, "Egypt Between a Religious and Civil State."[8] Huwaydi claims that both in the debate itself and in the writings and discussions that surrounded it, the title was alternatively translated and understood as "Egypt between a Religious and Secular State" and "Egypt between a Religious and Civil State." Although he maintains that the first choice of alternatives would not be contested by any of the participants in the debate, the latter would be, and was. According to Huwaydi, "despite the fact that the Islamist faction . . . objected to the title and their representatives requested that it be corrected to be more precise and more accurate in expressing that this is a case between the Islamists and the secularists, no one listened to them. All the different treatments [of the debate] kept describing the Islamists as calling for the religious state and the others as supporters of the civil state" (Huwaydi 1993, 184–85).[9] This distinction, and its implications for the Islamists' inclusion in the sphere of civil society, has been argued since the beginning of the civil society debate in Arabic. In a 1991 article appearing in the journal published by the Center for Islamic World Studies

8. Huwaydi has said that he prefers to be called a "moderate fundamentalist" *('usuli mu'tadil)* (Dwyer 1991, 81).

9. The argument Huwaydi makes here has been repeated by his close associate Muhammad 'Imara (1995, 162–68).

(the Islamist response to the well-established Center for Arab Unity Studies),[10] Bin 'Isa al-Dimni accuses secularists of hiding behind the concept of *civil* society to make an argument against *Islamic* society, which, he argues, is not civil society's opposite, but in fact "the *desired* civil society" (1991, 225–37, my emphasis). It is true that the concept of civil society has been explicitly used, particularly in North Africa and especially in Tunis, as a weapon to exclude the Islamists (Zghal 1992b, 438; also 1992a).

Huwaydi's response to the exclusion of the "Islamic" from the "civil" consists not only in providing an interpretation of the Islamic state as a civil state, but also in showing that the Islamist movement represents "a defense of civil society." Huwaydi approaches his subject slightly tongue-in-cheek. "If we want to maintain a good opinion of those who describe the Islamic state as a religious state and view it in contradiction to the civil [*madani*] state," he argues, the only option is "to provide them with the excuse" that they were led to error by their ignorance of the meaning and the history of the concepts they use (1993, 184). Huwaydi looks first at the concept of the religious state, which he argues is connected with the European experience of the state founded on the theory of the divine right of kings. According to this view, rulers "have powers from above which make their leadership a matter above questioning and criticism." In light of this understanding of the concept, Huwaydi recounts how "when someone said to me the other day—'you want a religious state'— my reply was both 'no' and 'yes,' because I consider that it is not a religious state according to the measure of the dominant meaning of this concept [that I seek], but it is religious in the sense that it is founded on the basis of a conformity to the principles of Islam." He continues: "Then I explained the matter as follows: the main difference between the reli-

10. The parallels between the two organizations are too stark to be accidental. In addition to the similarity of names—the Center for Arab Unity Studies (*Markaz dirasat al-wahda al-'arabiyya*) publishes the journal *al-Mustaqbal al-'arabi*, while the Center for Islamic World Studies (Markaz dirasat al-'alam al-islami) publishes *Mustaqbal al-'alam al-islami*—the latter organization, founded in 1991, even boasts a similar letterhead and design for the books it publishes.

gious state and the Islamic state is that the first is founded on the idea that God is the source of authority and in the second case, the Islamic state, God is the source of the law and the community [*umma*] is the source of authority. The leader has neither immunity nor infallibility but, rather, the law is above [higher than] the group and the ruler is in front of the others [the first one to whom law should be applied]" (1993, 185). Thus Huwaydi suggests a distinction between the source of authority and the source of law and community in Islam that, he argues, is not part of the Western experience where the religious state gave rulers "the status of infallibility and divinity that placed them in a class above their subjects and gave them the freedom to practice despotism . . . without accountability" (1993, 186). Like John Locke, Huwaydi seeks to refute the notion that political leadership is divinely sanctioned by God. But whereas authority in Locke's view is rooted in natural law and a natural community, Huwaydi attributes to the law and the Islamic community divine sanction: God has revealed the law that sustains and is sustained by the community. The problem with Arab liberals, in Huwaydi's view, is that they equate the Islamic state with a problem identified by and limited to Western liberals working in the Anglo-European context: the problem of rule by divine right.

Again, with more than a bit of sarcasm, Huwaydi argues that we can "excuse the Orientalists" who misunderstand the Islamic state in light of their own experience, but this excuse cannot work for "our own people" who argue similarly. Again, he argues that "if we are to keep thinking well of [these Egyptians]," there is only one possible explanation: ignorance. "They read about Islam, but they do not read Islam," that is, they have been reading too much of the Orientalist writings, rather than the works by Muslims and especially the fundamentals of Islam, the Qur'an and *sunna* (1993, 126). Huwaydi recounts the famous Islamic modernist Muhammad 'Abduh's rejoinder to the liberal thinker Farah Antun's similarly misinformed ideas about religious authority in Islam in 1902. In responding to Antun, 'Abduh argues that the Caliphate of the Muslims is not infallible, nor does it have a right to monopolize the interpretation of the Qur'an and *sunna*. Rather, 'Abduh maintains, the Muslim *umma* is the watchguard and must provide corrective advice when the leader deviates from the course. Further, this community has the right to remove the leader when it is in their interest. The ruler described by 'Abduh is, in Huwaydi's assessment, "a civil ruler in all respects," and he expresses some frustration that he is forced to repeat this same debate over ninety years later (1993, 187).

According to Huwaydi, 'Abduh's opinion was neither new in his own time, nor has it been contested by religious scholars in the period between 'Abduh's time and the present. While the latter part of Huwaydi's claim is not (and, I think, cannot be) substantiated, he draws from a great number of rich historical examples to support his claim that this view of authority is the predominant one in Islam. He begins first with a number of examples where the Prophet Muhammad—who Huwaydi argues "opened the door himself" to this interpretation—encouraged criticism and advice (1993, 188).[11] Again, Huwaydi expresses frustration that, despite the great number of well-known examples of the distinction between God's sovereignty and the authority of the community to question, correct, and remove their rulers, some (unnamed person) insists otherwise. He ends this chapter by asking, "how do we characterize this position? Ignorance, obstinacy, or a lie against Islam and Muslims?" (1993, 191). The chapter that follows, entitled "A Defense of Civil Society," begins in a similar manner: "The civil state is put in contradiction with the Islamic state which is called religious in a spectacle in Cairo, while the call for establishing civil society is one of the basic demands of the Islamic movement in Tunisia. This suggests a confusion [over the concept of civil society] that also needs clarification and liberation" (1993, 192). Once again he suggests that "it is necessary for those who claim the title of civil society in opposing the Islamists to understand

11. Among the *ahadith* (sayings, sing. *hadith*) that Huwaydi recounts is one in which when a man recalled a loan from Muhammad using harsh language, the Prophet's companion, 'Umar Ibn al-Khattab, became angry with the lender. Muhammad is reported to have said to 'Umar that he should "advise me to give the man his money back and advise the man to be patient with me."

what it is about which they speak"; and he says that the "newness" of the term excuses them from their ignorance of its meaning, though not from the "arbitrariness" they exercise in "tearing it from its determined meaning."

In contrast to the thinkers discussed in the previous chapter, Huwaydi devotes his time to drawing parallels between Western thought and Islamic thought. In an assertion of their similarities with the Islamic ideas he outlined in his previous chapter, Huwaydi discusses Locke's understanding of the "separation of power" in "Civil Government," Rousseau's ideas of the "sovereignty of the people" and the "political contract between the people and the ruling power," the revolt against tyranny in the French Revolution, and the contemporary notion that the presence of parties, syndicates, unions, interest groups, and *"ahaliyya* institutions" (in Kawtharani's sense) in society "reflects the vitality of the community" and provides a "balance to the institutions of the state" (1993, 193–94). He concludes that "there are no grounds for considering civil society a contradiction to the Islamic state." On the contrary, he argues, it is the secular state that has proven that it can be antithetical to civil society. "The example of the modern Arab state," he maintains, "is evidence of that. Most pursued the secularist route after independence in the course of trying to increase the central ruling power, which in turn destroyed the spaces of the various civil societies" (1993, 194). While rejecting the secular and the civil as embodied in existing Arab states, Huwaydi conflates the Islamic *umma* and civil society, asserting congruence between the Islamic and the civil, and between a particular form of community and society as such. This parallel is stated even more firmly in a number of other works by prominent contemporary Islamist political thinkers.

Islam Resides in the Group: That Is, in Civil Society

Despite the multiple discourses about the "Islamic state" and the persistence of despotism in Muslim countries, the vast majority of Muslim thinkers, jurists, and theologians have asserted the priority of the community *(umma)* over the government (Moussalli 1995, 80–81). The concept of the *umma* has a long history in Arab-Islamic political discourse.[12] In classical Arab and Islamic thought, *umma* was most often conceived as a somewhat abstract feeling of belonging to a community of believers. In the writings of Ibn Khaldun, the *umma* was tied to a concept of solidarity *('asabiyya)*, an expression of traditional forms of sociability, of which religion was the primary, but not sole, basis. In the modern context, the traditional *'asabiyya* has been fragmented by the establishment of the modern state in the Arab context, with the urbanization, the social upheaval, and the spread of competing secular and religious ideologies. The works of the great pan-Arabist theoreticians of the 1950s and 1960s (for example, Michel Aflaq) gave further importance to the notion of *umma*, infusing it with a more expansive sense of the greater Arab community/nation. More recently, Islamist thinkers have attempted to revive the more religious notion of *umma* that, while returning to the idea of a community without time or place, at the same time situates group solidarity in a new social and political category, in particular in the modern notion of civil society that is said to be the cornerstone of the Islamic state.

Interestingly, at least one scholar of Islamic history, Akram Diya' al-'Umari (1983), has referred to the Islamic community Muhammad established in city of Madina as *"al-mujtama' al-madani,"* the same phrase used for "civil society." Although this coincidence appears to be purely accidental, the author does intend to characterize the city of Madina during Muhammad's lifetime as consisting of a particularly *civilized* society in the sense that it was composed of Muslims coexisting with Jews and other non-Muslims (1983, 99–122). In addition, the social

---

12. *Umma* derives from *"umm"* (mother), yet according to one Muslim scholar, "means more than the mother-land in its geographical-territorial limitation. It means FAITH and CREED. *Ummat al-Islam* encloses the entire collectivity of the Muslims living anywhere regardless of their geographical boundaries" (Elkholy 1979, 173). So too, the Islamic *umma* is distinct from the Islamic state, in the sense of a political-legal system (1979, 177). According to Elkholy, the "password" for entering the community is "the acknowledgement of the one principle: the universality of the One God" (1979, 172).

structure is said to reflect society's diverse powers, which, 'Umari argues, were both acknowledged by the Prophet and reflected in the first Islamic constitution. According to 'Umari, that constitution tolerated a pluralism of religions and of ways of life and permitted the various segments of Muslims allied along tribal and geographical lines to be represented by their leaders, who could be called upon to act as mediators between the authorities and individuals when necessary (1983, 123–36).

In a more recent work, 'Abd al-Hamid al-Ansari, the former dean of the faculty of *shari'a* at the University of Qatar, attempts to conceptualize an "Arab-Islamic civil society" based on the first community of Muslims in the city of Mecca. According to Ansari, when the call to Islam began in Mecca, it was received by individuals exercising their free will in order to establish values guiding social relations ("specifying rights and duties among a plurality of religions and races, and according to the values justice, mutual agreement, the right to differ and freedom") and to confront an oppressive order in Mecca that was at war with those values. Most important, Ansari maintains that an Islamic civil society was established in Mecca before that society finally selected its state in Medina. In short, "the classical understanding of civil society—as prior to the state—conforms to the development of Islamic society which preceded the institutionalization of the state, and [affirmed] the priority of the social order system over the political order" (al-Ansari 2001, 103). It not only precedes the state in time and importance, "Islamic civil society," according to Ansari, "forms the center of gravity in the social structure" of the *umma*. Interestingly, just as Jabiri considers modern civil society (or *mujama' al-mudun,* the society of the cities) to be the antithesis of rural society *(al-mujtama' al-badawi),* Ansari asserts "Islamic civil society" as the antithesis of both *badawi* (rural or, here, Bedouin or nomadic) and *jahili* (ignorant, pre-Islamic) society.

Other arguments for an Islamic civil society are put forth using different examples from Islamic history, but for similar ends. For example, Muhammad Salim al-'Awwa, a prominent Egyptian lawyer and member of the Muslim Brotherhood, recounts the considerable debate and struggle over the nature and process for establishing political leadership when the Prophet Muhammad died without naming a political or religious successor. Muhammad had prescribed *shura* (consultation) as the method for making the choice. 'Awwa focuses on the society of this period where, he argues, tribes formed a social, nonpolitical structure for electing a political leader whose authority was considered contractual in nature. According to 'Awwa, the tribal structure functioned as a mediator for relations between individuals and the government. However, "what matters is that the community be able to exercise its free will in choosing or appointing the ruler," while the procedure they use for doing so "is left for the community to determine" ('Awwa 1989, 69–74).

Islamists also argue that the *'ulama* (Islamic scholars) are intended to control the state by providing guidelines based on the *shari'a* for individuals' exercise of their legitimate rights and duties. Legislation is to be formed by the social institution of religious scholars whose legitimacy is grounded in civil society, not in formal governmental or legal institutions—that is, its influence is said to be moral and thus beyond the coercive power of the state. As Khalid Ziyada succinctly puts it, "a look at Arab-Islamic history will lead us to notice the separation of the state from civil society and that the law [*shari'a*] is realized and lives in the group and not in the state" (1992, 132).

The Islamist appropriation of civil society in their discussion of the Islamic *umma* aims neither at establishing a diverse associational life, nor at reviving forms of public participation, nor at restoring some lost *civis*. Rather, this discourse seeks to restore solidarity among the Islamic community and to assert that group's authority as the source and basis of legitimate rule. The concept of civil society has been an important tool in advancing this project—a project with considerable political importance because it asserts the capacity to grant or withhold legitimacy to particular states. At the same time, the appropriation of civil society discourse in articulating this program has in turn forced a reinterpretation of Islamic ideas about political and social life. This reinterpretation is seen in the thought of Hasan al-Turabi (Sudan, b. 1932) and Rachid al-Ghannouchi, two important Islamists from the Arab region, not only because of the reinterpretation of Islamic fundamentals involved in their discussion of civil society, but also because of their roles as leaders of two major sociopolitical Islamist movements.

Islamic Civil Society and Political Reform:
Hasan al-Turabi and Rachid al-Ghannouchi

Turabi, the founder and ideologue of Sudan's Muslim Brotherhood and the holder of a PhD in constitutional law from the Sorbonne, is considered by some to be "the leading and most powerful fundamentalist thinker of contemporary Islamic movements" (Moussalli 1999, 90).[13] Turabi argues that, because the traditional Islamic state and society have disintegrated in the modern era, there is an urgent need for an interpretative approach founded on new foundations *(usul)* to build a new state and to renew society. In his book *The Renewal of Islamic Thought,* Turabi argues that religious thought is prone to either renewal *(tajdid)* or deterioration *(inhitat).* Islamic discourse has deteriorated in his view because it has become alienated both from the fundamentals of Islam and from the reality of peoples' lives (1993, 4). Instead of focusing on the roots or fundamentals *(usul)* as the source of jurisprudence as circumstances changed throughout history, Muslims have given undue attention to the specifics *(furu').* For Turabi, the former is eternal, while the latter is a human construction, yet Muslims' incorrect prioritization has led them to treat the specific, rather than the roots, as if they were of divine origin. As a result, Islamic thought has become obsolete and ill-suited for serving Muslim societies in the modern age. It is because of this deterioration, Turabi argues, that Muslims have been led to borrow non-Islamic sources, such as positive Western laws, instead of returning to the fundamentals of Islamic law *(shari'a).*

Thus Turabi identifies two sources of challenges confronting attempts to renew Islamic thought, one external and one internal: the in-

13. Turabi, a former speaker of parliament and head of the National Islamic Front, was considered by many to have been instrumental in the institutionalization of *shar'ia* law in northern Sudan and a close ally of President 'Umar al-Bashir during the early part of his rule. However, in 1999, the president imposed a state of emergency, disbanded parliament, and accused Turabi of trying to undermine his authority. As a result, Turabi has been subject to periods of detention and imprisonment and now leads the opposition party, the Popular National Congress.

vasion of foreign values into Islamic societies and the insistence on blindly following traditions *(taqlid)* (1993, 52). In Turabi's view, what is needed is a renewal *(tajdid)* of Islamic thought that takes into account modern conditions while remaining grounded in the divine text. In order to deal with the profound issues facing modern Islamic society, the doors of *ijtihad* (individual reasoning, technique for deducing laws and theology) must be swung wide open. Turabi locates this task of *ijtihad* not in the state, nor primarily among the jurists *(fuqaha)* or traditional Islamic scholars *('ulama)*, but in society where Muslims participate through consultation *(shura)* and the formation of social consensus *(ijma')* (El-Affendi 1991, 170–71).[14]

In his early writings (1971; 1987), Turabi cites the mosque as the place where the true spirit of Islamic democracy is exemplified. Formed by ideological bonds and unified by social and political orientations, he considers the mosque a prototype for the larger Islamic *umma,* pointing in particular to its basis in communal solidarity and cohesive forms of organization, communication, and leadership. Turabi argues that the mosque also exemplifies the democratic character of the Islamic religion in the approach that Muslims take in determining who will lead the prayer: prayer leaders cannot be forced on the people, but must be selected by them. In addition, in the context of the mosque, all believers are equal before God and each other, regardless of differences among them in class, race, and gender. In Turabi's view, this principle of equality should serve as an example for the political realm. In a 1973 pamphlet, translated into English in 1991, Turabi applies the principle to women by drawing upon the example of the second caliph, Umar bin al-Khattab, who allowed women to perform some public duties, to make a case for women's right to educate themselves, engage in business, and participate

14. Turabi has become increasingly inclusive in his more recent specifications of those Muslims who should take part in this process of *ijtihad.* Compare his early view that the *ijtihad* of qualified Muslims would be coordinated under the auspices and guidance of Islamic authorities in *The Renewal of Islamic Jurisprudence* (Turabi 1984) to his more recent view that "the Muslim people at large and not the select *ulama* are the authoritative interpreters of Islamic doctrine," quoted in El-Affendi (1991, 160).

in public life. He further argues that "the greatest injustice visited upon women is their segregation and isolation from the general society" (1991, 43).

More recently, Turabi has increasingly emphasized the community as the locale and source of ultimate political authority. Like 'Awwa and Ansari, Turabi argues that the *umma* draws a contract with an individual to whom power is delegated to lead the community and organize its affairs. The main Qur'anic discourse, in his view, is directed primarily toward the people and, more specifically, to the individual rather than toward the state. Thus Turabi sets forth preconditions regarding the nature of institutions permissible under an Islamic constitution, most significantly limitations on the power and reach of the state. According to Turabi, the state's role should be confined to the task of laying down general rules that enable society to organize its own affairs.

Responding to the question "what would an Islamic government mean?" Turabi asserts that "the model is very clear; the scope of government is limited" (Turabi and Lowrie 1993, 22). However, in regard to the question of whether initially the government in Sudan must play greater role, Turabi is less direct in his reply. Although he restates that "ideally, the Muslims always look to minimal government, very much like the liberal tradition," he adds, "very much like the Marxist dream of a vanishing state" (Turabi and Lowrie 1993, 23), suggesting that in a manner similar to that suggested by Marx, an Islamist government would use law and policy to reform society and then subsequently withdraw. As to his own role in government, Turabi responds, "I'll say I'll have a role in society rather than in government. I want to assert the fact that society is the primary institution in Islam rather than the state" (Turabi and Lowrie 1993, 23–24).

According to Turabi, in the Islamic state power lies with society, not the governing apparatus: "the government is also limited not only as to function but as to power" (Turabi and Lowrie 1993, 24). At the same time, the form that power takes should not be confused with the form of power idealized in liberal notions of democracy, public participation, and political representation. Turabi does maintain that "the most fundamental institution" in Islam is "public opinion," what he identifies as the imperative to enjoin what is right and forbid what is wrong *(al-amr bil-ma'ruf wa al-nahi 'an al-munkar)*. Yet power lies not with the people in the sense of their will or interests, but in the *shari'a* (Turabi and Lowrie 1993, 24). Turabi emphasizes a spirit of consensus *(ijma')*, which he says unites Muslims. This consensus must be derived from the contemporary *shura* of the people who represent the divine will (1993, 20, 73, 132–33). According to Turabi (and most other Islamists), the Qur'an envisions Islamic society as an active society. However, Turabi understands that activism not in a participatory or even associative sense, but active in the sense that individuals take it upon themselves to correct what is improper and promote what is proper according to the *shari'a* in society at large. The authority of government is limited by Islamic law, which he characterizes as a "detailed constitution" and higher law. The difference Turabi emphasizes between *shura* (consultation) and democracy (as government of people) is that "the higher law in Islam is so intensive that the legislature has much less to do or say" (Turabi and Lowrie 1993, 25).

However, there is also much less for the people to do or say about politics proper (outside the realm of morality), given that the average person has no direct access to political office, and *shura* (consultation), upon which the governing consensus must be based, is confined to civil society. This is because unlike secular democracy, which acknowledges no authority higher than popular sovereignty, *shura* recognizes and is subject to God's sovereignty, which Turabi sees as comprehensive and sufficient for governing political life: "The legislature, the Congress or Parliament or whatever, is not sovereign at all. The *shari'a* governs so much. Sometimes the rules are categorical and certain and you can do very little about them. Sometimes there are principles that guide you and control you, but there is a lot to do within these limits" (Turabi and Lowrie 1993, 25). This limitation on what a representative body can do is a guarantee of the supremacy of the religious will of the community" (Turabi 1983, 244). What *shura* and democracy have in common in his view is the principle that political sovereignty belongs to and is exercised by the people, who are free to articulate or voice preference regarding an appropriate course of action, set of rules, or even representative bodies—though Turabi cautions that they are not free to break any fundamental Qur'anic principles (1993, 68–80).

Turabi's focus on civil society, understood as an Islamic *umma* united by the recognition of God's sovereignty, serves to focus attention away from the way in which the freedom of society to choose its interests, rulers, and representative bodies might be compromised in an Islamic state. Furthermore, Turabi claims that *shura* in Islam must cover not only the relationship between the state and society, but must include all the institutions of society, even the family. Each sector must work to advance consultation in public and private life (1993, 68–71). Turabi says that he is less concerned with the Islamic state becoming a repressive institution (the fear that he, like Huwaydi, associates with Western political thought), than with the possibility that "Muslims will give too little space to the state and have too little regard for it" (1993, 52).

The Sudanese government with which Turabi has been affiliated has hardly been limited in the sense he describes, but rather has met its society's secessionist movements and demonstrations with widespread human rights abuses and national security acts such as that enacted in 1995, which provided agents of the government with wide-ranging and largely unsupervised powers (Lawyers Committee for Human Rights 1996). More recently, Turabi himself has suffered oppression at the hands of the ruler whom he once helped to establish power and rule. Now a part of the opposition, he has again looked to society in calling for the *umma* to rise up against this "dictator." Perhaps most problematic in Turabi's assertion of a democratic state and a pluralist civil society is the lack of specification of the way in which popular participation in projects of renewal and interpretation *(ijtihad)* of the *shari'a* might be meaningfully realized. As pointed out earlier, Turabi's Islamic polity lacks those institutions that connect civil society with the state. So long as there exists no agreement, or process for reaching agreement, on the meaning of the *shari'a,* which is supposed to be the basis for the evaluation of government action, it is impossible to limit that government, let alone to differentiate legitimate from illegitimate policies and actions by the regime.

Rachid al-Ghannouchi, a former philosophy teacher and the current leader of the Nahda (Renaissance) Party in Tunisia makes some bolder strides toward addressing those issues Turabi neglects. Ghannouchi has even less affection for the state as such than Turabi, and he is even more strident in his focus on the task of developing a strong civil society to counter state hegemony by limiting the sphere of its activities. No doubt the different circumstances in which these individuals live and the different statuses of their respective movements dictate this variation in emphasis: Turabi wavers somewhat precariously between providing the ideological force behind the ruling power in Sudan and being considered a threat to the ruling power, while Ghannouchi lives in exile from his home, Tunisia, and his party is banned from participation in Tunisian politics. Nonetheless, their ideas about Islamic state and society are quite similar—so similar, in fact, that the two were able to publish a book together (Ghannouchi and Turabi 1981).

Like Turabi, Ghannouchi argues that the texts of the Qur'an and *sunna* and the command for consultation *(shura)* are the founding canons of authority in the Islamic state (1993, 109). He argues that the former sources preserve the Islamic consensus, while *shura* is the apparatus through which that consensus is substantiated and developed. However, Ghannouchi further specifies that the political legitimacy of the political system must be tied to its provision of freedom for political parties and different elements of civil society to compete peacefully over social political and ideological agendas. In response to Islamists who see this proliferation of modern forms of social and political organizations, such as parties and civil groups, as divisive to the *umma* and in conflict with God's sovereignty *(hakimiyya),* Rachid al-Ghannouchi propounds the concept of the *dini* (the religious, the sacred, or the absolute) and the *siyasi* (the political, the profane, or the relative) and the idea that Islam includes *faragat,* spaces left for humans to fill in accordance with the respective needs and exigencies of time and context (Tamimi 2001). Within this space, Ghannouchi maintains that the people can and should exercise democratic powers and practices. "Today," Ghannouchi argues, "the concept of civil society is associated with non-governmental organizations, which seek—as mediators between the state and the individual members of society—to improve and bolster the intellectual, spiritual and moral standards of these members and of the community as a whole. The purpose of these organizations is to achieve as much self-power of intervention and, when necessary, to mature into a force to influence the state and supervise its performance." Ghannouchi continues: "This conception concurs with the role of the *umma,* the society Muslims established more than fourteen centuries ago. As a society founded to a large extent on freedom and voluntary cooperation, where authority is not repressive, and having regard to relations among its individual members, traditional Muslim society is a model of civil society" (2000, 107). Ghannouchi's support of freedom of association runs deep enough that, unlike most Islamists, he claims that he is willing to accept even parties that profess atheism, such as the communist party (Ghannouchi and Turabi 1981, 34–35). The political system must permit free elections to representative institutions. If all this takes place, he argues, the Islamist movement will lend its support and legitimacy to the system, as the popular authority grounded in God's governance is the highest authority in society.

Despite Ghannouchi's argument in favor of permitting atheist political parties, he is no secularist. He is quite clear that "there is no future of a political group that wants to govern on the basis of refusing the rule of Islam . . . because this society is of an Islamic nature. . . . [The secularists] have to give up their hopes of changing the nature of Islam to 'Christianity,' meaning a set of beliefs that bears no relationship to the running of society's affairs" (1993, 16). Ghannouchi deems a "secular democratic regime" to be the "second best alternative for Muslims" as they work to establish an "Islamic *shura* (consensual) stem of government" (2000). This belief suggests that his acceptance of secular and atheist civil associations and parties is also part of a "second best" means of achieving a "first best" solution, a solution that ultimately might exclude such associations and parties. So too, he specifies that "the president of the Islamic state must be a Muslim, a good Muslim" (1993, 160). It is important to remember that civil society for Islamists such as Ghannouchi is not *merely* a mediating force that curbs and checks state power. It also is specified as the realm that "seeks . . . to improve and bolster the intellectual, spiritual and moral standards" of the community. As such, "this conception concurs with the role of the *ummah*" (2000, 107). Ghannouchi views both the society and the state as grounded in the comprehensive unity of Islam *(tawhid)*, which should be the source of its values. As such, the leader of the state and at least the majority of society must be "good Muslims." Rather than religion's providing a point of distinction between state and society, Ghannouchi views Islam as the bond that holds these two realms together. According to Ghannouchi, the Islamic state is not a theocratic state: its ruler does not enjoy a divine mandate or a privileged religious status, but rather is elected by the people to carry out an agreed-upon "contract" between himself and the nation (Ghannouchi and Turabi 1981, 33–34). The nation, according to this contract, is to be ruled by Islamic law *(shari'a)*. If the ruler violates this contract, the nation, being the source of authority, has the right to replace him. In fact, "not only does the Islamic faith permit a Muslim to resist despotism and rebel against it, but it makes it incumbent upon him to do so" (Ghannouchi 2000, 115). This perspective is in stark conflict with the conventional perspective of the relationship between the governed and the government in Islam, where anarchy is perceived to be a greater evil than tyranny, and thus Muslims are instructed to accept any ruler who can maintain the *'umma.* According to Ayubi, "The Sunnites tend to look at the state as the organizer of their religious affairs. In their traditional theory, the ruler is the implementer of the Word of God; and in this capacity obedience is due to him from every believer. . . . Little space is allowed for disagreement: consensus *(ijma')* is a cardinal principle. . . . The culture is assimilationist in spite of diversity, giving an impression of unity and harmony to be derived from the comprehensive translation of religion into public policies. Opposition to the state is therefore almost tantamount to abandoning the faith; it is not only to be condemned by society but is also to be prevented by the state" (1992, 83–88).

Ghannouchi maintains that "the first Islamic society" constitutes the original civil society. The "civility" of the Islamic religion provided the source of the "transition" from the "natural association of the clan," based on the "legitimacy of power and necessity," to "a community whose members associate together voluntarily, and in which relations are governed by law" (2000, 110, 111). "True civility is found in Islamic society, because belonging to it is not founded on instinct or fear" but, rather "on faith which individuals embrace freely" (2000, 107). Although "civility" and "civil society" are associated with "the Western liberal tradition," Ghannouchi locates in modern, secular Western societies a "profound potential for *tawahhush*" (wildness, savageness) (2000, 15).[15] According to Ghannouchi, while in Islamic societies "faith," not the state, "keeps the peace," "in Western civil society the prevention of *tawahhush*, or the maintenance of civilized standards, requires the dedication of enormous material resources in order to compensate for the erosion of the influence of religious deterrents" (2000, 117). Further drawing an image of "wildness" in Western civil society, Ghannouchi likens the effect of secularism to a story of two beasts, "the bear and the fly," where in trying to kill a fly, "the bear ended up killing his fellow bear whom he intended to rid of the annoying insect" (2000, 120). Ghannouchi's point seems to be that while secularism aimed at freeing individuals from various forms of oppression, it ended up killing off all those things binding the individual to God and humanity. Again, Ghannouchi develops this notion of the increasing savagery found in the West: borrowing an expression used by the Tunisian writer and Nahda Party ideologue Muhsin al-Mili, Ghannouchi claims that secularism ultimately brings about "the death of man" because it views him as merely a body and confines itself to man's material needs and, in the process, denies man one of the most important features that distinguishes him from other creatures and forms the basis of the solidarity that binds him to his fellow man: his "metaphysical dimension" (2000, 120). As a result, Ghannouchi concludes, secularism has developed into the "antithesis of civil society," which requires forms of altruism, solidarity, and community.

Ghannouchi's conception of civil society relies upon Western liberal political institutions, supported by an Islamic community and infused throughout with an Islamic ethos. Even though many aspects of Islamist notions of civil society bear close resemblance to especially Arab liberal conceptions—for example, in terms of civil society's role vis-à-vis the

15. The editor of the book in which Ghannouchi's article appears notes that "*tawahhush* is derived from the Arabic word *wahhasha* (to be unable to warm or reconcile, or to be alienated or become estranged). *Tawahhush* is the return to a wild or savage state, to barbarity."

power of existing states—what Arab liberals and socialists fear about civil society when spoken through the mouths of the Islamists is that it will not be seen for what it really is. The fear is that this Islam, once legitimated as the source of political and social norms, will prove repressive for individual liberties, especially for non-Muslims, nonpracticing Muslims, Muslim minority groups, and Muslims with new or different interpretations of their religion. Women from all of those categories also express a particular concern about Islamic rule. Aware of this concern, both Turabi and Ghannouchi have asserted women's right to participate in civil society and public life. As is discussed in chapter 7, one Islamist woman, Heba Raouf Ezzat, has exerted particular effort to ensure a central role for women in an Islamist civil society.

Hasan Hanafi's "Reflective Islamic Approach"

In his articulation of what he terms a "reflective Islamic approach" to civil society, the Egyptian philosophy and liberation theorist Hasan Hanafi identifies two opponents: the "radical [Islamic] fundamentalists" who "reject the very idea of civil society as alien to Islam" and the "radical . . . secular, Westernized alternative." He deems his own approach the "reformist or modernist alternative," which is based upon the conviction that the "ingredients of classical Islam" should be creatively interpreted, through *ijtihad,* to reflect "modern social needs" (2002a, 180).[16] So too, Hanafi maintains that the three approaches to civil society correspond

16. Hanafi, formerly an outspoken champion of secularism, now refers to himself as a "leftist Islamist" to signal his intention to articulate a "progressive," "liberal" perspective in accord with the Islamic religion. Hanafi (1993) distinguishes "traditional Islam," as "exemplified by the present Islamist groups," from "progressive Islam," as "exemplified by the Islamist left." He has come under considerable attack from Orthodox Islamists and the shaykhs of al-Azhar. For more on the politics of Hanafi's interpretation of Islam, see Browers (2004). Although my discussion of Hanafi's "translation" of civil society relies most heavily on an essay written in English, the ideas expressed in that work are found in Arabic. See, for example, Hanafi 1998. Because this essay has been widely circulated among English-speaking scholars as an "Islamic view of civil society," it seems useful to place it in the context of other debates taking place in Arabic. Hanafi's same essay also appears in Hashmi (2002).

with various Islamic societies. Afghanistan represents the radical fundamentalist view for Hanafi, because of the "strict application of Islamic law" to all sectors of politics and society there such that civil society is stifled under a "military dictatorship." Lebanon, according to Hanafi, represents the radical Western view to the extent that its society is based on the minimization of sectarianism, the maximization of citizenship, and a balance of power between state and society. Hanafi seems to suggest that neither the state nor society in Lebanon is based on Islamic laws, values, or institutions. The "middle course" is one he locates in most states in the Muslim world, "where we find a balance between civil society and the dictates of medieval Islamic law. In the public sphere, the rules of civil society are maintained: citizenship, equality of all in front of the law, the constitution, freedom of expression, democracy, pluralism, and the like. In the private sphere, such as family law, the *shari'a* is maintained since it is one of the sources of civil society" (2002a, 171–72). Hanafi acknowledges that even among the states pursing the "middle course" the reality is that "civil society in its fullest sense is still far from realized."

The shortcoming of the third course is that it balances rather than integrates the two extremes: fundamentalism continues to unduly influence the private sphere and secularism maintains the public sphere. Hanafi's aim, then, is to develop a conception of civil society that is most suitable for a truly Islamic state, one that is less concerned with the "application of the penal code or the observance of external rituals," and more aimed at implementing "the spirit or intent of the law *(maqasid al-shari'a)*." According to Hanafi, "a state that pursues this spirit may not replicate all the institutions associated with Western civil society, but it will foster and protect many of the values that underlie it" (2002a, 172).

In many respects, Hanafi's articulation of civil society is similar to that of Wajih Kawtharani. Like Kawtharani, Hanafi points to many institutions in Islamic history and theory that "played roles analogous to those institutions of civil society," in that they were "independent from political authority" and maintained a system of "checks and balances in society." Hanafi pays particular attention to the *'ulama*'s checks on the interpretations of law employed by the wielders of political power; the *diwan al-mazalim,* "a tribunal to which every Muslim could go and complain against any form of injustice done to him directly by the ruler or the ruler's agent"; the *awqaf* (religious endowments; plural of *waqf*), which supported scholarship; the Sufi orders *(tariqas)*, which "played extremely important mediating roles between families or tribes and the state"; and the institution of *hisba* (guardianship), which was charged with "supervision of the application of law in society, especially in the marketplace, against treachery, mishandling monopoly, usury, exaggerated profits, and the like" (2002a, 174–75). Also similar to Kawtharani, Hanafi is clear that while these autonomous institutions do go some way toward balancing the power of the state, "civil society is not a panacea for all the problems of state and society" (2002a, 183). Both Kawtharani and Hanafi seek to articulate an authentic but liberal and democratic understanding of politics. The point of difference between Kawtharani and Hanafi is really primarily one of emphasis as they outline their diagnosis of where the real problem lies and where the solution is to be found. Whereas Kawtharani views a lack of democracy as the problem and called for a liberal, democratic state—albeit in line with Islamic history and values—Hanafi understands an "inauthentic," "conservative" interpretation of Islam as the problem, and a "reflective" reinterpretation of that tradition as the solution.

Elsewhere, Hanafi characterizes his method of interpretation as "phenomenological." What he means by this is that all meanings exist in relation to particular, concrete, historical existence. As such, he places human beings and their needs at the center of his interpretation in order to reconstruct "Islamic culture at the level of consciousness in order to discover subjectivity. Instead of being theocentric, it becomes anthropocentric. [It] provides the method for analyzing lived experiences and describing the process of linguistic pseudo-morphology" (1988, 231). Hanafi's interpretation of Islamic texts aims at what he himself has characterized as an Islamic equivalent to Latin America's liberation theology.[17] While it is clear that Hanafi draws from socialist traditions of thought, he situates his own work within the Islamist ideological tradi-

---

17. Hanafi (2002c) provides a summary of his understanding of his own role in the founding of "a social phenomenology applied to the Muslim world."

tion: "I have followed the intellectual path mapped out by Sayed Qutb, whom I consider one of the early Islamist leftists." And he offers his program as an alternative to less progressive interpretations of Islam (Sayed 2002). In response to those who lay emphasis on Islam as "submission," Hanafi maintains that the term *aslama* yields "a double act of negation and affirmation" as it asserts a surrendering to God but rejects the yielding to any other power and states his intention as reasserting "the other aspect of Islam, intentionally hidden, namely the rejection, the opposition, and the revolt, taking into consideration the actual needs of the Muslim Masses. . . . The ambiguity of the word Islam is consequently a reflection of the dual socio-political structure of society: Islam as submission both to the political power and to the upper classes, and as revolt by the ruled majority and the poor classes" (2002a, 184). Hanafi seeks to contribute to a revolutionary religious consciousness aimed at facing modern conditions of inequality, poverty, underdevelopment, domination, westernization, and alienation. His interpretation of Qur'anic passages asserts the necessity of "the implementation of social justice and the foundation of an egalitarian society," one based on public ownership of such things as "agriculture, industry, [and] mining," given that verse 59:7 dictates "What God has bestowed on His Apostle (and taken away) from the people of the townships—belongs to God, to this Apostle and to kindred and orphans, the needy and the wayfarers" (2002a, 186–87). Hanafi's Islamic society is also one in which the "application of the Law is an individual and societal commitment," and in fulfilling that commitment, "the scholars of the law" play a central role as the "guardians of the city." According to Hanafi, these scholars "are the educators of the people and the conscience of the rulers. They can denounce the tyrants and mobilize the masses. Their words are substantiated by their deeds. Their ideas correspond to their feelings. The revolution of Transcendence [what Hanafi calls God] is a revolution of Thought, of Knowledge and of Science" (2002a, 189).

Although in some respects Hanafi's thought has remained remarkably consistent over most of his long and prolific career as a writer and theorist of Islamic ideology, one detects a shift in his thought. John L. Esposito and John O. Voll note a shift from his early years, "as a student and a young intellectual, [when] he saw the major challenge coming from the communists, and then possibly the secular leftists," to a critical perspective in the 1980s that "was aimed at the 'Islamic fundamentalists' and 'ritualists' who represented, from Hanafi's perspective, the forces of repression and obscurantism" (Esposito and Voll 2001, 71). One also detects another more recent shift in Hanafi's thought most prominent in the time period that comprises the focus of the present study. While in the past Hasan Hanafi has characterized his position as part of the "Islamic Left" and quite intentionally drawn upon socialist ideals in a manner similar to Christian liberation theologies,[18] more recently he has placed greater emphasis on ideals more closely associated with liberalism, such as rights-based freedoms and pluralism as well as a liberal understanding of civil society. So too, one detects a decrease in the revolutionary tenor of Hanafi's writings among those sectors of civil society that are to engage in the necessary revival and reform. The "scholars of the law" who in 1988 are called to "denounce the tyrants and mobilize the masses" are described in the 2002 essay as "Muslim intellectuals and modernist scholars practicing *ijtihad,* creatively linking ageless concepts of a just and virtuous society with the modern ideals of civil society" (2002a, 188). In the place of a "mass mobilization for the defense of mass interests" and "a belief-system of opposition" (1995, 108, 146), he has increasingly sought a "middle course" aimed at "developing and implementing pluralistic and representative conceptions of state and society from within the Islamic tradition" (2002a, 187). The unity *(tawhid)* Hanafi describes is "faith in the unity of God and the unity of His Creation [that] helps to unify Islamic societies, despite their great social, cultural and economic diversity" (2002a, 177).

Islamist Civil Society in Opposition: A Shift from the *Khalifa* Ideal or a New Democratic Realism?

Many analysts ask whether the attention Islamists are giving to democracy and civil society represents a transformation in their thinking or

18. Hanafi (1981) published one issue of a journal announcing the foundation of the "Islamic Left."

merely a shift in their strategy. According to the 1989 program of Algeria's Islamic Salvation Front (FIS), the organization seeks "the consolidation of the ideals of justice, liberty, and democracy," but maintains it "cannot take place without an organization that will take charge of all demands and needs (material, moral, and spiritual) in order to strengthen resolve according to the demands of renewal and the requirements of the movement" (Islamic Salvation Front of Algeria 2002, 273). How do democratic institutions fare in such an all-inclusive organizational structure? It is well known that the FIS founder and chairperson, ʿAbbasi Madani (b. 1931), claims to support democracy, pluralism, and elections (Moussalli 2001, 64) while his deputy chairperson, ʿAli Belhaj (b. 1956), rejects democracy as an alien concept, a Western evil, and a heresy. But even Belhaj advocates *shura* "as a political duty that Islam imposed in order to eliminate tyranny" (Moussalli 2001, 61). Yet one must be clear that *shura* in Belhaj's view is compatible with the absences of elections once an Islamic government is in place, as he has been infamously known to repeat: "When we [the FIS] are in power there will be no more elections because God will be ruling." The Program's plan suggests a compromise between the two positions. While it calls for the adoption of *shura*; "the equality of political, economic, and social opportunity"; "guarantees freedom of expression, encourages self-criticism and sets out the accountability of all institutions and organizations"; and the "reassess[ment of] the electoral code in order to guarantee the free arbiter of the Umma and safeguard its rights to express its will legitimately and according the Shariʿah" (Islamic Salvation Front 2002, 278–79), FIS characterizes the program it offers as "successive steps that need to be taken, taking into account the spirit of the times" (Islamic Salvation Front 2002, 276), and lacks a discussion of the status of this political program if times change, for example, if the result is successful election of FIS. This was precisely the worry of many after FIS electoral victory in 1991.

Nonetheless, at the turn of the twenty-first century the willingness of a number of Islamist groups and parties to work within existing electoral systems—often with democratization prominently featured in their political platforms—is readily apparent. For example, the Muslim

Brotherhood in Jordan has participated in elections since 1989 and has become an outspoken advocate for further democratic reforms in the country. In a statement explaining why the Brotherhood chose to boycott the 1997 elections in Jordan, the Muslim Brotherhood pointed to the "deterioration of democracy" owing to the changes in voting and press laws in the country and claimed that "they believe that their decision of boycotting the 1997 parliamentary elections is necessary to establish democracy and protect the homeland." The statement is also interesting for the articulation of the Muslim Brotherhood's understanding of democracy's three "bases": (1) elected representative governing institutions, (2) a free press and freedom of expression, and (3) "political pluralism and parties." According to the Brotherhood, the government undermined these bases through the institution of a "One Man One Vote Law," the temporary press laws, and the "arbitrary and unjustified arrest" of opposition party members and candidates (Society of the Muslim Brothers 2002, 302–3).

It has been noted that "one question that has divided Muslim scholars over the ages is whether an Islamic state precedes an Islamic society or vice versa. . . . [Will] the state impose Islamic norms so as to create an Islamic society, or will a society made up of pious and observant Muslims *nolens volens* beget an Islamic state[?]" (Chehabi 1996, 146). Many Islamist groups do appear to have undergone a notable shift of political strategy by the 1990s. For example, according to Nizar Hamzeh, "while there are still pockets of virulent militancy, notably in the south, developments indicate that Hizbullah, who led a military *Jihad* (holy struggle) in the 1980s against Israel, the West, and all those who opposed its vision of an Islamic Lebanon have entered a new phase since 1989; this phase might be called the phase of 'political jihad.' . . . Increasingly, the early revolutionary Iranian model has been overshadowed by a more participatory one which led to the party's participation in Lebanon's political system. The party has concentrated more on the ballot box than on bullets and military victories" (Hamzeh 1992, 321). In a later article, the same analyst suggests that "even if we consider the use of the ballot box by the leadership of Lebanon's Islamists as tactical or opportunistic, there is reason to believe that the process of local politics will transform this opportunistic commitment to a more substantive one" (Hamzeh 2000, 739). There is a vast literature in political science that supports Hamzeh's suggestion that political inclusion or participation can result in political moderation.[19]

Huwaydi, Turabi, Ghannouchi, and Hanafi all share a call for the revitalization of civil society as a way of strengthening Islamic society and providing for good Islamic governance. Other Islamists, such as the Egyptian writer Muhammad Salim al-'Awwa, have more explicitly called on the fortification of civil society as a means of freeing society from the grip of the state and its unrepresentative institutions (1993, 19). In some respects, the Islamists discussed here offer an interesting point of contrast with the Arab liberals discussed in the previous chapter. Civil society is here prioritized over democracy, whereas Arab liberals argued that a democratic ethos and process were a necessary basis for the formation of a truly civil society. And procedural aspects of democracy (a rule of law and access to elections) appear to take precedence over more substantive notions. Not surprisingly, whereas Arab liberals viewed a democratic ethos—neither necessarily religious nor secular—as the prerequisite for the success of democratic action and processes, Islamists looked to Islamic values as both the prerequisite and the desired outcome of a democratic process.

In other respects, however, these Islamists share much with those liberal thinkers who bracket the discussion of secularism or explicitly draw upon religious institutions in conceptualizing hybrid or *ahli* forms of civil society. Just how close these two perspectives have become is apparent in a recent study by Sayf al-Din 'Abd al-Fattah Isma'il, an Egypt-

19. The many versions of this hypothesis are surveyed in Schwedler (forthcoming). Although rejecting a simple and "neat" causal relation between inclusion and moderation, Schwedler's work both argues and provides evidence for some ideological moderation on the part of the main Islamist groups that organized into political parties and vied for space in a pluralist system during Jordan's and Yemen's "stalled" democratic experiments. However, her analysis suggests that moderates are likely to become more moderate as a result of increased interaction in plural political spheres, while suggesting there is no evidence that radicals become more moderate.

ian political scientist whose works claim to offer an "Islamic perspective" on various political topics (1989; 1998). In a study that he wrote in collaboration with al-Habib Janhani, a professor of economic and social history in Arab and Islamic society in Tunisia, Isma'il attempted to articulate an authentic Islamic concept that combines the *ahli* and *madani*, a "symbiotic reading" *(qira'a mutakafila)* of *al-mujtama' al-madani* and *al-mujtama' al-ahli* (Janhani and Isma'il 2003, 64). According to Isma'il, the form of civil society most appropriate to Muslim societies is one that encompasses what he terms "the institutions of the nation [*umma*]" (Janhani and Isma'il 2003, 97). Here he specifies various Islamic institutions that historically stood opposed to the institutions of political power, such as the *'ulama*, the mosque, *ifta* (the issuing of legal opinions), *waqf* (charitable institutions he deems particularly important in securing the financial independence of the *'ulama*), and the extended family. Isma'il departs from liberal thinkers, such as Kawtharani, by basing his Islamic liberalism not on an ethic of tolerance, nor even individual responsibility, but on a notion of community responsibility.

Certainly the Islamist emphasis on civil society as the locus of the preservation and perpetuation of Islamic values is reflected in the strategy of the Islamist movement. In discussing Egypt, one author notes how

> during the last two decades the Islamic movement has created large numbers of private voluntary organizations, including a few which run major schools, hospitals and charitable institutions. However, the main focus of the movement has been upon formal grass-roots associations, avoiding formal institutions since these tend to be controlled and monitored by the state. In particular mosque-centered associations have acquired considerable importance in, and influence over, the lives of people. By providing at nominal fees urgently need community-based social services such as kindergartens, medical clinics and social assistance to the poor which the state is unable to provide or does so inadequately, those associations have become highly effective agents in Egypt's civil society. (Zaki 1995, 63).

When Egyptian President Husni Mubarak held a much-publicized "national dialogue" in 1994, the Muslim Brotherhood was refused official representation. In response, the son of Brotherhood founder Hasan al-Banna and general secretary of the Lawyers' Union, Ahmad Sayf al-Islam Hasan al-Banna, argued that, though excluded as a political party, they could still be included as a representative of civil society. Instead, the government resorted to the repression of the group. The repression of the Muslim Brotherhoods in Egypt and the Sudan and of the Nahda Movement in Tunisia may attest to their success in mobilizing civil society, as Zaki suggests, but it also represents a more recent setback in their ability to actualize their strategy. It is in this context that a Muslim woman has addressed Islam's strategy for political change by rethinking the civil society idea itself in a way that refocuses attention on the family and women. To the extent that she is successful in doing so, she precludes the exclusion of women from the realm of civil society—and from a central role in the *umma*—on the part of the Islamists as well.

In a book examining the interrelations of the concepts of civil society and fanaticism, Dominique Colas argues that religious discourse formed the background against which the public sphere in early modern Europe emerged (Colas 1997). Perhaps the Islamist institutions that have carved out a space in Arab society, and the Islamist ethos that is shared by many Arabs, will prove a precursor to the emergence of civil society in this region as well. Or conversely, perhaps the dominance of the civil society in Arab political thought will provide the opportunity—or even reveal the necessity—for Islamists to join in the building of a civil sphere that is defined both more broadly (in the sense that it is not confined to those who adhere to particular religious practices) and more narrowly (in the sense that it exists within the framework of the modern state) than the classically conceived notion of an Islamic *umma*.

6

The Civil Society Debate and
New Trends in Arab Socialist Thought

Another freedom fighter bides the time from his houseboat
—Fu'ad in Abdel-Malek,
A Study of the Vernacular Poetry of Ahmad Fu'ad Nigm[1]

Arab Socialism: Crisis and Marginalization

The fall of the Soviet Union was a decisive event for socialist forces throughout the world and certainly Arab socialism is no exception.[2]

1. This line, written by Ahmad Fu'ad Nijm (Egypt, b. 1929), is from a song performed by Shaykh Imam 'Isa (Egypt, 1918–1995), entitled "Farewell to Che Guevara." Abdel-Malek translates the lines as "Latter-day freedom fighters, in houseboats." The poem continues: "What can you say, may your riches stay on, Guevara is dead" (Abdel-Malek 1990, 152). Shayk Imam was a blind singer of leftist political protest songs who put many of Nijm's poems to music. Throughout the 1970s, Shaykh Imam and Nijm were the icons of political dissent in Egypt.

2. For the purpose of this chapter and following the common self-identifications in contemporary Arab discourse, I use the appellation of "socialist" to designate a broad category of individuals who occupy both the Marxist and the socialist/nationalist trends in Arab political thought. However, the differences between these two are important and, when appropriate, will be indicated. Marxism appeared in the eastern Arab region in the beginning of the twentieth century before spreading to North Africa in the middle of that century and was an important influence on both Arab nationalist-socialist and universalist socialist and communist trends in the Arab context. Arab national-socialism began in Syria with the pan-Arab movement, and led to the formation of the Ba'thist parties now in power in Syria and Iraq and the Nasirist movement in Egypt. In 1940, a Syrian Christian, Michel Aflaq, and a Syrian Sunni Muslim, Salah al-Din al-Bitar (1912–1980),

Much of the political discourse of Arab nationalism, socialism, and Marxism, with its focus on social and economic justice, "popular" democracy, the revolutionary party, and Frontal politics, has given way to a more "liberal" discourse of pluralism, human rights, and civil society. Individuals and movements identified as socialist have been in power and "lost" over the course of the last several decades: the socialists have lost much of whatever claim they might have once had to represent the masses, and the people Arab socialists claim to represent have changed as well. As many socialists have come to realize, they cannot reconstruct their identity irrespective of the present reality, in which two factors in particular demand their attention.

---

founded the party of "Arab Resurrection" *(al-ba'th al-'arabi)* on the principles of "one nation with an eternal message." The Ba'th party merged with the Arab Socialist party of Akram al-Hawrani (b. 1914) in 1952 to become the Socialist Arab Resurrection Party *(hizb al-ba'th al-'arabi al-ishtiraki),* not only linking socialism and nationalism, but declaring the latter to be the former's truest expression. The Ba'th became further radicalized through its competition with the Arab communist parties, which rejected the theories of pan-Arabism, advocating a program that included "the redistribution of wealth, the national ownership of public utilities and resources, the limitation on ownership of land, social insurance, labour legislation, the establishment of free trade unions, and the guarantee of a minimum standard of living" (Hourani 1983, 357). In Egypt, Jamal 'Abd al-Nasir also moved toward a fusion of pan-Arabism and socialism, also in response to competition with communism (as well as both influenced by and in competition with Ba'thism), in addition to the imperatives of social conditions in Egypt and the attraction of the Soviet model of development. Despite the latter's adoption of such forms of political organization as democratic centralism, the single party, the economic conception of history (phases of development, stages of society), and the analysis of imperialism, some commentators have questioned these party-states' commitment to and understanding of socialism. For example, Ayubi (1992) argues that socialism was an "afterthought" and "strategic device" for Arab regimes that found it useful to create organizations parallel to their Soviet or East European counterparts during the cold war. Further, the Nasirists, for example, have found it politically useful to insist upon their differences from Marxism and communism on principled as well as pragmatic grounds (Salmawi 1993). There remain many Arab communists who are virtually indistinguishable in their thinking from communists in Europe. But when I intend to refer more broadly to the diverse strains of socialism and communism, I opt for appellation of "left" or "leftists."

The first factor is the strength of the Islamist movement. The Islamists form the main opposition group in most contemporary Arab societies, as well as the largest opposition bloc in most parliaments that allow such representation. In attempting to deal with this new political reality, Arab socialism is seeing a growing political and intellectual split among their ranks. On the one hand, many socialists in a number of countries are opting for the state, while, on the other hand, some socialists, seduced by the popular impact of the Islamists, are trying to woo the Islamists (Jabar 1997, 91).

Intellectually, this first trend of Arab socialism (that of opting for the state) continues to look to the Nahda heritage with its concern for modernization and state-building as an intellectual source for progressive economic, social, and political reform. Politically, although in many countries the political apparatus has become increasing isolated and authoritarian, these socialists view the state as the last bastion of rationality against the rise of religious fundamentalism, and thus join it in the effort to counter, confront, or eradicate the Islamist threat. At the same time, Faleh A. Jabar, an Iraqi communist who has been in exile since 1978, notes that the nationalist wing of Arab socialism, which has been in power in many countries (for example, Egypt, Algeria, and Tunisia), in particular, has "made a U-turn in terms of socio-economic, regional and even international policies. In countries where there was a strong corporate-state economy, often built in the name of a particular form of Arab socialism, there was a fast, downhill move toward economic liberalization (deregulation) or privatization (the sellout of the state sector) or both. The tilt from corporatism to commercialization was coupled with a leaning toward, if not an alliance with, the West" (1997, 91).

Many of the more doctrinaire Marxist parties reflect a similar shift, which has brought this traditional oppositional bloc closer to the state. This shift is seen most clearly among the communist parties in Tunisia and Algeria, who not only shifted toward liberalism but also reflected this shift by eliminating any reference to Marxism or socialism in the names of their parties (Jabar 1997, 100). The communist parties in Algeria and Tunisia reveal the same tensions involved in the shift toward liberal discourse as the nationalist/socialist states, demonstrating a reluctance to adopt a fully liberal stand in light of their concern over the threat, whether potential or real, of an Islamist takeover. Thus both branches of the left (communist and Arab socialist) in these countries have to some extent proved willing to ally politically as well as ideologically with existing secular states.

On the other hand, as the opening speeches of the four "Nationalist-Islamist Conferences" that have been held to date by the Center for Arab Unity Studies in Beirut between 1994 and 2004 attest, a number of left-leaning Arab nationalists have come to the conclusion that at least some Islamist groups and individuals can be nationalized (Arabized) and rationalized (Center for Arab Unity Studies 1995; 1999; 2004a; 2004b). There are many trends in Islam, and these socialists find that if they are willing to shelve the question of secularism they are able to find plenty of meeting points with many of the Islamists.[3] Further, Arab nationalists likely have some political strategic interests in allying themselves more closely with the predominant oppositional force in the region. According to the Islamist historian Basheer Nafi, the roots of the Arab Nationalist-Islamic Conference lie in

> the fundamental changes that the Arab state and politics experienced after the third Arab-Israeli war of 1967. The 1967 defeat was not only seen as the ultimate failure of the Arab state but also signaled the beginning of the end for the alliance between the ruling clique and the Arab nationalist intellectual. For the great majority of Arab intellectuals, disengagement from the state's bankrupt project looked now as the only way for survival. . . . While the Arab nationalist intellectual joined the forces of opposition, the state entered the postnationalist age in which ideological authoritarianism was replaced with self-serving policies of limited political openness. . . . [A]s the distance between the Arab intellectual and the state evidently increased, the intellectual's discourse grew more and more to resemble that of the Islamist. (Nafi 2000, 111–12)

3. Alexander Flores discusses this "opportunism and accommodation" in the context of the Egyptian left (1997, 90–93).

The most recent dialogues reveal the trajectory of this alliance since the first conference theorizing the nationalist-religious ideology relation was held in 1989.[4]

The most striking change is that, although the first such meeting in September 1989 was entitled "National-Religious Dialogue" *(al-Hiwar al-qawmi al-dini)* (Bishri 1989), the four later conferences were specified as dialogues between nationalist and Islamic thinkers *(al-Mu'tamar al-qawmi al-islami)* (Center for Arab Unity Studies 1995; 1999; 2004a; 2004b). Despite some continuity among the participants, less effort was exerted at the later conferences to account for the plurality of religions in the region, while the central importance of Islam as a regional political force is duly acknowledged. In general, there is a shift from the "National-Religious" and the "National-Islamist" conferences—and even a shift between the first and second "National-Islamist" conferences toward including fewer university professors and more heads and members of movements, parties, and organizations, as well as professionals, predominantly lawyers, doctors, and politicians. Further, the backgrounds of the participants in the 1997 conference are less readily known from the names and, in a number of instances, it is difficult to differentiate the representatives of Islamism from those representing nationalism. The exceptions to this are of course the number of well-known Islamists, most significantly the secretary-general of Hizbullah, al-Sayyid Hasan Nasrallah (b. 1960), whom Khayr al-Din Hasib (1998), the president of the Center for Arab Unity Studies, describes as "the representative of the new discourse of the Arab movement." As the opening remarks of the various conferences attest, Arab nationalists/socialists and the Islamists unite around the Palestinian issue, around relations between the United States/West and the Arabs, and, to varying extent, around the issue of democracy, understood as antiauthoritarianism.

The overture to Islamist forces is not confined to the Arab social-

---

4. A closer reading of the conference proceedings reveals a more complex interaction than merely a shift toward Islamism on the part of Arab nationalists. I discuss these conferences at greater length and depth in a forthcoming work.

ists/nationalists, but is also becoming increasingly common among historically doctrinal Marxist-Leninists who, with the Islamists, maintain an oppositional status vis-à-vis the state. The attempt to attract a broader base is seen in the Palestinian Communist Party's decision in the winter of 1991 to change their name to Palestinian People's (Sha'b) Party, symbolic of their anti-Israeli nationalism, which joins them with Islamic fundamentalism (Jabar 1997, 106).[5] Significantly, the program of the Second Congress, which took the decision to change the party's name in October 1991, is absent of any specific mention of Marxism (Sharif 1997, 67). In fact, one prominent Palestinian socialist sociologist, Salim Tamari (b. 1945), notes that "in common with many reformed socialist parties in the last few years, [the Palestinian People's Party] recognizes what it is against rather than what it seeks. The new party is neither communist nor Leninist. It is hardly even socialist. In its political preamble it defines itself as a movement struggling for independence, democracy, progress, social justice and a socialism 'congruent with the specificities of the Palestinian realities' " (Tamari 1992, 17). Among the most important of those "realities" is the resurgence of Islam. Tamari identifies "openness to religion and religious membership" as one of the main attributes of this reformulated party.

However, a number of Arab intellectuals on the left, wary of allying themselves too closely with either the state or the Islamists, are attempting to use the loss of the Soviet model as an opportunity to reconstruct a new non-Soviet vision of Arab socialism. Most of these intellectuals are critically appropriating much of what is considered liberal discourse (pluralism, human rights, civil society), but are also returning to the works of Marx and other socialist thinkers. In the process, many are (re)discovering the works of the Italian thinker Antonio Gramsci. As early as 1987, Peter Gran wrote that "while the Arabs have yet to produce a Gramsci, the questions which Gramsci raised in the 1920s are now quite freely raised in the *Ahali* newspaper in Cairo, in 'Jumblatist' circles

---

5. A notable exception to this trend of groups downplaying their overtly communist and Marxist elements is the Communist Party in Iraq, which remains one of the country's most prominent political forces.

in Lebanon, in the Islamic left of the Ayatollah Muhammad Baqr al-Sadr and Hasan Hanafi, and in academic writings" (1987, 92). A former deputy secretary-general and veteran member of the Lebanese Communist Party's Political Bureau, Karim Muruwwa (b. 1930), commented in September 1993 that "our theoretical resources are not confined to Marxism-Leninism, but have been expanded to encompass the whole range of Marxist thought—Kautsky, Rosa Luxemburg, Gramsci, Mao, etc. We need, of course, to develop the theory in order to cope with the changing world" (quoted in Jabar 1997, 101).[6] The same position was expressed in the Iraqi Communist Party's draft program published in 1991. As Muruwwa's comment suggests, Gramsci is not the only intellectual source of Arab socialists' reconsideration of their theories. Nor does Gramsci necessarily represent the predominant source or trend for that movement. Rather, I focus on the turn to Gramsci for two reasons. First, the work that has come out of this turn is, in my view, some of the most theoretically innovative, because it requires the incorporation of a number of new concepts and a reconsideration of many old ones. In this sense, it may possess the potential for contributing to a revival of socialist thought, perhaps even a "post-Marxist" socialism, in the Arab region.

The second reason for the focus on Gramsci has to do with the second important factor that Arab socialists face in the current context: the prevalence of a discourse about civil society, both internationally, since the transformations in East and Central Europe, and increasingly in the Arab region as well, as the number of nongovernmental organizations continues to grow. Gramsci provides the predominant entryway for an Arab socialist qua-socialist reconsideration of their position vis-à-vis the civil society debate. In fact, Arab socialists were fairly late overall in entering the civil society debate. Discussing Tunisia, the socialist sociologist Abdelkader Zghal notes that "since the legislative elections of April 1989, and particularly since the Declaration of the Nahda Party directed against the program reforming religious instruction books [in November of that same year], all of the political sides—except the farthest left—

---

6. For an outline of Muruwwa's careful proposals for dialogue with religious parties, see Ismael and Ismael (1998).

used the concept of civil society to mobilize their sympathizers together" (Zghal 1992a, 44). Not surprisingly in light of the Marxist tradition prior to Gramsci, Arab Marxists saw "civil society" initially as a bourgeois liberal term. For Marx, civil society *(bürgerliche Gesellschaft)* refers to the bourgeois economy of producing and consuming individuals and is productive of contradiction and conflict, an entity to be transcended and reproduced at a higher level of social development (Poulantzas 1973). Both the form and the content of civil society are "bourgeois." As a result, in the Marxian tradition of political thought, the notion of a "socialist civil society" has been viewed as an oxymoron. As Ghassan Salamé has noted, "falling back on Marx [in defining civil society] is no help" particularly in the Middle East "since he saw civil society as the society which a particular actor, the bourgeoisie, historically produced." As this Arab sociologist notes, "looking for the Arab or Persian bourgeoisie at the origin of established states would not be a very useful enterprise" because that state in this region is "artificially created" by colonialism (1994, 12–13). Within the discourse of Arab socialism, Marx's definition of civil society remained restricted in scope as an actor in the conflicts of the modern period and received little in the way of theoretical attention until very recently.

The fact that the socialist history of thought, unlike the history drawn on by Islamists and statist forces in the Arab region, possesses a distinct understanding of one conceptualization of civil society (the Marxist notion of civil society as bourgeois society) may provide an explanation for why socialists have resisted standing under the banner of civil society, that is, uncritically accepting the normative dimensions commonly attributed to the concept in current discourse. Ironically, the discovery of civil society as an important concept originally came from within Arab socialist discourse in the 1970s by some intellectuals who had come to view the Soviet state as a repressive mechanism of the party bureaucracy and sought alternative views of the party, the state, and society in socialist systems, such as the thought of Gramsci (Labib 1992).

According to the Tunisian sociologist al-Tahir Labib, the Arabs' relationship with Gramsci dates back to at least the 1970s. In fact, *The Modern Prince* was translated into Arabic in 1970, and a number of other works were translated shortly thereafter. However, Labib maintains that most of this relationship has been one of Gramsci's "presence by his absence" in which a "profession of ignorance has preceded any rare reference to him" (1992, 62). Until recently, very few Arab scholars had actually read Gramsci's writings. In addition, until the past few years the few references to Gramsci were limited to his concepts of "hegemony," "the organic intellectual," and "the historic front," with little if any reference to Gramsci's notion of civil society. The early studies of Gramsci also remained limited to only a very few. It was only in the late 1980s to early 1990s, and after other intellectual currents (for example, liberal and capitalist) began to propagate the term, that some Arab socialists began to show a serious interest in philosophical debates about civil society.

At least part of the reason for the neglect of Gramsci can be explained by the third challenge the Arab socialists face in addressing the problems of contemporary politics: their Leninist heritage. Labib notes that "Gramsci's influence was not present in the writings of the Arab communists loyal to the Soviet Union" (1992, 64). Historically, Arab Marxists have preferred the Third International, and reflected a Leninist version of democratic centralism and a political strategy based on a "war of maneuver" led both by "revolutionary specialists" and by bureaucratic cadres. The Bolshevik legacy of Arab socialism has meant its intellectuals tend to subsume the interests of society in general within those of an abstract proletariat, which has made it difficult to develop creative strategies of mass mobilization and to reach wider sectors of the public (such as merchants, housewives, and professionals) who do not have sufficient proletarian credentials. To a considerable extent this inclination remains apparent, even in the writings and discussions of Gramsci's work. At the same time, what one finds in the most recent Arab discussions of Gramsci is an attempt to move, think, and create beyond the Third International. Inspired by Gramsci, some Arab socialists have begun to explore strategies for propagating their political perspective through mass-based organizations—in Tamari's words, strategies for moving "from Frontist politics to civil intrusions" (1992, 19).

The remainder of this chapter examines recent trends in Arab socialist thought, focusing in particular on a number of studies of Gramsci's work, beginning with the proceedings of the 1990 conference in Cairo on Gramsci and the issue of civil society in the Arab region, and continuing with more recent writings in Arabic. Arab socialist intellectuals' discussions of Gramsci in these literatures are characterized as having passed through two phases. The first involves the (re)appropriation of Gramsci's ideas as a way of gaining a foothold in the discourse of civil society that dominates much of contemporary Arab political thought. The second phase moves toward a more critical assessment of the current Arab civil society and an attempt to formulate a strategy for changing that reality in light of Gramsci's thought.

Phase 1: Arab Socialism's Search for an Inroad to the Civil Society Debate

In November 1990, the Center for Arab Studies in Cairo and the Arab Group for Sociology (based in Tunis) organized a conference entitled "Civil Society in the Arab World in Light of Gramsci's Thought" (Rashid 1992b). Although almost two-thirds of the participants came from Egypt (not surprisingly, since the conference was held in Cairo), it also included scholars from Tunisia, the Sudan, Lebanon, Algeria, Iraq, and Palestine, in addition to two scholars from Italy and one from the United States. In her opening remarks, professor of French literature at Cairo University and conference rapporteur Amina Rashid offered some preliminary answers to the question that she noted most of the participants had raised: "Why Gramsci?" "Why are the Arab Studies Center and the Arab Group for Sociology celebrating this fighter, agreed by all to be truly great, but seen by many as incompatible with prevailing progressive thought, a thinker whom some see as a radical socialist whereas others consider him to have revised the interest in Marxist thinking?" (1992b; 1992a). The most superficial reason suggested by Rashid is the celebration of the centenary of Gramsci's birth (b. 1891).

However, Rashid suggests two more significant reasons for the gravitation to the thought of Gramsci: "First, we believe that the great thinkers in the world comprise a part of our heritage of struggle as socialist thinkers critical of the prevailing order and established thought. Second, and fundamentally, in our struggle to understand our current stumbling Arab reality we see in the thought of Gramsci a model for struggle that knows how to broach especially the universality of concepts and the specificity of his Italian heritage in the totality of the principle of the world-historical movement" (1992a, 9–10). By arguing that Arab socialism and Gramsci share a common heritage, Rashid indirectly identifies one of the main tasks of the socialists' entry into the civil society debate: finding a foothold within historical narrative about civil society that addresses the movement in both its "universality" as a socialist movement and its "particularity," that is, its need to address the current Arab reality. Zghal more explicitly voices a similar awareness of this task by pointing out that Gramsci lived in historical circumstances "that required thinking about a new question, within an old intellectual model"; Arab thinkers live in a similar context: civil society and its relationship to contemporary reality must be considered within the Marxist tradition (1992a, 52). However, Zghal also suggests that the problems facing Arab society in some respects more closely resemble at least one issue Adam Ferguson faced: "How can we keep our civilizational path toward the division of labor and military specialization [and] from transforming into a tyranny and despotism? How does civil society protect itself from the danger of the militarization of its political order?" (1992a, 48). Although it is doubtful that Zghal is calling for a citizen militia, as Ferguson does, his reference to the question of the militarization of the political order suggests one concern that Arabs face that is not addressed by Gramsci, one perhaps that is better addressed by liberalism than by the Marxist tradition. Unfortunately, Zghal does not carry through this comparison.

In the current context, Arab socialists have found that the return to Gramsci involves, in part, reclaiming this thinker as their own, that is, as a thinker in the Marxist tradition of which they are a part. In his contribution to the conference, Labib notes that, in contemporary Arab political thought, Gramsci is often not considered to have any particular relationship with, nor necessary distinction for, the Marxists: civil society, organic and traditional intellectuals, and ideological hegemony are concepts cutting through different forms of rhetoric. He has incited non-Marxists as well as Marxists. Gramsci's concept of civil society in particular has often been confused in the mix of Western political thought with liberal theories of civil society (Labib 1992, 68; Bishara 1998, 210). In addition, Labib cites an Islamic magazine in Tunis, *"mustanir"* (1984), that devoted a number of pages as well as its cover title to Gramsci. He also recounts how in response to this appropriation of Gramsci by the Islamists, the progressive journal *"Atruhat"* published the proceedings of a meeting in which one of the participants lamented the fact that "those firmly with Marxism were late in their discovery of Gramsci while [Rachid] al-Ghannouchi, the leader of the Islamic movement in Tunisia, applies Gramscian ideas, since he knows how to invade civil society."[7] The former chief of the military arm of Egypt's Muslim Brotherhood, 'Ali 'Ashmawi, seems to confirm the left's fears in his claim that the Brotherhood's current strategy was to infiltrate and dominate the institutions of civil society (Kamal 1994). Commenting on this remark, another Egyptian thinker characterized this as the Brotherhood's "Gramscian strategy" (Zaki 1995, 119). Labib notes that while "certainly we do not always need to read Gramsci to invade civil society, it is certain that Islamists in the example of the culture of Ghannouchi know Gramsci well" (1992, 68–69).

Thus Labib attempts to reassert Gramsci's Marxist-Leninist credentials by drawing attention to the fact that the Italian thinker wrote in the context of prison and thus the reader of his *Notebooks* must look "between the lines" for what is not mentioned by name, such as references to Marx and Lenin (1992, 66). Labib also argues that Gramsci already has an influence and presence among the Arab left via the writings of the Lebanese Marxist Mahdi 'Amil (1936–1987). Although 'Amil seldom cited Gramsci directly, Labib argues that 'Amil provides an example of an Arab thinker who "can be considered to have been inspired by or to have appropriated from Gramsci." In fact, Labib maintains that, in light of 'Amil's deep knowledge of Gramsci, his "undeclared Gramscism appears more deeply influential than other Gramscians who perhaps more frequently claim him and repeatedly cite him, without comprehension and

7. Labib refers to a 1988 issue of *Atruhat* that I have been unable to locate. Ghannouchi was sentenced to eleven years in jail in 1981 by Habib Bourguiba's government, but was released in 1984 and is now living in Europe as a political exile.

thorough study" (1992, 66). 'Amil viewed the Lebanese state as consisting of a "financial caste" allied with forces of "political feudalism" that engaged in pre-capitalist relations of production and practices politics via a system of fiefs and sects (1979). The state in turn "reproduced" the sects in a political form by consecrating the role of confessional representation in all state institutions.

In addition, a number of papers presented at this conference are concerned with articulating Gramsci's form of Marxism as a progressive project that to a significant extent corresponds with the concerns of socialists in the contemporary Arab world. Rashid, for example, identifies two basic questions that she argues provided the starting point for Gramsci's revolutionary perspective of civil society: (1) Why did the revolution begin in backward Czarist Russia and not in the industrial developed West as Marx and Engels predicted? (2) How can the particular historical experience of Italy, and especially its intellectuals, help better understand the limits of progress and revolution in light of the division of the country into a thriving industrial north and a backward peasant south still under the control of the cultural hegemony of traditional society? (Rashid 1992a, 10). According to Rashid, these two questions correspond with Arab socialists' preoccupation with appalling class disparities, a retreating state in terms of social services, the overall decline of socialism as a political force coupled with a growing Islamist influence both at the level of the masses and at the level of the state, and continuing foreign occupation, as well as an increasing dependency on and hegemony of foreign organizations and a general absence of democracy.

Rashid notes how Gramsci formulated his concept of civil society in light of his consciousness of the danger of institutions of the state ideology that supplement its instruments of repression (the army, police, courts, and the laws) by means of persuasion: the media, education, propaganda, and so forth. "Gramsci studied its particular influence in thwarting the activities of the opposition and insurgency and in creating a modern 'myth' that nourishes the dreams of the masses and replaces the interests and aspirations in the world with a false alternative while the repressive state remains basically in the underdeveloped world." Here Rashid asks, "what is the true role of the ideological apparatus in the

Arab world? What is the condition of civil society in it, between the enduring traditional organizations and the components of dependency from the 'developed' world in the garb of technological ideologies? And what is the possibility of developing other ideals and institutions to create circumstances for helping to free the Arab people?" (1992a, 10).

In sum, based on this conference, it is possible to identify at least three justifications given by Arab socialists for their recent turn to Gramsci's political theory and in particular to his version of civil society.[8] First, Gramsci is a Marxist, but an alternative kind of Marxist who adapts the ideas of Marx to his own situation: the Italian context. Many Arabs find Gramsci's context for working out his concept of civil society (the backwardness of the south or "The Southern Question") more relevant than the British context where more "liberal" notions of civil society were conceived.[9] An Iraqi professor of literature at the American University in Cairo, Firyal Jabburi Ghazul, articulates this appeal of Gramsci most explicitly, describing the Italian's writings as "texts with which we can enter into dialogue because they deal with issues of concern to us. Although they were written more than half a century ago in Italy, the concerns, aspirations, and debates contained in them appear to me parallel to our own, Arab and international concerns today" (1992, 136). Second, Gramsci's writings on intellectuals both contribute toward an understanding of the persistence of the Islamic movement (through his concept of the traditional intellectual) and provide one possible vision to bridge the gap between socialist intellectuals and the people they claim to represent (through his concept of organic intellectuals). Third, Gramsci's concept of civil society, unlike the predominant (Tocqueville-

8. At the same time, the return to Gramsci in a post-Soviet Union context is not devoid of critique: for many socialist thinkers Gramsci still poses a "Leninist problematic" with the idea of the "New Prince" in the form of a "Revolutionary Party" (Traboulsi 1998).

9. The first of these explanations is emphasized by Sadiq Jalal al-'Azm (1998b). See 'Azm's (1998a) own critical analysis of civil society, which draws from the theories of Hegel and Marx. Some aspects of this work are discussed at greater length in chapter 4.

inspired, Putnam-revised)[10] conception of civil society (found in the writings under the direction of Augustus Richard Norton in English and Saad Eddin Ibrahim in Arabic), sees a potentially negative, as well as a potentially positive, role for this level of social activity. Many of the recent findings emerging from the works of Arab political scientists are confirming the more ambiguous relationship between civil society and democratization (with social and economic equality) in the Arab region. For example, the liberal Lebanese political scientist Paul Salem argues that his study of the incivility of Lebanese civil society brings him "to a vision . . . close to that of Gramsci, who viewed civil society as simply reinforcing the reach and subtle power of governing elites rather than as an emancipation of nonelite interest and perspectives" (1998, 10). These three justifications correspond to the main facets of the Gramscian-inspired rethinking of Arab civil society: (1) the analysis and critique of the postcolonialist state; (2) the analysis and critique of the Islamist movement; and (3) the critical conception of Arab socialism's role—actual and potential—in Arab civil society.

Phase 2: Gramsci-inspired Rethinking of Arab Civil Society

The Modern State and Islam in the Maghrib

According to Labib, "the Maghribis [specifically, scholars from Morocco, Tunisia, and Algeria] were the first to venture into 'Gramscism' " (1992, 66). This assessment is certainly true of Gramscian interpretations of the postcolonialist state and its relationship to society. Of the scholars attending the Cairo conference, the Tunisian sociologist Abdelkader Zghal is one of the Arab intellectuals who began in the late 1970s to draw on Gramscian ideas at length in his work. In an essay originally published in French in 1977, Zghal uses Gramsci's concepts of a "historic bloc" and

10. Putnam's central variable is "civic engagement," "civic community," or "civic tradition," rather than civil society, but the terms are often used interchangeably in subsequent work and in social science discourse. Putnam's conception refers to horizontal interpersonal networks in society, "like neighborhood associations, choral societies, cooperatives, sports clubs, mass-based parties and the like" (1993, 173).

"civil society" to answer the question of why so many Algerian peasants refused to take up the land they were assigned by the postcolonialist state's agrarian reform plan (1985). This work is of interest not only because of its early date, but also for its continuity with Zghal's later discussions of Gramsci and civil society.

Zghal describes the notion of "historic bloc" as a situation of an "alliance" between, on the one hand, "a social structure" or "classes," and on the other hand, the two aspects of the superstructure: "an ideological superstructure—the 'civil society' or ideological direction—and a political superstructure—the 'political society' or domination (state apparatus)" (1985, 332). Zghal argues that the two aspects of the superstructure are relatively autonomous. This means that "a radical and rapid change on the level of the political society (revolution or independence)" does not necessarily correspond to "a total and immediate collapse of the civil society." Rather, "the intellectuals of the Old Regime continue to influence the new civil society in gestation." However, Zghal takes this argument one step further by asserting that "the organic intellectuals of the new historic bloc cannot escape contamination by the ideology of the traditional intellectuals (those of the Old Regime)" (1985, 333). In short, Algerian peasants resist the land distributed to them by the ruling class because they have yet to adopt the nationalist ideology of that class.

In his writings during the 1990s Zghal transfers his argument from a discussion of Algerian peasants to an explanation of the Islamist movements in Tunisia, Algeria, and Morocco, and what these movements reveal about the postcolonialist state. Beginning in the 1980s, a number of groups that form parts of the Islamist movements in these countries began to accept the "rules of the game" of the modernizing state, which meant a multiparty system (including communists) with elections. Rather than merely explaining the Islamist strategy as a manipulation of the system (although he suggests it is that to an extent as well), Zghal places the movement in the context of the ideology and dynamics of the national liberation movement and the institutional of that movement in the context of the Tunisian nation-state—that is, in the context of the ruling hegemony. He argues that the Islamist movements are "a parasite on the rationalist ideology and a reaction to the establishment of nationalism as it was applied in each country" (1992b, 466). The state, for its part, "still clings to the rationality of absolute rule despite having known the principle of political pluralism." In the context of his own country, Zghal argues that the exiled leader of the Tunisian Islamist movement al-Nahda, Rachid al-Ghannouchi, is "the illegitimate son of [Habib] Bourguiba,"[11] the leader of Tunisia's independence struggle and the country's first president, just as "Bourguiba was the illegitimate son of the Third and Fourth French Republics" (Zghal 1991, 217). "However," he clarifies, "both are above all products of Tunisian civil society, well entrenched within the long tradition of exchange between the two shores of the Mediterranean and continuing the reformist tradition of political men such as Kheireddine [Khayr al-Din al-Tunisi] and of the ulema such as Tahar ben Achour [Tahar bin Ashur, 1879–1973]" (Zghal 1991, 211).

While president of Tunisia, Bourguiba sought to modernize cultural practices, including reducing the influence of religion on society and guaranteeing the rights of women, economically, in marriage, and in social life; and in so doing he offended a large part of the public who remained tied to their own traditions. However, during the period of confrontation between the nationalists and the colonial powers, Bourguiba defended women's wearing of the veil and even declared as heretics Tunisians who willingly acquired French citizenship. Ghannouchi, on the other hand, opposed what he criticized as Bourguiba's process of Westernization in the name of religion, while at the same time identified his own movement as more akin to the European Renaissance in a Muslim context than to a fundamentalist movement. He also contends that in seeking to reform their societies, Islamists are committed to social justice, human rights, pluralism, and an end to dictatorships. Zghal points to a speech Ghannouchi gave to American Muslims in which he advised them to be faithful to their country, to assimilate its language and culture, and not to live isolated and withdrawn into the Muslim community (1991, 209). Thus, whereas the leader of the modernizing nationalist movement has politicized the religious, the leader of the Islamist movement distinguishes between notions of citizenship and religious confes-

---

11. The aged and allegedly incompetent Bourguiba was deposed in 1987.

sion. In fact, Zghal locates Ghannouchi's wider appeal not among the more traditional classes, but among "the more or less Westernized new social periphery [who are] fighting against the feeling of depersonalization and social marginalization" (1991, 217), hence the source of what Zghal refers to as the "illegitimate" relationships between these political forces.

More important, Zghal uses these understandings of a historic bloc and the autonomy between the two aspects of the superstructure—civil society and political society—in order to explain the flawed states that currently exist in these countries. His main thesis here, as in his contribution to the conference "Civil Society in the Arab World and Its Role in the Realization of Democracy" in Beirut (1992), is that the new ruling order founded at independence broke down traditional relations but did not succeed in establishing a modern framework that recognized the individual and the individual's membership in a modern society. Even in Tunisia, which has, Zghal argues, perhaps the best organized civil society in the Arab region, society as a whole continues to privilege the idea of the community over that of the individual. The political decision to weaken traditional authority was easy to put into effect because of the strength of Tunisian civil society institutions that were favorable to this policy. However, since independence, as the state has seized more and more power, by taking over more domains of civil life and blocking the emergence of notions of the individual with laws and practices at the political level, civil institutions have been "suffocated."

The Algerian sociologist Ali El-Kenz explains the failure of the postcolonialist state in a related way that more explicitly draws upon Gramsci's notion of hegemony. According to El-Kenz, "the dominant groups emerging from the decolonization movements in the Arab World have given clear priority to the command function [direct domination] at the expense of the hegemony function" (1991, 77). Paradoxically, despite its mass base, the Algerian nationalist movement lost any possibility of cultural hegemony over these masses because of its success in enslaving the intelligentsia—this success led to the state's loss of both the intelligentsia and civil society (1991, 26). El-Kenz argues that this loss deprived the postcolonialist state of "the organic intellectuals . . . who might have breathed into it the life that civil society carries within itself, nationalist . . . thought, ran out of breath and was transformed into a dead language composed of crude slogans deprived of meaning" (1991, 77–78; see also Karru 1992).

For Gramsci the concept of "historic bloc" refers to a specific unity between the "base" and the "superstructure" in a given social formation that is, simultaneously, a form of thought-in-action such that popular beliefs acquire the solidity of material forces (1997, 377). But, as with much of Gramsci's terminology, the expression "historic bloc" had several meanings. In the sense that Zghal and Labib use it, "historical bloc" indicates the way in which a hegemonic class combines the leadership of a bloc of social forces in civil society with its leadership in the sphere of production. Gramsci also uses the phrase to refer to a counter-hegemonic group seeking to circumvent the privileging of one dimension of totality over another. Importantly it presupposes the unity between objective and subjective forces so that "man is to be conceived as an historical bloc" or the political party as subject of history or collective personality that acts "progressively" or "regressively" in relation to the historical movement. The latter notion of historic bloc is addressed by Arab socialists in their discussions of the intellectual.

The Intellectual—Traditional or Organic?

Intellectuals and their role in political and social change have long been discussed in Arab political thought. In an article first published in 1988, the socialist Egyptian literary critic Ghali Shukri (1935–1998) noted that although Gramsci's notions of the "organic intellectual" and the "collective intellectual" can be found in Arabic writings since at least the 1970s, his notion of the "traditional intellectual" has not provided a model of reference for the Arab thinkers. Shukri quotes Gramsci's statement that "[the formation of] traditional intellectuals is the most interesting problem historically" (Gramsci 1997, 17). "These words," Shukri claims, "are words worthy of our interest as ones who live in the vicinity of the *'salafiyya'* phenomena in contemporary Arab thought" (1992, 56). In fact, he continues, "it is as if [Gramsci] spoke of the 'contemporary *salafiyya* intellectual' in Arab culture." Further, while most analysts study the Salafiyyun movement as a collection of events, personalities of texts, the need exists, in Shukri's view, for a deeper study of the relationship between the movement's economic structure and traditional intellectuals.

Although at least one of the Cairo conference participants notes having read Shukri's article (Labib 1992, 67), the only individual there to heed Shukri's call for a sustained study of the relationship between economic structure and traditional intellectuals in the Arab region is the American scholar Peter Gran. In his paper entitled "Gramsci's Concept of the Traditional Intellectual: Appropriateness for Studying Modern Egypt," Gran maintains that Egypt is a country in which the strategy of hegemony and the important social institution of the traditional intellectual closely resemble those in Gramsci's Italy (1992). To illustrate his argument, Gran analyzes the Shaykh of al-Azhar, the president of the prominent Islamic university in Cairo, as example of a traditional intellectual in Gramsci's sense.

However, the paper that created the most controversy at the conference, if we are to judge by the report of the discussions that accompanied the paper presentations (Fawzi 1992b), questions the Gramscian categories of the intellectual. Although making almost no use of "traditional" or "organic" as descriptors, the well-known Palestinian cultural critic Faysal Darraj begins his paper by analyzing the way in which popular religion is the extension of official religion, and how the two are interconnected via traditional culture (1992). In response, the Egyptian sociologist Ahmed Kamal 'Awwad asks, "In so far as the traditional intellectual is able to penetrate into common sense and popular wisdom, what is the role of the organic intellectual?" (Fawzi 1992b, 321). The manner in which Kamal posed the question and the dismay it reveals suggests disagreement regarding the source of the organic intellectual's "organicity" and the traditional intellectual's "traditionalism." However, Kamal's question does raise an important issue: if we are to identify an intellectual's "organicity" by virtue of the extent of his or her penetration of "popular discourse" (as does Fawzi 1992a), "popular culture" (as does Darraj 1992), or "civil society" (as does El-Kenz 1991), the Islamists may more aptly fit the category than the socialist intellectual. One commentator at the Cairo conference rightly cautions that "we must study the social, economic, and political circumstances of the intellectual before we can describe the religious intellectual as traditional or that Marxist intellectual as organic" (Fawzi 1992b, 321). Yet it is precisely this characterization (the Islamist as traditional intellectual, the secular socialist as organic intellectual) that appears to be the underlying presumption of this conference.

Only conceived as such does the inclusion of the controversial Egyptian scholar Nasr Hamid Abu Zayd (b. 1943) among the conference participants makes sense. While a professor of Arabic studies at Cairo University, as a result of his "untraditional" application of modern literary methods of interpretation to religious texts, Abu Zayd was accused of apostasy in 1992, and hounded and brought to trial by Islamists. In 1995 a court declared him an apostate and dissolved his marriage on this basis.[12] Although Abu Zayd's erudite work has clearly important implications for secularist thinking in Muslim contexts, prior to this occasion Abu Zayd was considered neither particularly political nor socialist, and certainly was not known outside of his very specialized academic circle. As one commentator on his work notes, "the implications of what [Abu Zayd] wrote had to be teased out, someone had to bell the cat, for the stuff of his book was not streetcorner reading" (Ajami 1998, 216). Abu Zayd's contribution to the conference shows no particularly Gramscian influence, never cites the thinker nor uses Gramscian language. It is most concerned with exposing the "middle ideology" of the Islamic theologian Abu 'Abd Allah al-Shafi'i (767–820) as a political fabrication. One could certainly read into this piece an understanding of Shafi'i (the founder of one of the four main schools of religious law, or *fiqh*, in Sunni Islam) as an organic intellectual who put forth a particular ideology in order to establish a hegemony in the diverse and rapidly growing Islamic empire during the early years of the religion's spread. Yet, without considerable reinterpretation (and perhaps still with it) Abu Zayd's 1992 contribution remains a scholarly work that uses historical and ideological context in a way that is not particularly Gramscian nor intimates any particularly Gramscian or Marxist intentions.

12. For a fuller analysis of Abu Zayd's thought, see Browers (2004).

Nevertheless, Gramsci's account of the traditional intellectual re-mains underdeveloped in discussions of the Islamist movement. One possible reason for this lack of development might be the fact that in Gramsci's work one form of the traditional intellectual is found in the type of philosopher who emerges within the university, largely apart from mass society, while it is the organic intellectual who emerges within and maintains a connection with a fundamental social group (Gramsci 1997, 6, 12). The fact is that most socialist intellectuals who discuss Gramsci, although their sympathies and preoccupations may be opposi-tional and working-class, still find themselves in the role of traditional intellectuals—that is, within the academy and socioeconomically sepa-rated from the working class. Most of them are not in a position where they find it difficult to be involved in some kind of meaningful prac-tice—either by circumstance or choice. Shukri lived in exile until 1986, during which time he was either a student or academic, albeit a very pro-lific literary critic as well. Abu Zayd, who, with his wife, has left Egypt for a position in the Netherlands, has not proved to be an effective force in appealing to any secular instincts the masses may harbor, let alone seemed to have contributed to the emergence of a popular secular cul-ture in the region.

The problematic view of the organic-traditional distinction held by many of the conference participants may reveal as much of the ambigu-ity in Gramsci's conception as it departs from it. Darraj's response to the questions raised by his paper is more consistent with Gramsci's under-standing of these characterizations, yet also demonstrates the limitations of the organic/traditional distinction, specifically in the context of Egypt:

> In regard to the traditional intellectuals and the organic intellectuals, their existence is connected with the existence of classes formed histor-ically. . . . The existence of the bourgeois as a distinct class . . . [or] that of a working class distinguished historically and having an actual po-litical and cultural personality permits us to speak of an organic intel-lectual. In this framework I presented Shaykh [Muhammad] al-Sha'rawi because he forms a powerful case of confusion. He is a Shaykh accepted by the deprived and oppressed popular masses and he

is also accepted by the ruling power. In this situation he forms a hybrid intellectual. He is a hybrid intellectual because of the hybridism of the social classes. (Fawzi 1992b, 323)

Shaykh Sha'rawi (1911–1998), a popular Egyptian preacher, held many high-profile positions, including president of al-Azhar, head of graduate studies at King 'Abd al-'Aziz University in Mecca, and minister of *Awqaf* (religious endowments) in Egypt (1976–78). However, he is most widely known for his radio and television broadcasts from Egypt, including appearances on Egypt's first Islamic discussion television program, *Nur 'Ala Nur* (Light on Light). According to Darraj, there is presently no homogenous bourgeois class nor a homogenous working class in Egypt. So too, the Egyptian state is hybrid because it permits an Islamic intellectual, Shaykh Sha'rawi, to act as the intellectual of its ruling power, yet also permits secular practices and party pluralism, characteristics that Darraj suggests would not be permitted were Islam truly a hegemonic force in Egypt.

The papers presented by Darraj, Fawzi, and, to some extent, Abu Zayd focus on scrutinizing those aspects of mass culture that present both the support for and the alternative to this hybrid culture. Darraj and Fawzi in particular focus on scrutinizing what they refer to as "actual knowledge" or the "general sense" or "common sense" of the oppressed. The issue, as Darraj states it, is how to "transform popular mass culture to a new form of knowledge productive of real political influence that brings Marxism to its successful realization" (1992, 95). The "revival of the positive social actor [effective social actor]" is identified as the foremost goal in the summary of the conference discussion (1992, 317). Yet this social actor's task is described as being engaged in a dual critical act: the critique of the dominant bourgeois culture and the critique of the dominated masses. The latter leads Fawzi and Darraj to suggest the need for a critique of "folklore" and "popular religion." The problem, Darraj argues, is that "popular culture is a crude tool" for the intellectual. "It is possible for the general sense to dangle between critical awakening and fatalism. Folklore has been an expression of the needs and philosophy of the people" as much as it has been a form of "cheap profit and intellectual abuse" in the hands of popular religion. Popular culture has created in Shaykh Sha'rawi a television star and a religious leader who detests medicine and electricity, yet praises the American army in the Gulf War. Sha'rawi was host of *Shaykh Sha'rawi Talks*, a widely watched television talk show that explained Islamic principles in simple terms and spoke in a colloquial Arab dialect. Darraj also refers to the shaykh's *fatwa* (legal opinion), which banned organ donations and transplants after death as blasphemy, and his attack on electricity as against human nature because it turned night into day and made people "active at night." Sha'rawi also supported the assistance of the United States and other foreign parties in confronting Iraq in the Gulf, citing examples of the Prophet Muhammad's use of non-Muslim assistance to achieve his goals. Darraj himself seems to alternate between affirming Gramsci's understanding of "the new prince," the collective party that acts as the ethical and cultural reformer, and dismay at Gramsci's utopian faith in the working class as a force that can give expression to a unified philosophy. Yet Fawzi underscores the already existent distinction between religious hegemony and popular rhetoric about religion. The task in his view is to appeal to the latent secular and progressive instincts among the masses and to take hold of the tools of hegemony that support such a worldview in popular culture (1992a, 128).

Toward A Progressive Role for Arab Socialism: A Critique of Self and Civil Society

Since the Cairo conference of 1990 socialist scholars in the Arab region have further studied Gramsci's writings and have had additional time to reflect on the role of civil society within their own contexts. As a result, a more incisive critique of civil society has formed and a more sophisticated analysis of its possibilities may be beginning to emerge. A number of these writings have been published in an Egyptian monthly magazine entitled *al-Yasar* (The Left), published by the twenty-two-year-old National Progressive Unionist Party *(Tagammu')*, a national united front combining Marxists, Nasirists, and others. The list includes, more recently, "progressive Islamists." In July 1998, this party decided on the first changes in their program since 1980. Among the main issues that dominated the discussions was "the redefinition of socialism following the collapse of the Soviet Union." In their report on the discussions, socialism was defined as "a renewable and sustained program to emancipate humanity comprehensively . . . [and] the system most capable of managing society and economics and ensuring productivity and social justice." The party's platform affirmed their "rejection of a theocratic state and theocratic parties," and upheld "civil society and the state, based on a civil constitution and civil law" (Farag 1998). Although many of the changes in this platform reveal an appropriation of various liberal ideas, they also reflect the Gramscian view of the party as the unifier of different classes and intellectuals throughout civil society. That is, among socialist intellectuals, the party maintains a central role, at a time when the party's role as an organizer of political alliances with its own autonomous ideological identity is declining or rejected among Arab neoliberals and Islamists.

Prior to these discussions Farida al-Naqqash published an article in the magazine, entitled "A Civil Society or a Socialist Opposition?" in which she identifies a growing phenomenon among current and former socialist activists. The article is framed by pictures of Ahmad Fu'ad Nijm, Saad Eddin Ibrahim, Samir Amin (b. 1931), and Gramsci and opens with the following image: "Whenever I am invited to one of these select conferences held by intellectuals specialized in establishing organizations or groups which have adopted the appellation of the institutions of civil society, I find myself while at the doorstep of the hotel unconsciously recalling the line from the song of the deceased artist Shaykh Imam 'Issa that Ahmad Fu'ad Nijm wrote 'In Farewell to Ghifari': 'Another fighter bides the time from his houseboat' " (Naqqash 1996, 78). Nijm and Naqqash refer to Abu Dar al-Ghifari (d. 652), an important figure for Arab Marxism. He was a companion of the Prophet Muhammad and reputably a rebel against the privileges and hoarding of wealth on the part of Mecca's mercantile elite. Early Egyptian Nasirists and Marxists sought the roots of Arab socialism in the teachings of Ghifari and he remains an important source in all attempts to "authenticate" this movement. The choice of pictures appears quite intentional in that it displays a range of options for Arab socialists. Ahmad Fu'ad Nijm, an important poet and activist of early Arab Marxism, represents the heyday of socialist activity.

Saad Eddin Ibrahim represents a former socialist (of the Arab social-ist-nationalist stripe) who has more recently championed a decidedly Western-style liberalism and its corresponding form of civil society. In his influential article, Shukri criticizes Ibrahim for his role as an "organ-izer of the coercion that the ruling class exercises over the subordinate classes by means of the state." Shukri points out that, while head of the Arab Thought Forum in Amman, Jordan, an organization with close ties to the then Crown Prince Hasan, Ibrahim wrote an article (1984b) enti-tled "Crossing the Fissure between the Intellectuals and the Decision Makers in the Arab World," which argues that society provides a bridge between the "prince" and the intellectual (Shukri 1992, 59–63). Despite the critique Ibrahim has suffered from the left for his ties to various sta-tist forces, the Egyptian state felt sufficiently threatened by Ibrahim and his Cairo organization, the Ibn Khaldoun Center for Development Stud-ies, to arrest them in July 2000. In May 2001, Ibrahim was sentenced to seven years' imprisonment for receiving foreign funding without au-thorization and disseminating false information abroad. The sentence was overturned on appeal by the Court of Cassation and sent back to the State Security Court for retrial. In July 2002, the State Security Court again convicted Professor Ibrahim. In December 2002, the Court of Cas-sation overturned his sentence for the second time. A final retrial took place on February 4, 2003, before the Court of Cassation, which decided on March 18, 2003, to acquit Ibrahim and his codefendants. The process of trial, overturn, and retrial seems to confirm the view of those who ar-gued the charges were politically motivated.[13]

The figure who represents a more critical view on normative, liberal conceptions of civil society like those espoused by Ibrahim in Naqqash's 1996 article is the Egyptian-born Marxist Samir Amin. Amin is a Marx-ist economist of importance in the Arab world and beyond. He is cur-

---

13. An account of the trial, assessment of the politics behind it, and analysis of its implications for Egyptian civil society are provided by one of Ibrahim's defense lawyers, 'Abd al-Qadir Hashim (2003).

rently director of the Third World Forum in Dakar, Senegal. It is also apparent in the context of the article that Gramsci represents a possible alternative conception.

Naqqash mourns the fact that she "no longer meets a socialist intellectual who has not began, or planned to begin, establishing one of these [civil society] organizations, which must then conform entirely with a type of expert mission that America, the new world order and the institutions of international funding have launched with the aim of substituting [their agenda of] work for the protection of the environment, local services, women's organizations and the human rights of the individual, for [the traditional socialist agenda of] the rights of peoples, which in a previous period, were axes for the national liberation movement and social progression of the third world" (Naqqash 1996, 78). Although Naqqash maintains that there is no real contradiction between the freedom of peoples (the socialist project) and the right to freedoms and interests of individuals (the cause championed by these civil society organizations), "the actual practice leads to the existence of a gap between, on the one hand, 'socialist' political activity that aims at changing the existing reality to something better, which struggles out of necessity with the IMF and World Bank, considering it a tool for the hegemony of the great capitalist centers over our nation and, on the other hand, the task of civil society and the defense of human rights that has expanded its area of operations in an unprecedented manner under the shadow of the Europeans . . . without any corresponding change in the structure of the antagonistic political and legal structure of freedoms at the core" (Naqqash 1996, 78).

Naqqash argues that the bulk of the civil society movement is composed of socialist intellectuals who have established human rights organizations connected with various international funding bodies. The great majority of these individuals came from the ranks of the student movements and the progressive politics of the communists and Nasirists of the 1970s. She maintains that they ceased political activity for many reasons, "such as the violence of the police pursuit that exhausted some of them and made them prefer safety or to plunge into work and pursue professional success, or the lack of satisfaction with the pursuits and practices of the existing socialist parties, not to mention the resounding collapse of the socialist system" (Naqqash 1996, 78). This assessment of the civil society movement is confirmed by Sana' al-Masri's recent study of nongovernmental organization (NGO) activity in Egypt. Masri's 1998 work details the vast number of socialists who make up Egypt's NGO membership and skillfully traces the strings attached to donations and funds.

What Naqqash sees as occurring consists of no less than "the sabotaging of the socialist vanguard intellectuals in a distinct manner by sinking them in the illusion of activism without real activism or at least restricting to a minimum their activity as combatants." She attributes this "cyclone" of foreign funding as the rich north using "institutions to cleanse their conscience of the burdensome feeling of guilt resulting from the intense exploitation that the great capitalist centers enacted upon the southern countries and their peoples" (1996, 78). Naqqash quotes the Egyptian sociologist Samir Amin as saying that civil society "complements the role of the state and plays a basic role in the reproduction of the condition of a social alliance that safeguards the state of mutual harmony only when it is agreement on democratic political practice on the one hand, and an agreement on a respect for the laws of capitalist administration of the economic sphere, on the other." Samir Amin adds that "[w]e are not in need of a civil society that plays this role" (Naqqash 1996, 79). According to this view, the activists working in civil society end up "offering services that increase the need for them and for the withdrawal of the state, while decreasing state expenditure on these services, in accordance with the will of its financier." But the task of these socialists is not in any way connected with a program of political change: "The absence of a socialist political project or even socialist literature is one of the conditions of the financiers of these projects, since they are often on guard against anything that will anger the Egyptian government because it simply supports its program of structural adjustment" (Naqqash 1996, 79).

Naqqash claims that her critique is "not aimed at the former socialist fighters who moved to the other side when they became defenders of capitalism." Rather, she claims to be addressing those "socialists who still trust that socialism has a worthy future via the role of the conscious organized masses, creators of history who were yesterday in need of their intellectuals, their vanguards, not as actors for the good who pity them, sympathize with their hopes and rush to provide services for them, without acting to change the landscape or formulate a critical consciousness, but as socialist political fighters, committed responsible organic intellectuals—in Gramsci's expression—capable via the institutions of civil society of enacting ideological dynamism and political opposition" (Naqqash 1996, 79). Thus Naqqash provides the first intimations of not only those combatants who have been lost to the hegemony of civil society, but also of the unrecognized and untapped power Arab socialism has owing to the fact of the vast number of them who head these civil society organizations.

Naqqash's article demonstrates both the promising and the unfinished nature of Arab socialists' attempt to appropriate and adapt Gramsci's concept of civil society to their context. Unfortunately, she does not take the next step and articulate precisely what it means to build civil society organizations, staffed by socialists, as part of a revolutionary project. Naqqash does indicate one significant barrier to the move from a civil society staffed by socialists to a civil society as the ground of revolutionary activity that is unique to the current Arab and international context. Naqqash creates a distinction between those who control the instruments of domination (political society, the [Egyptian] state) and those who control the instruments of hegemony (civil society institutions, that is, international organizations and other forces of globalization). But, again, the implications of this development remain undeveloped.

This critical stance toward civil society in the tradition of Gramsci was continued in the next issue of *al-Yasar*. Yusri Mustafa notes that the expression "civil society" has in recent years "passed from pen to pen as a truth, a discovery and sometimes as a 'problematic' " (1996b, 67; also 1996a). Mustafa argues that "this widespread circulation [of the term] corresponds with the national and well-ordered inclination toward the operations of the market mechanism and the substitution of private monopoly in the place of public monopoly." Mustafa turns alternatively to Gramsci as a thinker who framed the issue of civil society as a "problematic."

Although Gramsci continues to preserve the Leninist heritage, particularly Lenin's ideas regarding the seizure of state power and his comprehensive view of the instruments of social change, that is, that fundamental view of the idea of the ruling vanguard party oriented toward the sum of revolutionary activities, at the same time and as a result of the reality of Western societies, he provides a model for revolution that differs from the model of the October Revolution. In this context Mustafa quotes Gramsci's distinction between Russian society and Western societies: "In Russia the State was everything, civil society was primordial and gelatinous; in the West, there was a proper relation between State and civil society, and when the State trembled a sturdy structure of civil society was at once revealed. The State was only an outer ditch, behind which there stood a powerful system of fortresses and earthworks: more or less numerous from one State to the next, it goes without saying—but this precisely necessitates an accurate reconnaissance of each individual country" (Gramsci 1997, 238). Mustafa interprets Gramsci's intention in this passage as distinguishing between, on the one hand, revolutionary strategy aimed against a power without civilizational and social supports and, on the other, a strategy aimed against a power having these supports. "In the second situation, the struggle must take place within civil society (meaning the cultural front). The attainment of state power necessitates embarking upon specific struggles aimed at seizing the fortress that fortifies the state behind it" (1996b, 67).

Mustafa focuses on Gramsci's realization that it was no longer possible to carry out revolution in Italy following the pattern of the Bolshevik revolution. Socialist forces were confronted by a far more complex process because these societies were increasingly differentiated, and, as a result, a political revolutionary process could not be achieved by a single act. The war of position is a form of political struggle that is possible in periods where there exists a relatively stable equilibrium between fundamental classes, that is, when frontal attack or war of maneuver is impossible. Mustafa argues that "this concept [the war of position] is distinguished by the fact that it opens the door to resources that correspond with the forces of social change in every society. It is a general concept in so much as it highlights the plethora of strategies of opposition and change . . . incorporating multiple and diffused movements over the whole of society" (1996a, 71). This strategy centers on building the broadest possible mass movement, using all possible means of getting in touch with the masses and seeing the progressive side in different expressions of rebellion and resistance.

In these articles, Mustafa, like Naqqash, does not delve into the practical implications of this Gramscian strategy for any particular political context. Gramsci maintained that each revolutionary strategy must be adapted to and worked out in, take into account, and adequately respond to the specificities of each particular political-cultural context. Mustafa, like the intellectuals at the 1990 Cairo conference, draws parallels between the situation in Italy and the situation in many parts of the Arab region. However, Naqqash demonstrates, the instruments of hegemony—that is, the instruments of civil society—are more global today than in Gramsci's time. At the same time, the left is both less organized (as a group) and more favorably positioned (at the heads of civil society institutions) than in Gramsci's Italy.

While Arab socialism has succeeded in locating a promising inroad into the civil society debate and in forming an incisive critique of the role of this realm of associational life, the hard work of formulating a workable strategy for changing contemporary Arab reality remains incomplete. At the same time, this debate is ongoing among the left. A more recent collection of writings edited by Mustafa and published by the Arab Research Center in Cairo and El Taller Organization in Tunis continues the critique of intellectuals' roles in civil society and the lack of an effective response to issues of "impoverishment" *(ifqar)*—both intellectual and economic—in the Arab region (Mustafa 2002). Yusri Mustafa and other intellectuals at the Arab Research Center continue to insist on the theme of democratization in the region and that democratization must be fundamentally tied to development that targets the lowest classes.

And there are indications that the leftists, working under the banner of "civil society," are engaging authoritarianism openly in even some of the more oppressive contexts. After the death of Syrian President Hafiz al-Asad and the succession of his son Bashar in 2000, the regime instituted a limited process of political and economic liberalization during a period now referred to as the "Damascus Spring." A "Civil Society Committee" was formed by various left-leaning intellectuals, journalists, and activists, which began to hold lectures and forums, usually in private homes. According to one analyst, "a subversive civil society resurgence, akin to Latin America's in the early 1980s or Eastern Europe's in the late 1980s, seemed imminent" (Haddad 2001). However, by early 2001, the Syrian regime began to crack down on these civil society forums. In addition, the civil society activity itself had begun to reveal "internal squabbles." According to one observer, those involved in these forums had lost the "art of association" after "nearly two decades of being silenced" by an authoritarian regime: they had become "accustomed to working alone, writing alone and criticizing alone" (Haddad 2001). It remains to see what sort of impact this fledgling civil society will have there (or even whether such a civil society actually exists, as Sadiq al-'Azm [1998a] has suggested, in an undeniable fashion).[14] So too, the verdict is still out on whether we are witnessing the emergence of a post-Marxist-Leninist form of socialism in Syria or elsewhere in the Arab region—that is, a way of viewing political change that both maintains Arab socialism's position in the international socialist tradition and adapts itself to the new re-

---

14. Among the most high-profile of such migrations to Islamism from the more decidedly socialist wing of Arab nationalism are Tariq al-Bishri (Egypt, b. 1933), 'Adil Husyn (Egypt, 1932–2001), and perhaps most dramatically the Palestinian thinker Munir Shafiq, who converted to Islam from Greek Orthodox Christianity to become a prominent Hamas ideologue. Among the most significant (and doctrinaire) Marxist intellectuals to shift toward a focus on civil society is Tayyib Tizini, whose most recent work, albeit critical of much civil society discourse (especially that which he sees as imposed by and in the interest of foreign powers), ultimately embraces the idea that a national democratic dialogue must begin in Syria, and that the "band of intellectuals" who first sounded the call for "civil society" in Damascus have already contributed toward such a dialogue (see Tizini 2001, especially the work's final chapter).

quirements and realities of the Arab region. But it is clear that at least some leftist activist-intellectuals in the Arab region have decidedly shifted away from state-centered sociopolitical reform without abandoning socialist ideals or trading socialism for an Islamist oppositional frame.

7

Gender and Its Absence in Arab Debates over Civil Society

Why is there an absence of women, as researchers and thinkers, at this forum? And why was not one of the papers assigned to a woman? Is it because Arab women do not have their great intellectuals and thus are only invited as mere listeners or commentators? This phenomenon reveals, in my view, the failure of [male] Arab intellectuals to understand the basic problem that stands before civil society and their failure to discern true democracy and its basic preconditions

    . —Nawal al-Sa'adawi, "What Is to Be Done? A Discussion Circle"

As a number of social science researchers have begun to refute the designation of Islam or "Islamic attachments" as the explanatory variable for the lack of democracy in the Middle East (Tessler 2003; Braizat 2003), a new explanation has emerged to take its place. According to more recent analysis based on the same World Values Survey data cited in this book's introduction, although the Arab region demonstrates high levels of appreciation of democratic rule and of rejection of totalitarian rule, it clearly ranks among the lowest in the world with respect to the value placed on women's civil and political participation, as well as tolerance for other forms of differences among individuals and groups. Thus the conclusion is put forth that there is not an "Islamic democracy deficit" so much as there is an "Arab democracy deficit," and the latter is explained, not by a lack of desire for democratic political structures, but by a dearth of democratic values. Ronald Inglehart and Pippa Norris point specifically to attitudes regarding divorce, abortion, gender equality, and gay rights as the real, measurable difference between "Western and Islamic societies" (2003). This theme is not limited to Western scholars, but has been articulated by the Arab researchers who penned the 2002 Arab Human Development Project, placing "women's empowerment" with freedom and education as the three most significant "deficits" facing the Arab region. Many scholars have used these studies to base claims that the real explanation of the "democracy deficit" lies in a lack of values of civility and tolerance for difference—most starkly, tolerance for women and homosexuals (Inglehart and Norris 2003).

Occupying the Gender Gap

In light of the varied and controversial character of Arab debates over democracy and civil society, one should not be surprised to find that even the most widely accepted conceptions of these notions have been subjected to further interrogation by those who find themselves excluded or marginalized by the debate. These challenges dissuade too easy conclusions about "absences" and go some way toward revealing the character of existing "deficits" and their amelioration.

Addressing the 1992 CAUS conference on "Civil Society in the Arab World and Its Role in the Realization of Democracy," Nawal al-Sa'adawi (Egypt, b. 1931) pointedly asks, "Why is there an absence of women, as researchers and thinkers, at this forum? And why was not one of the papers assigned to a woman?" She quickly dismisses the notion that there are not great female intellectuals in the Arab world and concludes instead that the absence of women "reveals the failure of [male] Arab intellectuals to understand the basic problem that stands before civil society and their failure to discern true democracy and its basic preconditions" (Sa'adawi 1992, 837). Sa'adawi discerns a very real lack in Arab intellectual debates, even those seeking democratization, participation, and political reform. Of the eighty-eight participants at the Beirut conference, only seven were women, two of whom served as paper commentators, while the remainder attended merely as listeners. The only conference debating civil society in the early 1990s that succeeded in fully incorporating women into their proceedings was one organized by the Center for Arab Studies in Cairo (Rashid 1992b). Of this conference's thirty-four participants, eight were women, all of whom presented papers and one of whom directed and edited the proceedings. However, focusing on "The Issue of Civil Society in Light of Gramsci's Notebooks," the Cairo participants revealed even less of an interest in theorizing how men and women are differently situated vis-à-vis civil society. The issue of gender is fully subsumed under issues of class at this socialist forum. Clearly things are not so simple as adding women (or democracy or civil society, for that matter) and stirring.

At least a few of the male participants at the CAUS conference discussed the status of women in Arab society, either as "sisters of men" and out of concern for not depriving society and the Muslim Brotherhood of women's capabilities and energies (Habib 1992, 334); to point out the "strategic place of women in the confrontation between the west and the Maghrib" (Zghal 1992b, 444, 452–53); in recognition of the historical model of women's groups as "peaceful" forces for change (in regard to women's rights) in Gulf countries (Baqir Najjar 1992, 572–77); or to assert Islam's affirmation of the rights of women ('Ariyat 1992, 724). The discussion of women by the more Islamist participants is interesting. While secular Arab nationalists, modernists, and reformers, such as Qasim Amin (Egypt, 1863–1908), often used women as markers of the modern or regressive nature of the community, and Islamists have used women as markers of cultural authenticity or, alternatively, as markers of the decadence and immorality (or *jahiliyya*) of the community, in this context Islamists use women to imagine the Islamic community as liberal.[1] In all such cases, women's behavior is constrained through the gendered constructions of these discourses (whether in the name of the nation, progress, authenticity, Islam, or liberation), even through those that imagine an emancipated status for women. "Women's projects" or "women as projects" appear only to create or reinforce stereotypes of what constitutes a "women's issue."

In this sense, women are clearly targeted as objects of social control in these political debates, a fact that does not pass unnoticed by Ilham Kallab (Lebanon, b. 1953) when she accuses Muhammad al-Sayyid

---

1. For a critique of the patriarchy underlying Qasim Amin's 1992 call for the liberation of women, see Leila Ahmed (1992, esp. 144–68).

Habib's claim that "the Muslim Brotherhood believes it important that women participate in parliamentary and syndicate work whenever personal conditions are so conducive" (Habib 1992, 335) of constituting "an ember that burns only in its place"—that is, of talking about women only to avoid a truly substantive engagement with the issues of women's status and gender relations (Kallab 1992, 336). Habib is an Asyut University professor, former parliamentarian, and member of Egypt's Muslim Brotherhood. Kallab senses a dichotomy between hidden and expressed views, between "that which is perceived [by women] and that which is decreed against women." It is this, Kallab maintains, that confines women's protest to a request for reconsideration, literally and substantively, of interpretating traditional texts, questioning their legality, only to replace these with other interpretations of the same texts.

What about the bulk of the remaining discourse on civil society, where neither women nor gender-conscious discussions appear? How do we conceptualize an absence? We should not make the mistake of using gender as a synonym for women. As Terrell Carver has pointed out, often the concept of "gender" is used as "loosely synonymous with 'sex' and lazily synonymous with 'women' " such that woman are marginalized as a problematic, and men, males, and masculinities remain "where they have always been, doing pretty much what they like" (1998, 18, 19). Rather than designating one sex, gender is best viewed as a structural, pervasive feature of how we order social life. As such, gender reflects not just male or female, but relations between genders.

Less readily apparent masculinities and male interests and perceptions are revealed in the discourse that defines civil society as a sphere of rational, competitive, self-interested individuals. Carver points out how "the 'abstract individual' exemplifies an absence of pregnancy or other female bodily characteristics that arguably play a major role for females in self- and social-identity formation, and in the formation of political interests" (Carver 1998, 23). So too, this "monotonically singular, unreproductive and apparently sexless" individual, is unbound (in public at least) by expectations regarding the prioritization of family roles or by dependency on others to marry, travel, or open businesses, as well as lacking privilege achieved via the capacity to control the marriage, travel, business practices, and even citizenship (through inheritance), of others (Joseph 2002).

This "male in disguise"—or, perhaps better, "patriarchy in disguise"—is found in imaging civil society as a space of absolute freedom or equality of opportunity, when it is a space characterized by the unequal division of power and hierarchically organized groups, based on gender, class, ethnicity, and religion. Kallab points out the masculinity of much of what passes for civil society in her response to Habib: "In the presence of all this male rhetoric that I have heard, I sensed that history, society and the law are men—by the way—and that women have no place in the structure of religious society as portrayed by man: except as supplementary, judged, subdued, illicit, if not absent" (Kallab 1992, 336).

Certainly many women fail to appear both in political society and in civil society in more material senses as well. According to the Inter-Parliamentary Union (1999), women's participation in Arab parliaments remains the lowest worldwide. Even in places like Egypt, where the women's movement has been strong historically, scholars have documented a decline in women's political participation as both candidates and voters over the past two decades (Kandil 2002). Although many women suggest that "in a region where the formal political sphere has been confined to men . . . civil society has provided many Arab women with the space through which to confront and address their political, social and economic marginalization" (Hamad 2002, 22), data collected by Amani Kandil and Sarah Ibn Nafisa in Egypt attest to the marginality of women's participation since the 1960s in precisely the types of non-governmental organizations Ibrahim asserts as the basis of civil society (1995, 95–101). Noha El-Mikawy maintains that "most working women in Egypt are in the informal sectors of agriculture and services, where work is characterized by long hours, bad pay and non-existent organization" (1999, 78). In addition, whereas women in the informal sector are rendered invisible by their dependence on household economic units, women in the formal sector remain dependent on the family connections and educational privileges that enabled their gains. The neglect of informal institutional arrangements in favor of more organized civil society groups helps to reinforce women's marginalization from formal social policies and maintains their subjugation to men.

To the extent that the concept of civil society is appropriated from a universal liberal discourse, it tends to obscure the fact that so much real experience of actual individuals depends upon how they are situated within structures of difference in society. On the other hand, to the extent that concessions are made to such things as culture and religion—in this case, especially, to conservative Islamist demands that "civil society" be decoupled from "secular society"—the notion runs the risk of further marginalizing those who are disadvantaged by existing gender structures (as well as constructions based on religion, ethnicity, and sexual orientation). For example, 'Abd al-Hamid Ansari maintains that an Islamic civil society was established in Mecca before that society finally selected its state in Medina, and, as such, civil society is understood as prior to the state in both time and importance. "Islamic civil society," according to Ansari, "forms the center of gravity in the social structure of the umma" (2001, 103). Wajih Kawtharani suggests that the formulation that presents a more "authentic" and thus more "possible" form of a modern civil society is the one that has its basis in *al-mujtama' al-ahli*, the informal network of relations based in the more primordial associations of kinship, tribe, village, and religious communities (1992).

It is often suggested that women find participation in civil society easier to negotiate than participation at the level of the state, owing to the relative nearness to those realms traditionally associated with women (private, domestic, familial). Yet women in civil society find themselves divided along the lines of political ideology, class, and interest groups, rather than united by a common goal (Bizri 1995, 151). Further, in the context of the contemporary Middle East (as elsewhere), both state and civil society are complex terrains—fractured, conflictual, threatening spaces that are as much a source of oppression as they are spaces of opportunity for struggle and negotiation. Also, from the perspective of women, civil society often occupies a slippery terrain as not-quite-state and not-quite-family. Women have often turned to the state to protect them from the tyrannies of their families, just as they have sought refuge in the family against the tyrannies of the state. Action at the level of civil society can as often mitigate as mediate both forms of appeal.

Relocating the Family in Civil Society:
Ezzat's Islamic Feminism

Heba Raouf Ezzat (b. 1965), the Egyptian political scientist who, between 1992 and 1997, wrote a weekly column called *"Sawt al-nisa"* (Women's Voice) in the weekly Islamist opposition newspaper *al-Sha'b* (published by a coalition of the Muslim Brotherhood and the Labor Party until it was shut down by the government in May 2000), offers a unique interpretation of civil society. Like Turabi and Ghannouchi, Ezzat articulates her support for a form of "direct democracy . . . where the state is marginal and civil society is strong" (Negus 2000). Yet her central concern lies in incorporating the family into contemporary discussions of civil society. In an article based on her doctoral dissertation, Ezzat draws upon political science, sociology, anthropology, feminist theory, and Islamist sources to offer what she calls an "Islamist perspective on the role of the family in political change."

Ezzat begins her discussion by reviewing the study of the family in the Western social sciences. According to Ezzat, whereas Western schools of anthropology and sociology "study the family as a 'traditional' social unit" present in undeveloped tribal and kinship-based societies, the family "as a 'social unit' does not enter in as a subject of political studies" and "it is rare that books of political science include a chapter on the family" (1995, 11). Ezzat claims that the lack of attention to the family reached its height during the behavioralist phase in (particularly American) political science, which focused on individual behavior, as well as in the trends that have "brought the state back in" after World War II and in the "post-behavioralist" phase of the 1980s (1995, 12–16). As attention turned to civil society in the second half of the eighties and the first part of the nineties, Ezzat argues, rather than refocusing interest onto the family, civil society "remained studied within the context of the relationship of society with the state and the tools of relations between them. It was an expansion of the approach and not a change of its methodological nature."

In the end, the recent focus on civil society has highlighted the two problematic dichotomies that Ezzat locates in Western political thought and that she seeks to get beyond by returning to a more authentic notion of Islam and Islamic society that captures the political aspects of the family and the political role of the mother in that realm. The first problematic dichotomy that Ezzat identifies is that between the state and society: "Despite the interest of western thought in the relationship between state and society [in general], and the increase of writings in recent years about 'civil society' in particular, its studies remained centered around the very same institutions—like parties, elites and groups—all of which are institutions subject in one form or another to the legal system said to have hegemony, while the family is viewed as a 'patrimonial institution' and outside the study of this 'civil society' " (1995, 17–18). This argument echoes feminist critiques of the public-private distinction in Western liberal thought. Feminists criticize the attempts of such early modern thinkers as John Locke to deny the legitimacy of the divine right of kings without challenging the right of men to rule over their families. In disputing the analogy between a king's authority over society and the father's authority over the family, Locke argued that the two spheres— political and domestic—were separate and distinct. Whereas political power was deemed to emanate from men (the governed), patriarchal authority in the family was deemed divine, natural, and beyond the scope of the state. In other words, because the family exists outside of the realm of state laws and state hegemony, it does not enter into discussions regarding relations between the state and civil society, nor is it subject to the legal system that regulates these spheres.

Ezzat further accounts for the neglect of the study of the family by returning to the same dichotomy between religious and civil society that Huwaydi took up in his discussion of the 1992 Cairo International Book Fair debate. Ghannouchi has similarly noted that "the concept of civil society has been used to counter religious practice" and as "a weapon against the Islamists" (2000, 109–10). Ezzat argues that, understood through the lens of this dichotomy, civil society cannot account for the family. The family is "connected in western reality with what is 'religious' and [religion] is placed in opposition with 'what is civil' [*madani*] in the modern secular perspective" (1995, 18). In other words, the more recent focus on civil society, rather than bringing the family into the purview of political science, as Ezzat suggests it should, has served to further alienate it from that study owing to the "secular bias" of its conception.

Given that the social and political implications of the state-society dichotomy for the family are not discussed by political science, Ezzat turns to sociology. She finds there "a study that interprets the hegemony of the state as a system, institutions and tools, is not born overnight, but it occurs incrementally through the expansion of the space of duties that the state undertakes and the shrinking of the space relative to different social institutions, especially the family" (1995, 18). Ezzat maintains that "the family in its traditional extended form has a role as a productive unit in the framework of a solidarity-type social system." Ezzat is sufficiently well versed in Western culture to understand the difference between Western and Arab conceptions of the family. As a result, she fairly consistently and very consciously refers to the Arab family as an "extended family" in her essay to draw attention to what is unique about the resources available in Islamic society. She notes how, with the Industrial Revolution and the entry of women into the labor force, the productive role of the family was transformed: "It did not take long before the family lost its role in social cultivation [*tanshi'an*]" (1995, 19). Schools and educational institutions took over the role of social upbringing; modern health institutions took over the role of health care and care of the elderly; psychologists took over the role of counseling. As a result, the family has been reduced to the role of "preparing food and washing clothes."

Here Ezzat begins to develop an understanding of the acculturative *(tanshi'ani)* role of the family that can perhaps best be described by the German philosophical term *Bildung*. Koselleck draws connections between *Bildung*, cultivation (especially self-cultivation), civilization, and civil society (1994, 13). In his *Philosophy of Right*, Hegel's notion of *Bildung* involves an educational structure that moves from a "natural" family education to the civil education of bourgeois society in which the family is replaced as educator. Within civil society we experience many different ways in which our civil relations have truths beyond their immediate bourgeois appearance. These constitute our experiences of culture that, for Hegel, re-present the relation between persons and the universal. As Ezzat's discussion continues, the metaphors of child rearing, the development of the citizen, and the cultivation of the land begin to blend together, and her distinct vision of the "political mother," or what contemporary theory might term "maternal feminism," begins to emerge.

Ezzat applies her understanding of maternal values to the liberal public-private distinction. In fact, Ezzat identifies four levels in Western liberal thought: (1) "the public," which is the realm of politics and the state; (2) "the social," which is the arena of interaction between state and civil society; (3) "the private," which consists of the organizations of civil society; and (4) "the personal," which is related to the individual and the family (1995, 24. Ezzat argues that the problem with these distinctions is not only that they are imprecise and that human actions tend to overlap across the categories but, more important, their relevance remains "limited and relative [and] hinders the development of a good method for understanding the role, reality and social position of the family." In reality, she continues, "the opposition and contradiction between the public and private is [*sic*] not so clear in all political societies but, rather, there exist societies that do not know this problematic at all" (1995, 24–25). Because of the extended nature of the family in some societies, Ezzat maintains that "the identification of the woman with reproduction, child rearing and bearer of responsibility for the household does not result in the diminishing of her social function" in such societies. In this sense, the sphere of the family has a public—social and economic—character in Islamic societies.

Ezzat turns next to a discussion of the family and politics in the Islamic perspective in which she does not merely accept the heritage *(turath)*, but she takes a critical view. Ezzat argues that the political writings of Muslim philosophers during the Middle Ages also suffer from an unwarranted focus on the state and a tendency to consider the family a special realm of jurisprudence outside of the framework of politics. "Even

Ibn Khaldun who is distinguished by his sociological method . . . focused in his analysis on the Caliphate and monarchy, on which he based definition of politics. This produced a neglect of society—and, thus, the family, which is one of its main structure—in the traditional method of Islamic political analysis" (1995, 26).

As a result, Ezzat, like Turabi and Ghannouchi, finds it necessary to return to the "fundamentals" of Islam—the Qur'an and *sunna*—to find the "true" perspective on the family and politics and Islam. She finds there that "the Islamic perspective differs fundamentally from the Western view in regard to the family," which leads her to conclude that the public-private dualism "only appears in Islamic society with the increased degree of secularization" (1995, 26, 30). Here, as in all of her writings, Ezzat understands herself to be using the same tools of interpretation as the *'ulama* to reach different conclusions: "the aim is to change the paradigm from within" (El-Gawhary 1994, 26–27). In a number of contexts, Ezzat has stressed the importance of incremental change that is pursued "from the inside" (Lawyers Committee for Human Rights 1996; Ezzat 1999). Thus, although Ezzat's view has much in common with feminist critiques of liberalism, she criticizes the expression "Islamic feminist" as well as the application of the term to her, arguing that "feminists are secularists who are fighting male domination," whereas she believes "women's liberation should rely on Islam" (El-Gawhary 1994; also Ezzat 1999). In contrast, she emphasizes that her views present an Islamic view [*ru'ya islamiyya*] of women and their role in society.

Ezzat's argument relies upon locating similar institutions and values at the levels of state, society, and the family in order to show that Islam, as a comprehensive and completely just way of life, does not require a public-private distinction to protect the individual or society from the state and its laws. According to the Islamic principle of *tawhid* (oneness, unity), rules that apply in the political arena should also be valid for the family and vice versa. She maintains that "in the Islamic perspective, the family is a small model for the *umma* and the state. The head of the family corresponds to the Imamate or the Caliphate at the state level: the *shari'a* governs it and it is run by *shura*" (1995, 31).

Like Turabi, Ghannouchi, and Huwaydi, Ezzat identifies consultation as the main Islamic dynamic within the political processes. However, unlike the male Islamists, she emphasizes that this same value is meant to be dominant in family relationships as well. *Shura* should characterize man-woman relationships within the family structure and relations—"you can't have a totalitarian patriarchal system in a family in Islam" (El-Gawhary 1994). Marriage is like voting for or choosing the *khalif* (the successor of the Prophet). The family should have a (male) head, but he should be chosen freely. The marriage contract resembles the *bay'a* or the oath of allegiance (1995, 31). If the leader is unfair, he loses his right to lead and just as people can withdraw their homage to their *khalif*, women can divorce their husbands. Ezzat also locates similar values and concepts in the state, society, and family. The marriage of a man and woman, the formation of a community, and the choosing of a leader *(istikhlaf)* "are to be governed by the values of mercy [*tarahum*], love [*mawadda*] and stability [*sukan*]" (1995, 27).

The concept of unity or oneness *(tawhid)*, which is said to be the basis of the Islamic community in that it unifies among the diverse aspects of life, Ezzat argues, also "represents a basic pillar in the philosophy of marriage": "Islamic legislation does not only order the relations between the man and woman within the family, but also creates between them a connection of unification into a perfect whole [*takamul*]" (1995, 28). She argues that the preservation of offspring, the community, and religion are all cultivated by both the community and the family in Islam. The family, the mosque, the *'ulama*, and the institutions of *waqf* and *hisba* (guardianship) are the main formations in Islamic societies, and what, in returning to her notion of *Bildung*, Ezzat calls the "natural nurseries of opposition against the inflation of the power of the state thus embodying the lines of defense of the community and individuals . . . for the preservation of the *shari'a*, that is, for the preservation of religion" (1995, 29–30).

Thus, when Ezzat turns to her discussion of "the family and political change," she has already introduced the idea that the family in Islam represents an important resource for social change. Again, she discusses the lack of the study of the family in political science research on political change and especially the more recent literature that posits an important role for civil society for bringing about that change. And once again she attempts to show that Islam recognizes that the family, and particularly the woman as bearer of the responsibility for the household, plays a particularly important role in cultural and social, and thus political, change. Ezzat quotes the Qur'an (13:11), which states that the first precondition of change is the "changing of the self": "God does not change a people's lot unless they change what is in their hearts" (1995, 38). Such change begins in the "natural nursery" of the extended family.

In good social science fashion, Ezzat illustrates her argument with the "case-study" of the Palestinian *intifada* (uprising) against Israeli rule. According to Ezzat, this example illustrates the inadequacy of studies of civil society in the Arab-Islamic region that fail to take into account the institution of the family: "The concepts that the researcher uses to define the referential framework for his understanding of phenomena stems from the focal point of the study. The concept of civil society, for example, removes the family (as a social unit) from its analysis. [As a result, such analysis] does not precisely interpret the Palestinian *intifada* which had the extended family its true basis, after which came the social institutions like the popular committees and groups, etc. The complete neglect of the family in the analysis reveals this gap between the analytical concepts widely used and the complex social phenomena in its Arab-Islamic context" (1995, 44). Ezzat maintains that the institution of the family plays a mediating role between individuals, local communities, markets, and the state. The family encourages the interdependence of formal and informal socioeconomic structures. Ezzat does not intend her emphasis on the family to suggest an underestimation of the influence of other forces and centers of power and authority, but only stresses the importance of "bringing the family in" and of the link that exists between public and private in the life of the poor in developing countries.

The Palestinian *intifada* presents a "real-life" example of the way in which society fulfils the roles of the state in the absence of representative ruling apparatuses and under the domination of a foreign system (the Israeli occupation). The agricultural Palestinians were forced off of or kept from (under curfew) cultivating their lands, so they began instead what Ezzat calls "the agriculture of nationalism," an educational solidarity and consciousness-building experience that took place within the context of the extended family. Activism also began to take root at the most personal level as "the family was the front that supported the human element in the *intifada* by raising the birthrate in Palestinian society to keep it demographically from extermination." As such, the extended family formed the only social unity that "the Zionist enemy did not plow in its 'closure' " (1995, 47). Ezzat notes the implications of this bringing the family into civil society:

> Notice that in so much as the extended family produced the rise and perpetuation of the *intifada*, the *intifada* produced a change in the nature of the responsibilities of the woman within and outside the family. The climate that the *intifada* created contributed to a higher level of politicization of the woman in Palestinian society just as the *intifada* produced a change in the consciousness of the Palestinian family of the issue of its nation and its participation in its liberation. A transformation occurred in the extended family such that the family solidarity reached its peak and the relations of neighbors improved and interactions between individual members of the Palestinian family increased despite circumstance hindering travel, strikes, and crises like the razing of some homes and the emigration. (1995, 47)

By the end of her essay, it becomes apparent that rather than just taking on secularism, Ezzat is attempting to saddle her opponents—who seem to be, alternatively, Western social science, secular liberalism, and perhaps some orthodox Islamic strands—with a much more equivocal identity of being anti-family or even anti-woman, by undervaluing both the family and women in studies of civil society and political change.

Secular Feminism and Global Civil Society

While Ezzat draws attention to the political role of the family in Arab society in order to highlight an often overlooked aspect of women's activism, a number of secular feminists suggest not only that "the most adequate defense against the forces of intolerance is the reinforcement of the secular state and the democratic rule of law" (Karamanou 2002; see also Moghadam 2002), but also that the focus on civil society to the neglect of the family is more likely to result in the neglect of the inequality of the latter realm, as well as of the recognition of the way in which patriarchal family structures are reproduced in the spheres of both civil society and the state. Even if difference-base oppression is acknowledged in the public sphere, much of liberal theory treats this as a corrective dysfunction of civil society, without reference to unequal private spheres. As Suad Joseph has pointed out, "patriarchy weaves together civil society, state, market and the family in Middle Eastern societies, subverting the separations and boundaries that Western theorists argue are necessary for democracy" (1996, 10). Struggles for gender equality best operate across often overlapping or continuous public-private spheres.

To some extent, Burhan Ghalyun captures this overlapping understanding of public and semipublic spheres in his conceptualization of civil society as a sort of "unofficial society," which encompasses all the economic, cultural, and religious institutions that fall outside the purview of ruling authorities and thus are able to act under conditions that permit them to expand their activities and compete with each other (1992, 738). According to Ghalyun, Arab civil society must be viewed as a hybrid of both communal and familial formations on the one hand, and voluntary, "modern," and "urban" civil associations on the other. So too, one might point to the many Arab socialist conceptualizations of civil society that, turning to Marx or Gramsci, frame the issue of civil society as a "problematic," though more from the perspective of class than gender (for example, Rashid 1992b; Mustafa 1996a; 1996b).

Certainly there is critical questioning and interrogation of the universalizing categories of liberal (and Islamist) discourses. Kallab suggests those oppressed and marginalized must "question the presence of their interests in the structure of civil society and regarding the meaning of democracy" (1992, 336). Toward this end, Kandil, executive director of the Arab Network for NGOs in Cairo,[2] presents an understanding of civil society that encompasses "a body of values and traditions based on ac-

2. The Arab Network for NGOs is an organization, founded in 1997, that aims at "strengthening the coordination among Arab Federations and NGOs working the field of human sustainable development." See their website at http//www.shabakaegypt.org.

ceptance and respect for others and on diversity which is reflected in a culture" (2002, 31). Understood as such, the particular and varied experiences of women and other differently situated individuals and groups must become a focus of study and activism. Kandil goes so far as to suggest that a process of critical reflection has already produced "qualitative changes" that can be discerned in women's activism. According to her analysis, early women's organizations "largely focused on social welfare, social service, and charitable endeavors while activities relating to developmental skills were limited." This focus shifted in the 1970s and 1980s to "women's economic role and the importance of providing women with economic resources such as loans and other tools of production" in order to fight women's poverty and expand their participation in socioeconomic development. In the past decade or so, women have become aware of the fragmented and limited impact these activities have had on women and gender relations. As a result, Kandil maintains, the emergence of a gender-conscious perspective "is likely to provoke a qualitative move towards the empowerment of women because it includes a radical, not a reformist, approach" (1999, 64–65). Such an approach would fight against gender oppression by seeking to understand not just those formal barriers to women's acting upon and within the institutions of civil society, how structural relations among various public and private institutions affect the concrete relations of dependence and autonomy in which women stand, ways in which the benefits of women's contribution are systematically transferred to men, how the current structures are enforced, and who controls the resources that produce and maintain them. As many secular feminists have further noted, such a gender-sensitive approach to civil society has global dimensions, as the mobilization of Arab women's organizations has been greatly facilitated by international donors and global civil society groups interested in women's issues (Hamad 2002, 26).

At the same time, the struggle in Arab political thought cannot be reduced to a struggle between global civility and local vestiges of incivility, nor to a struggle between advocates of Western liberalism and adherents to Islamic fundamentalism, nor between feminists and antifeminists. Ezzat and Kandil find themselves united in fighting patriarchal conceptions of civil society, but divided by their own particular understandings of that concept and the way in which it contributes to women's emancipation and democratization. Rather, the struggle taking place in Arab political thought is closer to that articulated by Michel Foucault in *The History of Sexuality*: "Are there no great radical ruptures, massive binary divisions, then? Occasionally, yes. But more often one is dealing with mobile and transitory points of resistance" (1985, 96). No ideational hegemony—whether patriarchy or liberalism—is able to impose itself as a monolith. The inability of even a liberal discourse that aspires to universal status to subsume the polysemy of the discursive field in Arabic is a condition of both politics and resistance. As such, counter-discursive practices usually remain "mobile and transitory" in form, "producing cleavages in a society that shift about, fracturing unities and effecting regroupings" (1985, 96). Without a precursory and concerted counter-posing discursive strategy, any challenge to hegemony cannot be sustained—it will lack the requisite ideological unity of the dominant *episteme* to efface the constructively integrated ideational aspects of existing hegemonic conditioning. Yet clearly such a possibility is not absent in Arab political thought. Whether or not the "gender and empowerment approach" suggested by Kandil can and will be further articulated by Arab intellectuals such that it succeeds in challenging patriarchal forms of difference-based oppression remains to be seen. But the existence of such a realm of theorizing should neither be denied nor dismissed. Both "democracy gaps" and "liberal constructions" reveal alternative fissures.

8

Conclusion

Transcultural Possibilities

Through the tragedies thus programmed by cultures, religions and ideologies, a new posture of reason, a more enabled imagination, an enlarged collective encompassing memory—a global civil society—appears to be emerging.

—Mohammed Arkoun, "Locating Civil Society in Islamic Contexts"

Civil Society is a Western dream, a historical aspiration; it is also, in the concrete form this dream has taken, part of the social history of Western Europe. . . . A characteristic of the history of transformation of the Western dream into a reality is that this metamorphosis is limited to the West. Civil society, for instance, does not translate into Islamic terms.

—Serif Mardin, "Civil Society and Islam"

Civil Society's Travels and Travails and the Impact on Arab Democratic Theorizing

Despite the dearth of democratic practice in the Arab region, civil society does not remain, in Serif Mardin's words, "merely a Western dream" and one untranslatable into "Islamic terms." Even in this corner of the world, individuals are both engaging and enlarging what Mohammed Arkoun deems a "collective encompassing memory." At the very least, among a broad and diverse sector of Arab intellectuals and activists, it is possible to detect a shared political language, insofar as they are increasingly deploying similar concepts—even as those concepts remain contested among, and differently located within, the existing ideological frameworks. It is also possible that, despite the existence of radical factions and violence undertaken by some groups in the name of Islam, the conflict is less about Islam against the West and its (secular) allies in the Middle East and more about diverse sectors of Arab society grappling with how to reform overreaching and unjust states and addressing the needs and shortcomings of their society.

Daniel Brumberg has pointed out that "Islam is a political *construct* that borrows from both Western and Islamic political thought." As a result, he argues, "to say that someone is Muslim tells us little regarding the person's view on politics" (2002, 109). However, telling us that he or she is liberal, Islamist, socialist, or a part of some other ideological tradition does go a long way toward identifying that person's political orientation and program. Brumberg rightly identifies the "greatest challenge" in studying Islamism in particular (though also true for other ideological groupings) "is not to figure out whether Islamism is 'essentially' democratic" but to see whether particular Islamists are "acting within a hegemonic political arena where the game is to shut out alternative approaches, or else within a competitive—let's call it *dissonant*—arena where Islamists, like other players, find themselves pushed to accommodate the logic of power-sharing" (2002, 112). While Brumberg is interested in competitive political systems established at the level of the state, such as the confessional system in Lebanon, his distinction can be applied to the arena of discourse as well. The question then becomes whether Islamists (or liberals or socialists) are focused on shutting out alternative systems of ideas or find themselves scrambling to be included in the discourse of civil society and democracy. The violent death of Faraj Fouda, the imprisonment of Saad Eddin Ibrahim and Matruk al-Falih, and the emigration and exile of scores of other intellectuals discussed here reveal the danger of the former. At the same time, the latter seems to be the case among at least some Islamist intellectuals, as they take great pains to literally find a place at the debate table of the Cairo International Book Fair by refuting the civil-religious dichotomy that frames the exchange. So too, Arab liberals adopt their own version of the same refutation by maintaining that what a modern, liberal society needs to be civil is not secularism but democratic values of tolerance, pluralism, respect for individual rights, and a limited state. Arab socialists who already have such a strong presence among many of the organizations that make up civil society in many countries also return to or find new roots for their thinking in Gramsci's writings as a way of both making inroads in the intellectual discourse of civil society and conceptualizing that sphere of thought and practice with a revolutionary potential.

While in some respects the lines between the advocates of liberal democracy and their opponents seem to have become more polarized, there is some indication that the number of thinkers in the latter category has been rapidly shrinking in the past few decades, as the polarization between advocates of secularism and advocates of Islamicization belies an underlying consensus about at least some of the ideational constellations that construct a liberal public sphere (democracy, civil society, citizenship). As noted by the Qatari researcher 'Ali Khalil al-Kawari, "Democracy [*dimuqratiyya*], or the rule of the people [*hukum al-sha'b*], is a banner raised over a very wide sphere today, despite the ambiguity that continues to surround the concept" (2000, 11). This admittedly imperfect but discernible consensus is apparent in the debates throughout the 1990s over civil society.

The fact is that the breadth of ideological groupings vying to claim civil society as most rightly theirs in the early 1990s has brought diverse traditions into dialogue with each other over the status of democracy, pluralism, the rights of minorities, and political and economic justice in their political programs. Despite the variation among particular conceptions of civil society there is broad agreement that enlarging a democratically engaged public sphere must be a priority for the development of the Arab region—even among those presumed the least likely of democrats: Islamists. As Mumtaz Ahmad points out, "there seems to have emerged a general agreement among mainstream Islamists that democracy is the spirit of the Islamic governmental system, even though they reject the *philosophical* assumption of Western democracy that sovereignty rests with the people" (1996, 30, my emphasis). The evidence provided here suggests that democracy is less peripheral to the concerns of an increasing number of Islamists than may have been the case when Ahmad made this claim—and that this emerging consensus includes other ideological groupings as well. Among leftists, who in their early

Marxist-Leninist history "justified the use of force in politics, discredited liberalism and democracy, encouraged violent revolution, justified state repression, legitimated social strife under the guise of class conflict, [etc.]" (Salem 1994, 148), one detects a refocusing of revolutionary activity away from frontal politics—and even party politics—and toward participation in civil society organizations, with the aim of creating of a counter-hegemonic force for confronting authoritarian practices at the levels of state and society, one that appeals to latent secular and progressive instincts among the masses. Among liberals, who in the Nahda period worried that empowering the unenlightened masses with truly democratic forms of government would lead to a loss of liberties and justice, democracy has become the priority surpassing even (remaining) concerns about the inclusion of (Islamist) parties who are feared to harbor undemocratic ideas. In one stark example of this transformation, a petition for "Political and Constitutional Reform in Egypt," signed by representatives from the Wafd, Tagammu', Nasirist, and Labor parties in 1999, united diverse forces in favor of the lifting of the state of emergency, the release of political prisoners, the holding of free and fair elections, the freedom to form political parties, free assembly, unrestricted expression in the media, and guarantees for the "independence of trade and professional unions, civic associations leading toward a civil society [mujtama' ahli] capable of contributing toward the building of democracy and progress" (Din et al. 1999).

Democracy, Civil Society, and Difference: Remaining Questions and Ongoing Debate

The most contentious discussions of civil society and democracy among Arab intellectuals have centered around a presumed tension between Islam and secularism: whether and to what extent the structures, organizations, values, and so forth seen to contribute toward the development or strengthening of civil society and democracy can be reconciled with or drawn from Islam; whether high levels of adherence to Islam promote or hinder civility, democracy, pluralism, modernity, and citizenship; or whether such values and institutions are fundamentally secular. In the earliest debates over civil society—its meaning, functions, sources, and existence—many Islamic thinkers problematized the "universality" of the concept, locating within it a secularist bias.

Yet, as the notion has been desecularized in favor of more "Islamic," "authentic," "pluralist" or "hybrid" conceptions of civil society (such as 'Abd al-Hamid Ansari's hyphenated *al-mujtama' al-madani al-'arabi al-islami,* Wajih Kawthrani and Matruk al-Falih's *al-mujtama' al-ahli,* and Burhan Ghalyun's *al-mujtama' al-hajin*), different problems for differently situated individuals and groups emerge. Many of these problems find their origins not in some presumed lack of democratic discourse in Arabic, but in the dominance of various liberal assumptions in that discourse. Even among the more critical appropriations of the notion, overall and with very few exceptions, the neoliberal discourse of civil society continues to base the remaining universalizing aspects of its discourse on the individual—understood as a rational, self-interested, full citizen—and on formal political and economic activities. The universal character of this citizen is called into question by what some deem its gender-class-ethnicity-race-religion (non-Muslim) blindness. Although a notion of tolerance is central to Arab liberalism, it tends to be a fairly limited notion conceptualized within the framework of interests of freedom of thought, such that one can be a secular or nonsecular Muslim, but with little attention to the many other forms of difference found in Arab society. In addition, the liberal conceptualization of civil society harbors assumptions about both the organizational character of civil society and the character of the individual who inhabits civil society, thus ignoring forms of participation in unofficial, informal, unpaid realms that remain essential for the reproduction of the official, formal, productive activities. Muslim and male interests and perceptions dominate much of the discourse of civil society, not only because so many of the intellectual forums are dominated by Arab and Muslim men—although this is quite clearly the case—but also because those engaging in this discourse fail to adequately address hierarchical relations between the Arabs and ethnic minorities, between Islam and religious minorities, and between genders.

Conceptual Change and Comparative Political Thought:
Toward a Transcultural View

This work began with a discussion of a body of literature that studies the ways in which concepts change over time before proceeding to present an analysis of that change across cultures. Yet this study of a "non-Western" context of political theorizing may be thought to have as much, if not more, affinity with the new literature characterized as "comparative political theory." While comparative philosophy has a bit longer history in the modern academy—dating at least back to the first East-West philosophy conference in 1939, which Gerald James Larson argues was "one of the formative events for the beginning of comparative philosophy as a field" (1988, 6)—the move to open up the subfield of political theory to comparative studies is a more recent phenomenon, perhaps not much older than the work undertaken by the scholars who came together in Fred Dallmayr's 1999 edited volume that bears the promising subtitle "Toward a Comparative Political Theory."

However, just as most (though by no means all) studies of conceptual change have limited themselves to one tradition, culture, or language, the writings of comparative political theory tend to treat non-Western works as "parallel developments" in the history of political thought. One of the great works of comparative philosophy written by a non-Western author takes this phrase as his title (Nakamura 1975). One of the early works to bear the title of "comparative political philosophy" describes its enterprise as "the study of substantive equivalence or *parallelism* in the development of different traditions of political philosophy" (Parel and Keith 1992, 7, my italics). As such, comparative work can tend to give the impression that the traditions compared developed independently of each other. Larson articulates a similar concern about comparative philosophy's "tendency to favor large, holistic boundaries of language, culture, and history; [and] a tendency to treat conceptual systems as 'entities' or 'things' that can be externally compared" (1988, 9). However the important "break" his volume represents in terms of "older conventional notions of what comparative philosophy represents" still underemphasizes the already existent transculturality of the works and ideas compared. The solution he suggests for the two tendencies he identifies consists not in looking at influences and exchanges of ideas *across* cultures or languages, but in highlighting the differences *within* the "wholes" of language, culture, and conceptual schemes.

However, a few recent works attempt to be not only comparative, but also cross-cultural. For example, Anthony Parel and Ronald Keith focus on "cross-cultural understanding in the threatening context of modernity" (1992, 8). A work comparing "Western" liberal democracy and Confucianism aims at "build[ing] bridges across a cultural gap" (Li 1999, 6). Similarly, Dallmayr's most recent work seeks "the proper modes of living and sharing together," amidst the "alternative visions" that occupy our increasingly "global village" (Dallmayr 1997, 421; 1998). A few of these works do often manage to incorporate the transportation and appropriation of ideas across cultures into their analysis, despite their claim to be "comparative" or the stated goal of articulating an "ethic" to guide interactions between "alternative visions." For example, Dallmayr's rich discussion of democracy in India suggests the existence of a cross-cultural response on the part of a number of thinkers (1996). Another good example is found in Roxanne Euben's discussions of Arab-Islamic "rationality" in the thought of Sayyid Qutb, which suggests a conscious, if not always direct, influence or interaction between "Eastern" and "Western" theorists of rationality (Euben 1995). Euben's book *Enemy in the Mirror* even more clearly presents Qutb's political thought as "a rebuttal of and antidote to [Western] rationalist discourse" (1999, 155). Nonetheless, Euben's analysis also tends to remain focused on drawing attention to "parallels" between the ideas of various Islamic thinkers and contemporary Western debates about the "crisis of modernity," a focus that obscures the varied and rich dialogues taking place within the Islamic setting as well as the ways in which the discursive settings of East and West overlap.

Part of the difference between the sort of approach I attempt to present and encourage here and these very promising works in the most recent comparative political theory seems to lie in the different ways in which the "encounter" is conceptualized—which itself has implications for the approach in that it influences what is taken into account or looked for in the analysis of the encounter. This difference is seen most clearly in Dallmayr's work *Beyond Orientalism,* in which he identifies seven "modes of cross-cultural encounter": conquest, conversion, assimilation/acculturation, partial assimilation/cultural borrowing, liberalism/minimal engagement, conflict/class struggle, and dialogical engagement. Dallmayr characterizes the first three (conquest, conversion, assimilation) as starkly hegemonic or hierarchical. The third, partial assimilation, takes place on a more nearly equal basis, but the "outcome," Dallmayr notes, "can be greatly varied," ranging from "the melting-pot syndrome" to "an ambivalent form of syncretism" or "a precarious type of cultural coexistence" to a "movement of genuine self-transformation." The fourth mode (liberalism/minimal engagement) tends toward isolationism, while the fifth (conflict/class struggle) is overly contentious and unstable. Dallmayr's mode of choice is the final mode, that of dialogical engagement and interaction, which he argues is best understood as a deconstructive dialogue, which respects otherness beyond assimilation.

Ideally, cross-cultural interactions would consist of each culture's viewing the others in a reflective and dialogic manner and thus acting as both the subject and the object of study in turn. However, because of the uneven social, political, and economic status accorded various "cultures," such a situation seldom, if ever, ensues. Conflict rather than cooperation is more often the norm. Studies focused on achieving cross-cultural, mutual understanding are only relevant to those discursive interactions that actors enter into with the intention of achieving agreement. More often, what takes place is that the intellectuals of the less-powerful, the "observed" cultures, themselves incorporate the concepts—categories and standards of intelligibility—of the dominant culture in their observation, understanding, and critique of their own cultures. This was certainly the case during the Nahda when, for the first time in their history, Muslims found themselves dominated—militarily, politically, and economically—by a colonizing Christian West. It is in that context that intellectuals in the Middle East began to raise questions based on an uneven comparison, such as: "What then are the causes of the malady experienced by Islamic nations?" (Amin 1992, 170); "If Islam was the first religion to address the rational mind . . . how is it that Muslims are content with so little?" ('Abduh 2002, 59); "How did it happen that the modern states came into existence only in Christendom?" (Gîkalp 1959, 222); and "Does Islam tolerate free, liberal institutions [and] [i]s it able to adapt itself to the demands of such institutions?" (Aghayev 2002, 229). It was in the broaching of these questions that we see the beginnings of modernist thinking in the Middle East. In a 1979 article that has been reprinted a number of times, the Egyptian thinker Hasan Hanafi attributes the "historical roots of the crisis of freedom and democracy in our *Zeitgeist*" to a lost ability to listen, discuss, and then move or progress beyond the current state or state of affairs. In the midst of the rise of political Islam, the political transformations in Europe, and the reach of globalization over the past several decades we see the onset of a new series of questions and issues being broached.

This is not to say that cross-cultural interactions need be characterized as the more hegemonic forms that Dallmayr identifies (conquest, conversion, and assimilation). Rather, the nature of conceptual change is such that cross-cultural encounters most closely resemble what Dallmayr calls "partial assimilation" when social and political concepts are involved; and the outcomes of such encounters can be as varied as Dallmayr describes. At the same time, what is often missed in many accounts of "[partial] assimilation" is the other half of this cultural borrowing: the activity and efforts on the part of those who translate and transport concepts cross-culturally, and in a way that leaves neither the concept nor its new home unchanged. It is this "agency" I seek to highlight in the present work through an analysis of translation as a distinct means of, or opportunity for, conceptual change and by "mapping" a particular case of the translation of "civil society" into Arab political discourse.

What Dallmayr terms "partial assimilation" has much in common with what I am calling "transculturation." Rather than an encounter that leads to an imperfect transformation, a "misreception" of ideas across cultures, or a situation in which one side loses (their language, history, or tradition), transculturation involves more complex processes of interaction, adjustment, and re-creation. As Pratt notes, "while subjugated peoples cannot readily control what emanates from the dominant culture, they do determine to varying extents what they absorb into their own and what they use it for" (1992, 6). This less unidirectional transformative process is what I attempted to describe in the first two chapters, through an analysis of the vast horizon of cultural material Arab intellectuals had to draw from in appropriating, approximating, and reconceptualizing democracy and civil society, and through an analysis of the internal and external factors that contributed to their recent focus on the civil society idea and the outcomes of this transcultural encounter. The transcultural nature of this intellectual activity was further illustrated through the various debates among Arab intellectuals over civil society and democracy that are analyzed here. It continues with the most recent feminist interventions in the debate.

However, there is another important facet of "partial assimilations," which lies in the fact that especially the initial encounter with a new concept is the freest, most fluid, and perhaps also the most "authentic." Hans-Georg Gadamer tells us that "we understand in a *different* way, *if we understand at all*" (1993, 291). One might also add that conceptual innovation is, in a sense, often the offspring of such "different understanding." When communication is impeded between different conceptual schemes, cultures, or languages, and when concepts are translated (intentionally or unintentionally), new opportunities ensue; or, to return to the analogy introduced in the introductory chapter, new opportunities arise when a new concept, like new technology, is put to different use in a new context, or when an old concept, like old technology, is put to new use.

As is apparent from the first discussions of civil society, the Arab intellectuals did not feel tied to any particular school of Western political thought and seldom felt compelled to "drop names" of particular theorists of civil society in making their points. Rather, they made use of concepts that they had come into contact with in a "partial," or sometimes even undeveloped, way and then looked to their own intellectual and ideological context and heritage for ideas that resonated with the new ones. As a result of this "partial assimilation," Wajih Kawtharani and Burhan Ghalyun were able to begin to develop theories about how a pluralistic and democratic movement could draw strength from or incorporate elements of traditional society. Sadiq al-'Azm could present an alternative vision of the way in which an Islamic ideology had been broken down and was being replaced by a bourgeois civil society, which, he argues, would have to be superceded by something else. Hasan Turabi and Rashid Ghannouchi could begin to see the Islamic *umma* as a broader concept in the sense of a public sphere in which both moral and democratic political authority would be invested and, at the same time, as the locale of a political strategy delineated by the context of an existing nation-state. Heba Raouf Ezzat could both further expand and further delineate that Islamic community that, respectively, encompasses the family as an important element in social change and women as an integral political actor in that social sphere. And Arab feminists could further question notions of civil society that rely upon conceptions of gender or liberal blindness to gender that they find problematic.

It seems to be at least in part a result of the left's rather late entry into the civil society debate that their assimilation of the concept appears less "partial" (in the sense that it is conceived in connection with Gramsci) and less incorporated as part of an actual political strategy (in comparison to the Islamists). Certainly when civil society is discussed as Gramsci's idea or Tocqueville's idea, one becomes bound to a particular notion. "Authentically" presenting Gramscian civil society can both enable and burden the presentation of authentic Arab or Islamic civil society. So too, opposing "civil societies" may run the risk of clashing over Gramsci and Tocqueville, for example, rather than clashing over the way in which "civil society" is really being used.

What is understood differently across cultures very often becomes a point of contestation. Gaining a truly cross-cultural perspective on the exchange of political and social ideas—that is, a perspective not only on the way in which one culture is dealt with by and deals with another or one aimed at articulating a better "ethic" to guide future interactions, but one that explores the travels and travails of political ideas as they cross boundaries of language and culture and are put to use in a new context—requires that we work in between critical conceptual histories and comparative political theory.

However, the same is true for intercultural studies. As one scholar has rightly pointed out, the real "clash of civilizations" in our time is not "between the West and some homogenous 'other' but between rival carriers of tradition within the same nations and civilizations" (Hefner 1998, 92). Many analysts have commented that the terrorism we witnessed in the United States on September 11, 2001, and throughout the world since that time springs from a "war of ideas" waging in the Middle East, as moderate and radical forces "struggle for hearts and minds of people within the region" (Tolson 2001, 22; Telhami 2001). In fact, Akeel Bilgrami claims, "What seems the best hope against the prophecy [of a 'clash of civilizations'] being fulfilled is the fact of a quite different kind of clash, one *within* the civilizations of which Huntington writes" (2003, 88). This book aims to provide evidence of such a clash within, as well as to contribute toward an increased understanding of some of the terms and stakes inherent in that internal struggle and the cross-cultural influences and opportunities put to use in the Arab context.

Glossary

❧

Works Cited

❧

Index

Glossary

'adala: justice

'adl: justice, just

ahl: kin, family, inhabitant, follower

ahl al-'asabiyya: solidarity groupings

ahl al-hal wa al-'aqd: literally, those who loose and bind; people of authority and stature in the community

ahl al-madina: inhabitant of the city

ahli: of or relating to kinship, familial, or other close relations

akh: brother

akhawiyya: brotherhood

'alam: world

'almaniyya: secularism

al-amr bil-ma'ruf wa al-nahy 'an al-munkar: the injunction to enjoin good and forbid evil

'amm: public

'asabiyya: solidarity, group loyalty

asala: authenticity; literally, steadfastness

aslama: he submitted

azma: crisis

badawi: Bedouin, rural, nomadic

bay'a: pledge, contract, agreement; oath of allegiance to a ruler

dawla: state, government, or the domain of politics

dimuqratiyya: democracy

dini: religious

diwan al-mazalim: council of acts of injustice

dunyawiyya: worldly, mundane, or temporal

fardi: individual (adj.)

faragat: spaces

fatwa: a formal legal opinion of a jurist on a point of law or legal question

fiqh: Islamic jurisprudence; literally, understanding or insight.

fuqaha: jurists

furu': specifics, branches

furu' al-fiqh: the body of positive rules for human behavior for *usul al-fiqh*

al-ghazw al-fikri: intellectual onslaught

hadariyya: civilizational

hadatha: modernity

hadith: report, account; a narrative that relates a prophetic tradition [*sunna*], that is, an utterance or action of the Prophet Muhammad

hakimiyya: the absolute sovereignty of God

hisba: guardianship, a device for enjoining good and forbidding evil *(al-amr bil-ma'ruf wa al-nahy 'an al-munkar)*

hukumi: governmental

al-hulul al-mustawrada: imported solutions

hurriyya: freedom

ibahiyya: laxity, permissiveness

ijma': consensus; one of the four sources of Islamic law; unanimous agreement of the *umma* on a regulation or of the leading *'ulama* on a legal question

ijtihad: exertion, independent judgment, creative intellectual effort; use of logical reasoning in elaborating and interpreting the *shari'a* to deduce laws from the Qur'an and *sunna*

ijtima': assembly, meeting

ikhwan: brethren

'ilm: science or knowledge

'ilmaniyya: rationalism

inhitat: deterioration

insaf: equity

insan: human

intifada: popular uprising

ishtirakiyya: socialism

al-ishtirakiyya al-'arabiyya: Arab socialism

islah: reform

al-islam huwa al-hal: Islam is the solution

isti'mar: imperialism

istiqlal: independence

jahili: ignorant (of Islam), pre-Islamic

jahiliyya: the pre-Islamic period; a state of ignorance (of Islam)

jama'a: group

jami': total

jama'i: collective

jami'a: university

jam'iyya: club

jihad: holy struggle

jumhur: multitude

jumhuriyya: republic

kafir: literally, ingrate; unbeliever, apostate, one who does not accept Islamic revelation

kalim: word

khas: private

khilafa: caliphate, succession

khulafa al-rashidun: the rightly guided successors of the Prophet Muhammad; refers to the first four caliphs: Abu Bakr, 'Umar, Uthman, and 'Ali, who were the companions of Muhammad. The period of their rule is regarded as an exemplar of Muslim society.

madina: city

al-madina al-jahiliyya: the ignorant city

al-madina al-jama'iyya: the social or collective city

madani: civil

mafhum: concept

majlis al-a'yan: senate

majlis al-nuwwab: house of representatives

majlis al-shura: consultative council

majlis tashri'i: legislative council

majlis al-umma: national council

maqasid al-shari'a: the spirit or intent of the law

masala muzayyafa: false question

maslaha: interest

maslaha 'amma: public interest

maslaha khassa: private interest

mu'asara: contemporaneity

mujaddid: renewer, one who renews

mujtama': society; literally, a gathering place or place of assembly

al-mujtama' al-ahli: civil society, traditional society

mujtama' al-badawi: society of the Bedouins

mujtama' hajin: hybrid society

al-mujtama' al-madani: civil society, civic society

mujama' al-mudun: society of the cities

mujtama' al-sahara: society of the desert

muwatin: citizen

muwatiniyya: citizenship

nahda: rising, awakening, renaissance

qawmiyya: nationalism

ra'iyya: subject; literally, herd or flock

raj'iyya: reaction

rif: countryside

salafiyya: pertaining to ancestors, the worthy successors *(salafiyyun)*; Islamic reform movement founded at the end of the nineteenth century

sha'b: people

sha'bi: populist

shari'a: literally, the way to "the water hole"; the revealed, canonical law of Islam

shirk bi-allah: attributing partners to God

shura: consultation, deliberation, taking counsel

siyasi: the political, the profane, or the relative

sukkan: inhabitants

sulta: power, authority, sovereign power

sunna: conduct, custom; the example of the Prophet Muhammad, inclusive of
sayings, actions, and silent approval, as recorded in the *hadith.* One of the
sources of *shari'a.*

tanshi'an: (human) cultivation

tanshi'ani: acculturative

ta'ifa: faction

tajdid: renewal, regeneration, revival; especially, revival of Islamic teachings

takfir: disbelief

taqlid: imitation, emulation, uncritical faith; acceptance of a traditional legal
position on mere authority without independent inquiry

tariqa: sufi order

tarayyuf al-mudun: ruralization of the cities

tawahhush: wildness, savageness

tawazun: balance

tawhid: unification; belief in the absolute oneness and unity of God

thawra: revolution

turath: heritage

'ulama: literally, "scholars"; used for traditional scholars in Islam, experts in *shari'a,* and loosely for those who perform religious duties

umma: community, nation; especially Muslim community

'uruba: Arabism

usul: fundamentals (of Islam)

usul al-fiqh: principles and sources of Islamic jurisprudence

wahda: unity

waqf: charitable religious endowment; plural, *awqaf*

watan: homeland

zawiyya: shrine or sacred location, often the former abode of a holy person or saint

Works Cited

'Abd Allah, 'Abd al-Khaliq. 1995. *al-Mujtama' al-madani wa al-tahawwul al-dimuqratiyya fi al-imarat al-'arabiya al-muttahida* (Civil Society and Democratic Change in the United Arab Emirates). Cairo: Ibn Khaldun Center for Development Studies.

'Abd al-Raziq, 'Ali. 1972. *al-Islam wa usul al-hukm* (Islam and the Fundamentals of Governance). Beirut: al-Mu'assasat al-'arabiyya lil-dirasa wa al-nashr.

'Abduh, Muhammad. 2002. "Laws Should Change in Accordance with the Conditions of Nations and the Theology of Unity." In *Modernist Islam, 1840–1940: A Sourcebook,* edited by Charles Kurzman, 50–61. New York: Oxford Univ. Press.

Abdel-Malek, Kamal. 1990. *A Study of the Vernacular Poetry of Ahmad Fu'ad Nigm.* Leiden: E. J. Brill.

Abu 'Amr, Ziyad. 1995. *al-Mujtama' al-madani wa al-tahawwul al-dimuqratiyya fi filastin* (Civil Society and Democratic Change in Palestine). Cairo: Ibn Khaldun Center for Development Studies.

Abu Zayd, Nasr Hamid. 1992. "al-Iydiyulujiyya al-wasatiyya al-talfiqiyya fi fikr al-shafi'i" (The Fabricated Middle Ideology in the Thought of Shafi'i). In *Qadayat al-mujtama' al-madani al-'arabi fi daw utruhat gharamshi* (The Issue of Civil Society in Light of Gramsci's Notebooks), edited by Amina Rashid, 161–86. Cairo: Center for Arab Studies.

Abu Jaber, Kamel S. 1966. *The Arab Ba'th Socialist Party: History, Ideology and Organization.* Syracuse, N.Y.: Syracuse Univ. Press.

Abu-Rabi', Ibrahim M. 1996. *Intellectual Origins of Islamic Resurgence in the Modern Arab World.* Albany: State Univ. of New York Press.

Aghayev, Ahmed. 2002. "Islam and Democracy." In *Modernist Islam, 1840–1940: A Sourcebook,* edited by Charles Kurzman, 229–31. New York: Oxford Univ. Press.

Ahmad, Mumtaz. 1996. "Islam and Democracy: The Emerging Consensus." *Middle East Affairs Journal* 2, no. 4:29–38.

Ahmed, Akbar S. 1992. *Postmodernism and Islam: Predicament and Promise.* London: Routledge.

Ahmed, Leila. 1992. *Women and Gender in Islam: Historical Roots of Modern Debate.* New Haven, Conn.: Yale Univ. Press.

Ajami, Fouad. 1998. *The Dream Palace of the Arabs: A Generation's Odyssey.* New York: Pantheon.

'Ali, Haydar Ibrahim. 1996. *al-Mujtama' al-madani wa al-tahawwul al-dimuqratiyya fi al-sudan* (Civil Society and Democratic Change in the Sudan). Cairo: Ibn Khaldun Center for Development Studies.

al-'Alim, Mahmud Amin. 1998. Interview with author. Cairo, Egypt. June 9.

al-'Alim, Mahmud Amin. 1997. *Qadaya fikriyya: min ajl ta'sil al-'aqlaniyya wa al-dimuqratiyya wa al-ibda'* (Intellectual Issues: For the Foundation of Rationalism, Democracy and Creativity). Issue 17/18 entitled "Lughatuna al-'arabiyya fi ma'rakat al-hadara" (Our Arabic Language in the Civilizational Battle). Cairo: Qadayat fikriyya lil-nashr wa al-tawzi'.

Alrawi, Karim. 1992. "University of the Extreme." *The Guardian,* June 23, 19.

'Amil, Mahdi. 1979. *Bahth fi asbab al-harb al-ahliyya fi lubnan* (An Inquiry into the Causes of the Civil War in Lebanon). Beirut: Dar al-Farabi.

———. 1984. *Azmat al-hadara al-'arabiyya am azmat al-burjwaziyya al-'arabiyya?* (A Crisis of Arab Civilization or a Crisis of the Arab Bourgeoisies?). Beirut: Dar al-Farabi.

Amin, Qasim. 1992. *The Liberation of Women and the New Woman.* Translated by Samiha Sidhom Peterson. Cairo: American Univ. in Cairo Press.

al-Ansari, 'Abd al-Hamid. 2001. "Nahw mafhum 'arabi islami lil-mujtama' al-madani" (Regarding an Arab-Islamic Understanding of Civil Society). *al-Mustaqbal al-'arabi* 272:95114.

The Arab Ba'th Party. 1962. "Constitution." In *Arab Nationalism: An Anthology,* edited by Sylvia G. Haim, 233–41. Berkeley: Univ. of California Press.

al-'Ariyat, 'Issam. 1992. "Munaqashat" (Debate). In *al-Mujtama' al-madani fi al-watan al-'arabi wa dawruhu fi tahqiq al-dimuqratiyya* (Civil Society in the Arab World and Its Role in the Realization of Democracy), edited by Sa'id Bin Sa'id, 723–26. Beirut: Center for Arab Unity Studies.

Arkoun, Mohammed. 1988. *Arab Thought.* New Delhi: S. Chand and Co.

———. 2002. "Locating Civil Society in Islamic Contexts." In *Civil Society in the Muslim World: Contemporary Perspectives,* edited by Amyn B. Sajoo, 35–60. London: Institute of Ismaili Studies.

Arslan, Shakib. 1965. *Limadha ta'akhkhara al-muslimun wa-limadha taqaddama ghayruhum* (Why Did the Muslims Fall Behind While the Others Advanced?). Beirut: Dar maktabat al-hayah.

Averroes. 1969. *Averroes' Commentary on Plato's Republic,* edited by E. I. J. Rosenthal. Cambridge, UK: Cambridge Univ. Press.

Avineri, Shlomo. 1969. *Karl Marx on Colonialism and Modernization: His Dispatches and other Writings on China, India, Mexico, the Middle East and North Africa.* Garden City, N.Y.: Doubleday.

al-'Awwa, Muhammad Salim. 1989. *Fi al-nizam al-siyasi lil-dawlat al-islamiyya* (On the Political System of the Islamic State). Cairo: Dar al-shuruq.

———. 1993. "I'adat bina al-dawla li-tanshit al-mujtama' al-madani" (Reconstructing the State to Activate Civil Society). *al-Hayah,* Aug. 3, 19.

Ayalon, Ami. 1985. "Semantics and the Modern History of Non-European Societies: Arab 'Republics' as a Case Study." *Historical Journal* 28, no. 4:821–34.

———. 1987. *Language and Change in the Middle East: The Evolution of Modern Arabic Political Discourse.* Oxford, UK: Oxford Univ. Press.

———. 2001. "*Muwatin.*" *Encyclopaedia of Islam.* Vol. 1. CD-Rom edition. Leiden: Brill.

Ayubi, Nazih. 1992. "State, Islam and Communal Plurality." *The Annals of the American Academy of Political and Social Science* 524:79–91.

———. 1995. *Over-stating the Arab State: Politics and Society in the Middle East.* London: I. B. Tauris.

al-'Azm, Sadiq Jalal. 1968. *al-Naqd al-dhati ba'da al-hazima* (Self-Criticism after the Defeat). Beirut: Dar al-Tali'a.

———. 1981. "Orientalism and Orientalism in Reverse." *Khamsin* 8:5–27.

———. 1998a. *al-'Almaniyya wa al-mujtama' al-madani* (Secularism and Civil Society). Cairo: Markaz al-dirasat wa al-ma'lumat al-qanuniyya li-huquq al-insan.

———. 1998b. Interview with author. Damascus, Syria. Jan. 27.

al-Azmeh, Aziz. 1996. *Islams and Modernities.* London: Verso.

Ball, Terence. 1988. *Transforming Political Discourse: Political Theory and Critical Conceptual History.* Oxford, UK: Basil Blackwell.

————. 1998. "Conceptual History and the History of Political Thought." In *History of Concepts: Comparative Perspectives,* edited by Iain Hampsher-Monk, Karin Tilmans, and Frank van Vree, 75–86. Amsterdam: Amsterdam Univ. Press.

Ball, Terence, and Richard Dagger. 2004. *Political Ideologies and the Democratic Ideal.* New York: Longman.

Ball, Terence, and J. G. A. Pocock, eds. 1988. *Conceptual Change and the Constitution.* Lawrence: Univ. Press of Kansas.

Ball, Terence, James Farr, and Russell L. Hanson, eds. 1989. *Political Innovation and Conceptual Change.* Cambridge, UK: Cambridge Univ. Press.

Becker, Marvin B. 1988. *Civility and Society in Western Europe, 1300–1600.* Bloomington: Indiana Univ. Press.

————. 1994. *The Emergence of Civil Society in the Eighteenth Century: A Privileged Moment in the History of England, Scotland, and France.* Bloomington: Indiana Univ. Press.

Bellamy, Richard. 1992. *Liberalism and Modern Society: An Historical Argument.* University Park: Pennsylvania State Univ. Press.

Bilgrami, Akeel. 2003. "The Clash within Civilizations." *Daedalus* 132, no. 3:88–93.

Bilqaziz, 'Abd al-Ilah. 1992. Ishkaliyyat al-marja' fi al-fikr al-'arabi al-mu'asir (The Problem of Referential Source in Contemporary Arab Thought). Beirut: Dar al-mantakhab al-'arabi.

Binder, Leonard. 1988. *Islamic Liberalism: A Critique of Development Ideologies.* Chicago: Univ. of Chicago Press.

Bin Sa'id, Sa'id. 1985. "al-Tayyarat al-falsafiyya fi al-fikr al-'arabi al-mu'asir wa al-mawqif min al-turath: mulahazat tamhidiyya" (Philosophical Tendencies in Contemporary Arab Thought and the Attitude toward the Heritage: Preliminary Observations). In *al-Falsafa fi al-watan al-'arabi al-mu'asir* (Philosophy in the Contemporary Arab World), edited by Ahmad Madhi, 93–100. Beirut: Center for Arab Unity Studies.

————. 1987. "*al-Watan* and *al-Umma* in Contemporary Arab Use." In *The Foundations of the Arab State,* edited by Ghassan Salamé, 149–74. London: Croom Helm.

————. 1992a. Introduction to *al-Mujtama' al-madani fi al-watan al-'arabi wa dawruhu fi tahqiq al-dimuqratiyya* (Civil Society in the Arab World and Its Role in the Realization of Democracy), edited by Sa'id Bin Sa'id, 9–29. Beirut: Center for Arab Unity Studies.

————, ed. 1992b. *al-Mujtama' al-madani fi al-watan al-'arabi wa dawruhu fi tahqiq al-dimuqratiyya* (Civil Society in the Arab World and Its Role in the Realization of Democracy). Beirut: Center for Arab Unity Studies.

Birah, Jhurj. 1995. *al-Mujtama' al-madani wa al-tahawwul al-dimuqratiyya fi suriya* (Civil Society and Democratic Change in Syria). Cairo: Ibn Khaldun Center for Development Studies.

Bishara, Azmi. 1998. *al-Mujtama' al-madani: dirasat naqdiyya* (Civil Society: A Critical Study). Beirut: Center for Arab Unity Studies.

al-Bishri, Tariq, ed. 1989. *al-Hiwar al-qawmi al-dini: awraq 'amal wa munaqashat al-nadwa al-fikriyya* (National-Religious Dialogue: Working Papers and Intellectual Roundtable Debates). Beirut: Center for Arab Unity Studies.

al-Bizri, Dalal. 1994. *Gharamshi fi al-diwaniyya fi mahall al-mujtama' al-madani min al-'arab* (Gramsci in Dialogue Concerning the Role of the Civil Society among the Arabs). Beirut: Dar al-jadid.

————. 1995. "al-Mujtama' al-madani: al-jam'iyyat al-nisa'iyya al-lubnaniyya" (Civil Society: Women's Groups in Lebanon). In *al-Mar'a al-'arabiyya: al-waqi' wa al-tasawwur* (Arab Women: Reality and Perception), edited by Fatima al-Zahra Azrawil and Dalal al-Bizri. Cairo: Dar al-mar'a al-'arabiyya lil-nashr.

Black, Antony. 2001. *The History of Islamic Political Thought: From the Prophet to the Present*. London: Routledge.

Borges, Jorge Luis. 1988. *Labyrinths: Selected Stories and Other Writings*. New York: W. W. Norton and Co.

Boullata, Issa. 1990. *Trends and Issues in Contemporary Arab Thought*. Albany: State Univ. of New York Press.

al-Braizat, Fares. 2003. "Muslims and Democracy: An Empirical Critique of Fukuyama's Culturalist Approach." *International Journal of Comparative Sociology* 43, nos. 3–5:269–99.

Browers, Michaelle L. 2004. "Islam and Political *Sinn*: The Hermeneutics of Contemporary Islamic Reformists." In *An Islamic Reformation?* edited by Michaelle L. Browers and Charles Kurzman, 54–78. Lanham, Md.: Lexington Books.

Brumberg, Daniel. 2002. "Islamists and the Politics of Consensus." *Journal of Democracy* 13, no. 3:109–15.

Brunner, Otto, Werner Conze, and Reinhart Koselleck, eds. 1972–97. *Geschichtliche Grundbegriffe: historisches Lexikon zur politisch-sozialen*

Sprache in Deutschland (Basic Concepts in History: A Historical Dictionary of Political and Social Language in Germany). Stuttgart: E. Klett.

Butalib, Muhammad Najib. 1987. "Qira'a fi al-qira'at al-jadaliyya lil-turath al-'arabi" (A Reading of the Dialectical Readings of the Arab Heritage). *al-Mustaqbal al-'arabi* 104:144–55.

Carver, Terrell. 1998. "A Political Theory of Gender: Perspectives on the 'Universal Subject.' " In *Gender, Politics and the State,* edited by Vicky Randall and Georgina Waylen, 18–24. London: Routledge.

Castiglione, Dario, and Iain Hampsher-Monk. 2001. "Introduction: The History of Political Thought and the National Discourses of Politics." In *The History of Political Thought in National Context,* edited by Dario Castiglione and Iain Hampsher-Monk, 1–9. Cambridge, UK: Cambridge Univ. Press.

Center for Arab Unity Studies. 1995. *Mu'tamar al-qawmi al-islami al-awwal: watha'iq wa munaqashat wa qararat al-mu'tamar* (The First Nationalist-Islamic Conference: Papers, Debates and Resolutions of the Conference). Beirut: Center for Arab Unity Studies.

———. 1999. *Mu'tamar al-qawmi al-islami al-thani* (The Second Nationalist-Islamic Conference). Beirut: Center for Arab Unity Studies.

———. 2004a. *Mu'tamar al-qawmi al-islami al-rab'i* (The Fourth Nationalist-Islamic Conference). Beirut: Center for Arab Unity Studies.

———. 2004b. *Mu'tamar al-qawmi al-islami al-thalith* (The Third Nationalist-Islamic Conference). Beirut: Center for Arab Unity Studies.

Chatterjee, Partha. 1990. "A Response to Taylor's Modes of Civil Society." *Public Culture* 3, no. 1:119–32.

Chehabi, H. E. 1996. "The Impossible Republic: Contradictions of Iran's Islamic State." *Contention* 5:135–54.

Cleveland, William L. 1971. *The Making of an Arab Nationalist: Ottomanism and Arabism in the Life and Thought of Sati' al-Husri.* Princeton, N.J.: Princeton Univ. Press.

Cohen, Jean L. 1982. *Class and Civil Society: The Limits of Marxian Critical Theory.* Amherst: Univ. of Massachusetts Press.

Cohen, Jean L., and Andrew Arato. 1992. *Civil Society and Political Theory.* Cambridge, Mass.: MIT Press.

Colas, Dominique. 1997. *Civil Society and Fanaticism: Conjoined Histories.* Stanford, Calif.: Stanford Univ. Press.

al-Dajani, Ahmad Sidqi. 1984. "Tatawwur mafahim al-dimiqratiyya fi al-fikr a-'arabi al-hadith" (The Development of Concepts of Democracy in Modern Arab Thought). In *'Azmat al-dimuqratiyya fi al-watan al-'arabi* (The Crisis of Democracy in the Arab World), edited by Saad Eddin Ibrahim, 115–42. Beirut: Center for Arab Unity Studies.

Dallmayr, Fred R. 1996. *Beyond Orientalism: Essays on Cross-Cultural Encounter.* Albany: State Univ. of New York Press.

———. 1997. "Introduction: Toward a Comparative Political Theory." *The Review of Politics* 59:421–27.

———. 1998. *Alternative Visions: Paths in the Global Village.* Lanham, Md.: Rowman and Littlefield.

———, ed. 1999. *Border Crossings: Toward a Comparative Political Theory.* Lanham, Md.: Lexington Books.

Darraj, Faysal. 1992. "al-Thaqafa al-sha'biyya fi siyasat gharamshi" (Popular Culture in Gramsci's Politics). In *Qadayat al-mujtama' al-madani al-'arabi fi daw utruhat gharamshi* (The Issue of Civil Society in Light of Gramsci's Notebooks), edited by Amina Rashid, 94–107. Cairo: Center for Arab Studies.

Darwish, Adel. 1992. "Obituary of Farag Fouda." *The Independent* (London), June 2, 14.

Dawisha, Adeed. 2003. *Arab Nationalism in the Twentieth Century: From Triumph to Despair.* Princeton, N.J.: Princeton Univ. Press.

Dawood, N. J. 1994. *The Koran, with Parallel Arabic Text.* London: Penguin Books.

DeLue, Steven M. 2002. *Political Thinking, Political Theory and Civil Society.* New York: Longman.

Den Boer, Pim. 1998. "The Historiography of German Begriffsgeschichte and the Dutch Project of Conceptual History." In *History of Concepts: Comparative Perspectives,* edited by Iain Hampsher-Monk, Karin Tilmans, and Frank van Vree, 13–22. Amsterdam: Amsterdam Univ. Press.

Derathé, Robert. 1950. *Jean-Jacques Rousseau et la science politique de son temps.* Paris: Presses universitaires de France.

Diamond, Larry. 2003. "Can the Whole World Become Democratic? Democracy, Development and International Policies." (Apr. 17). Center for the Study of Democracy, Paper 03–05, http://repositories.cdlib.org/csd/03–05.

al-Dimni, Bin 'Isa. 1991. "Bahthan 'an al-mujtama' al-madani al-manshud" (In

Search of the Desired Civil Society). *al-Mustaqbal al-'alim al-islami* 1, no. 4:225–37.

al-Din, Fu'ad Siraj, Khalid Muhi al-Din, Dhiya al-Din Da'ud, and Ibrahim Shukri. 1999. "Nida min ahzab al-'aml wa al-nasiri wa al-wafd wa al-tajammu' min ajl al-islah al-siyasi wa al-dusturi" (Petition from the Labor, Nasirist, Wafd and Tagammu' Parties for Political and Constitutional Reform). *al-Sha'b,* Sept. 3, 1.

Dwyer, Kevin. 1991. *Arab Voices: The Human Rights Debate in the Middle East.* London: Routledge.

Eberly Don E., ed. 2000. *The Essential Civil Society Reader: Classic Essays in the American Civil Society Debate.* Lanham, Md.: Rowman and Littlefield Publishers.

Ehrenberg, John. 1999. *Civil Society: The Critical History of an Idea.* New York: New York Univ. Press.

Eickelman, Dale F. 1998. "Inside the Islamic Reformation." *Wilson Quarterly* 22:80–89.

El-Affendi, Abdelwahab. 1991. *Turabi's Revolution: Islam and Power in Sudan.* London: Grey Seal.

El-Gawhary, Karim. 1994. "Voices: An Interview with Heba Ra'uf Ezzat." *Middle East Report* 191:26–27.

El-Kenz, Ali. 1991. *Algerian Reflections on Arab Crises.* Austin: Center for Middle Eastern Studies, Univ. of Texas.

Elkholy, Abdo A. 1979. "The Concept of Community in Islam." In *Islamic Perspectives: Studies in Honour of Mawlana Sayyid Abul A'la Mawdudi,* edited by Khurshid Ahmad and Zafar Ishaq Ansari, 171–81. Leicester, UK: Islamic Foundation.

El-Mikawy, Noha. 1999. "The Informal Sector and the Conservative Consensus: A Case of Fragmentation in Egypt." In *Women, Globalization and Fragmentation in the Developing World,* edited by Haleh Afshar and Stephanie Barrientos, 77–90. London: Macmillan.

Enayat, Hamid. 1982. *Modern Islamic Political Thought.* Austin: Univ. of Texas Press.

Esposito John L., and John O. Voll. 2001. *Makers of Contemporary Islam.* Oxford, UK: Oxford Univ. Press.

Euben, Roxanne L. 1995. "Islamic Fundamentalism and the Limits of Modern Rationalism." PhD diss., Princeton Univ.

———. 1997a. "Comparative Political Theories and Modernity, Islamic and Western." Paper presented at the American Political Science Association annual meeting. Washington, D.C.

———. 1997b. "Premodern, Antimodern or Postmodern? Islamic and Western Critiques of Modernity." *Review of Politics* 59:429–60.

———. 1999. *Enemy in the Mirror: Islamic Fundamentalism and the Limits of Modern Rationalism, A Work of Comparative Political Theory.* Princeton, N.J.: Princeton Univ. Press.

Ezzat, Heba Raouf. 1995. "al-Usra wa al-taghyir al-siyasi: ru'ya islamiyya" (The Family and Political Change: An Islamic View). *Islamiyyat al-ma'rifa* 191:11–47.

———. 1999. "Women and the Interpretation of Islamic Sources." (Oct.), <http://www.islam21.org/pages/keyissues/key2–6.htm>, 21st Century Trust.

Fakhru, Munirah Ahmad. 1995. *al-Mujtama' al-madani wa al-tahawwul al-dimuqratiyya fi al-Bahrayn* (Civil Society and Democratic Change in Bahrain). Cairo: Ibn Khaldun Center for Development Studies.

al-Falih, Matruk. 2002. *al-Mujtama' wa al-dimuqratiyya wa al-dawla fi al-buldan al-'arabiyya: dirasat muqarana fi ishkaliyat al-mujtama' al-madani fid aw tarayyuf al-mudun* (Society, Democracy and the State in Arab Countries: A Comparative Study of the Problematic of Civil Society in Light of the Ruralization of the Cities). Beirut: Center for Arab Unity Studies.

Farabi, Abu Nasr. 1963. "The Political Regime." In *Medieval Political Philosophy,* edited by Ralph Lerner and Muhsin Mahdi, 31–57. Ithaca, N.Y.: Cornell Univ. Press.

Farag, Fatemah. 1998. "Fresh Paint and a New Platform." *Al-Ahram Weekly,* July 30-Aug. 5, 3.

Farr, James. 1988. "Conceptual Change and Constitutional Innovation." In *Conceptual Change and the Constitution,* edited by Terence Ball and J. G. A. Pocock, 13–34. Lawrence: Univ. Press of Kansas.

Fawzi, 'Isam. 1992a. "'Aliyyat al-haymana wa al-muqawwama fi al-khatab al-sha'bi" (The Dynamics of Hegemony and Resistance in Popular Discourse). In *Qadaya al-mujtama' al-madani al-'arabi fi daw utruhat gharamshi* (The Issue of Civil Society in Light of Gramsci's Notebooks), edited by Amina Rashid, 122–31. Cairo: Center for Arab Studies.

———. 1992b. "'Urdh al-munaqashat" (Amidst the Debate). In *Qadaya al-mu-*

jtama' al-madani al-'arabi fi daw utruhat Gharamshi (The Issue of Civil Society in Light of Gramsci's Notebooks), edited by Amina Rashid, 317–29. Cairo: Center for Arab Studies.

Ferguson, Adam. 1995. *An Essay on the History of Civil Society.* New York: Cambridge Univ. Press.

Filali-Ansary, Abdou. 1996. "The Challenge of Secularization." *Journal of Democracy* 7, no. 2:76–80.

Flores, Alexander. 1997. "Secularism, Integralism, and Political Islam: The Egyptian Debate." In *Political Islam: Essays from Middle East Report,* edited by Joel Beinin and Joe Stork, 83–94. London: I. B. Tauris.

Foucault, Michel. 1985. *History of Sexuality.* New York: Vintage Books.

Fouda, Farag. 1987. *Hiwar hawla al-'ilamiyya* (Debate over Secularism). Cairo: Dar al-mahrusa lil-nashr.

———. 1988. *al-Haqiqa al-gha'iba* (The Absent Truth). Cairo: Dar al-fikr lil-dirasat wa al-nashr.

Frankel, Boris. 1983. *Beyond the State?: Dominant Theories and Socialist Strategies.* London: Macmillan Press.

Freeden, Michael. 1996. *Ideologies and Political Theory: A Conceptual Approach.* Oxford, UK: Oxford Univ. Press.

Gadamer, Hans-Georg. 1993. *Truth and Method.* New York: Continuum.

Gaffney, Patrick D. 1997. "Fundamentalist Preaching and Islamic Militancy in Upper Egypt." In *Spokesmen for the Despised: Fundamentalist Leaders of the Middle East,* edited by R. Scott Appleby, 257–93. Chicago: Univ. of Chicago Press.

Gellner, Ernest. 1979. *Spectacles and Predicaments: Essays in Social Theory.* Cambridge, UK: Cambridge Univ. Press.

———. 1981. *Muslim Society.* Cambridge, UK: Cambridge Univ. Press.

———. 1994. *Conditions of Liberty: Civil Society and Its Rivals.* London: Hamish Hamilton.

———. 1995. "The Importance of Being Modular." In *Civil Society: Theory, History, Comparison,* edited by John A. Hall, 32–55. Cambridge, UK: Polity Press.

Ghalyun, Burhan. 1990. *Ightiyal al-'aql: mihnat al-thaqafat al-'arabiyya bayna al-salafiyyat wa al-taba'iyya* (The Assassination of Reason: Arab Cultural Work between Salafiyya and Dependency). Cairo: Maktaba madbuli.

———. 1991. *Naqd al-siyasa: al-dawla wa al-din* (Critique of Politics: The State and Religion). Beirut: al-Mu'assasat al-'arabiyya lil-dirasat wa al-nashr.

————. 1992. "Bina al-mujtama' al-madani al-'arabi: dawr al-'awamil al-dakhiliyya wa al-kharijiyya" (Constructing Arab Civil Society: The Role of Internal and External Factors). In *al-Mujtama' al-madani fi al-watan al-'arabi wa dawruhu fi tahqiq al-dimuqratiyya* (Civil Society in the Arab World and Its Role in the Realization of Democracy), edited by Sa'id Bin Sa'id, 733–55. Beirut: Center for Arab Unity Studies.

al-Ghannouchi, Rachid. 1993. *al-Hurriyyat al-'amma fi al-dawlat al-islamiyya* (Public Liberties in the Islamic State). Beirut: Center for Arab Unity Studies.

————. 2000. "Secularism in the Arab Maghreb." In *Islam and Secularism in the Middle East,* edited by Azzam Tamimi, 97–123. London: Hurst and Co.

al-Ghannouchi, Rachid, and Hassan Turabi. 1981. *Harakat al-islamiyya wa al-tahdith* (The Islamic Movement and Modernization). Jerusalem: n.p.

Ghazul, Firyal Jabburi. 1992. "Manzur gramshi fi al-naqd al-adabi" (Gramsci's Perspective on Literary Criticism). In *Qadaya al-mujtama' al-madani al-'arabi fi daw utruhat gharamshi* (The Issue of Civil Society in Light of Gramsci's Notebooks), edited by Amina Rashid, 136–57. Cairo: Center for Arab Studies.

Gökalp, Ziya. 1959. *Turkish Nationalism and Western Civilization: Selected Essays of Ziya Gökalp,* translated by Niyazi Berkes. New York: Columbia Univ. Press.

Goldberg, Ellis, Resat Kasaba, and Joel S. Migdal. 1993. *Rules and Rights in the Middle East: Democracy, Law, and Society.* Seattle: Univ. of Washington Press.

Gramsci, Antonio. 1997. *Selections from the Prison Notebooks.* New York: International Publishers.

Gran, Peter. 1987. "Reflections on Contemporary Arab Society: The Political Economy School of the 1970s." *Arab Studies Quarterly* 9, no. 1:76–97.

————. 1992. "Mafhum gharamshi 'an al-muthaqaf al-taqlidi: salahiyyatuhu li-dirasat misr al-hadith" (Gramsci's Concept of the Traditional Intellectual: Appropriateness for Studying Modern Egypt)." In *Qadaya al-mujtama' al-madani al-'arabi fi daw utruhat gharamshi* (The Issue of Civil Society in Light of Gramsci's Notebooks), edited by Amina Rashid, 217–28. Cairo: Center for Arab Studies.

Habib, Muhammad al-Sayyid. 1992. "Munaqashat" (Debate). In *al-Mujtama' al-madani fi al-watan al-'arabi wa dawruhu fi tahqiq al-dimuqratiyya* (Civil

Society in the Arab World and Its Role in the Realization of Democracy), edited by Saʿid Bin Saʿid, 334. Beirut: Center for Arab Unity Studies.

Haddad, Bassam. 2001. "Business as Usual in Syria?" *MERIP Press Information Note.* <http://www.merip.org/mero/mero090701.html>.

Haddad, Yvonne Yazbeck. 1995. *Islamists and the Challenge of Pluralism.* Washington, D.C.: Center for Contemporary Arab Studies, Georgetown Univ.

Halima, ʿAbd al-Munʿim M. 1993. *Hukm al-islam fi al-dimuqratiyya wa al-taʿaddudiyya al-hizbiyya* (Islam's Judgment on Democracy and Party Pluralism). Amman: al-Sharika al-jadida.

Hall, John A. 1985. *Powers and Liberties: The Causes and Consequences of the Rise of the West.* Oxford, UK: Blackwell.

——. 1988. "States and Societies: The Miracle in Comparative Perspective." In *Europe and the Rise of Capitalism,* edited by Jean Baechler, John A. Hall, and Michael Mann, 20–38. Oxford, UK: Blackwell.

——. 1995. "In Search of Civil Society." In *Civil Society: Theory, History, Comparison,* edited by John A. Hall, 1–31. Cambridge, UK: Polity Press.

al-Hamad, Laila. 2002. "Women's Organizations in the Arab World" (English and Arabic). *al-Raʾida* 19, nos. 97–98:22–27.

Hampsher-Monk, Iain, Karin Tilmans, and Frank van Vree. 1998. *History of Concepts: Comparative Perspectives.* Amsterdam: Amsterdam Univ. Press.

Hamzeh, Nizar A. 1992. "Lebanon's Hizbullah: From Islamic Revolution to Parliamentary Accommodation." *Third World Quarterly* 14, no. 2:321–37.

——. 2000. "Lebanon's Islamists and Local Politics: A New Reality." *Third World Quarterly* 21, no. 5:739–59.

Hanafi, Hasan. 1979. "al-Juzur al-tarikhiyya li-azmat al-huriyya wa al-dimuqratiyya fi wujdanuna al-muʿasir" (The Historical Roots of the Crisis of Freedom and Democracy in Our Zeitgeist). *al-Mustaqbal al-ʿarabi* 5:130–39.

——. 1981. *al-Turath wa al-tajdid: mawqifuna min al-turath al-qadim* (The Heritage and Renewal: Our Position in Regard to the Ancient Heritage). Beirut: Dar al-tanwir.

——. 1988. *al-Din wa al-thawra fi misr: 1952–81* (Religion and Revolution in Egypt). Cairo: Maktaba madbuli.

——. 1991. *Muqaddima fi ʿilm al-istighrab* (Introduction to the Science of Occidentalism). Cairo: al-Dar al-fanniyya.

——. 1993. "Hiwar maʿ hasan hanafi: al-islam al-siyasi wa al-islam al-nafti"

(A Dialogue with Hasan Hanafi: Political Islam and Oil Islam). *Ikhtilaf: ma-jallat thaqafiyyat fasaliyya* 5:5–10.

———. 1995. "From Dogma to Revolution." In *Tradition, Revolution, and Culture.* Vol. 2 of *Islam in the Modern World.* Cairo: Anglo-Egyptian Bookshop.

———. 1998. *al-Din wa al-thaqafa wa al-siyasa fi al-watan al-'arabi* (Religion, Culture, and Politics in the Arab World). Cairo: Dar Qiba.

———. 2002a. "Alternative Conceptions of Civil Society: A Reflective Islamic Approach." In *Alternative Conceptions of Civil Society,* edited by Simone Chambers and Will Kymlicka, 171–89. Princeton, N.J.: Princeton Univ. Press; also in *Islamic Political Ethics: Civil Society, Pluralism, and Conflict,* edited by Sohail H. Hashmi, 56–75. Princeton, N.J.: Princeton Univ. Press.

———. 2002b. "Islam and Revolution." In *The Philosophical Quest: A Cross-Cultural Reader,* edited by Gail M. Presbey, Karsten J. Struhl, and Richard E. Olsen, 183–94. Columbus, Ohio: McGraw-Hill.

———. 2002c. "Phenomenology and Islamic Philosophy." In *Phenomenology World-Wide: Foundations, Expanding Dynamisms, Life-Engagements—A Guide for Research and Study,* edited by Anna-Teresa Tymieniecka, 318–21. Boston: Kluwer Academic Publishers.

Hashim, 'Abd al-Qadir. 2003. *Qadiyat d. sa'd al-din ibrahim wa mustaqbal al-mujtama' al-madani fi misr* (The Issue of Dr. Saad Eddin Ibrahim and the Future of Civil Society in Egypt). Cairo: Ibn Khaldun Center for Development Studies.

Hashmi, Sohail H., ed. 2002. *Islamic Political Ethics: Civil Society, Pluralism, and Conflict.* Princeton, N.J.: Princeton Univ. Press.

Hasib, Khayr al-Din. 1998. Interview with author. Beirut, Lebanon. Feb. 2.

Hefner, Robert W. 1998. "Multiple Modernities: Christianity, Islam and Hinduism in a Globalizing Age." *Annual Review of Anthropology* 27:83–104.

Held, David. 1996. *Models of Democracy.* Stanford, Calif.: Stanford Univ. Press.

Hermassi, Elbaki. 1983. "Le nouvel Etat et les résistances de la société civile." *Annuaire de l'Afrique du Nord* 22:417–21.

Hilal (Dessouki), 'Ali al-Din. 1989. "Nahw ma'ayir muhaddadat al-ittijah" (Regarding Definite Standards of Orientation). In *al-Ta'addudiyyat al-siyasiyya wa al-dimuqratiyya fi al-watan al-'arabi* (Political Pluralism and Democracy in the Arab World), edited by Saad Eddin Ibrahim, 337–42. Amman: Arab Thought Forum.

Hillal (Dessouki), Ali E. 1981. "Political Science in the Arab Countries: Some

Preliminary Observations." *Participation (The Newsletter of the International Political Science Association)* 5, no. 1:14–15.

Hinnebusch, Raymond A. 1995. "State, Civil Society, and Political Change in Syria." In *Civil Society in the Middle East.* Vol. 1, edited by Augustus Richard Norton, 214–42. Leiden: Brill.

Hourani, Albert. 1983. *Arabic Thought in the Liberal Age, 1798–1939.* Cambridge, UK: Cambridge Univ. Press.

———. 1989. *A History of the Arab Peoples.* Cambridge, Mass.: Harvard Univ. Press.

Huntington, Samuel P. 1996. *The Clash of Civilizations and the Remaking of World Order.* New York: Simon and Schuster.

Husayn, 'Adil. 1984. "al-Muhadidat al-tarikhiyya wa al-ijtima'iyya lil-dimuqratiyya" (The Historical and Social Limitations of Democracy). In *Azmat al-dimuqratiyya fi al-watan al-'arabi* (The Crisis of Democracy in the Arab World), edited by Saad Eddin Ibrahim, 199–242. Beirut: Center for Arab Unity Studies.

Husayn, Ashraf. 1996. "al-Mujtama' al-ahli fi zill al-takayyuf al-haykali" (Civil Society in the Shadow of Structural Adjustment). In *al-Mujtama' wa al-dawla fi al-watan al-'arabi fi zill al-siyasiyyat al-rasmaliyyat al-jadida: misr* (Society and State in the Arab World in the Shadow of The New Capitalist Policies: Egypt), edited by Samir Amin, 167–93. Cairo: Maktaba madbuli.

Huwaydi, Fahmi. 1992. "al-Islam wa al-dimuqratiyya" (Islam and Democracy). *al-Mustaqbal al-'arabi* 166:4–37.

———. 1993. *al-Islam wa al-dimuqratiyya* (Islam and Democracy). Cairo: Markaz al-ahram.

Ibn Badis, 'Abd al-Hamid. 2002. "The Principles of Governing in Islam from the Speech of [Abu Bakr] al-Siddiq." In *Modernist Islam, 1840–1940: A Sourcebook,* edited by Charles Kurzman, 93–95. New York: Oxford Univ. Press.

Ibn Batuta. 1969. *Travels in Asia and Africa, 1325–1354.* New York: A. M. Kelley.

Ibrahim, Saad Eddin, ed. 1984a. *Azmat al-dimuqratiyya fi al-watan al-'arabi* (The Crisis of Democracy in the Arab World). Beirut: Center for Arab Unity Studies.

———. 1984b. "Tajsir al-fajwa bayn al-mufakkirin wa sana'i al-qararat fi al-watan al-'arabi" (Crossing the Fissure between the Intellectuals and the Decision-Makers in the Arab World). *al-Mustaqbal al-'arabi* 7.

———. 1995. "Civil Society and Prospects for Democratization in the Arab

World." In *Civil Society in the Middle East.* Vol. 1, edited by Augustus Richard Norton, 27–54. Leiden: Brill.

———. 1998. Interview with author. Cairo, Egypt. June 28.

'Imara, Muhammad. 1980. *Tajdid al-fikr al-islami: muhammad 'abdu wa-madrasatuhu* (The Renewal of Islamic Thought: Muhammad 'Abduh and His School). Cairo: Dar al-hilal.

———. 1995. *Suqut al-ghuluw al-'almani* (The Fall of the Secularist Exaggeration). Cairo: Dar al-shuruq.

Inglehart, Ronald and Pippa Norris. 2003. "The True Clash of Civilizations." *Foreign Policy,* Mar.-Apr., 62–70.

Inter-Parliamentary Union. 1999. "Participation of Women in Political Life." Reports and Documents no. 35. Geneva: Inter-Parliamentary Union.

Islamic Salvation Front of Algeria. 2002. "All-Encompassing Program of an Islamic State." In *Modernist and Fundamentalist Debates in Islam,* edited by Mansoor Moaddel and Kamran Talattof, 273–300. New York: Palgrave.

Ismael, Tareq Y., and Jacqueline S. Ismael. 1998. *The Communist Movement in Syria and Lebanon.* Gainesville: Univ. Press of Florida.

Ismail, Salwa. 1995. "Democracy in Contemporary Arab Intellectual Discourse." In *Theoretical Perspectives.* Vol. 1 of *Political Liberalization and Democratization in the Arab World,* edited by Rex Brynen, Bahgat Korany, and Paul Noble, 93–111. Boulder, Colo.: Lynne Rienner Publishers.

Isma'il, Sayf al-Din 'Abd al-Fattah. 1989. *al-Tajdid al-siyasi wa al-waqi' al-'arabi al-mu'asir: ru'ya islamiyya* (Political Renewal and the Contemporary Arab Realtiy: An Islamic View). Cairo: Maktabat al-nahda al-misriyya.

———. 1998. *Fi al-nazariyya al-siyasiyya min manzur islami: manhajiyat al-tajdid al-siyasi wa-khibrat al-waqi' al-'arabi al-mu'asir* (On Political Theory from an Islamic View: The Method of Political Renewal and Experience of the Contemporary Arab Reality). Cairo: al-Ma'had al-'alami lil-fikr al-islami.

Issawi, Charles. 1956. "Economic and Social Foundations of Democracy in the Middle East." *International Affairs* 32, no. 1:27–42.

Jabar, Faleh A. 1997. "The Arab Communist Parties in Search of an Identity." In *Post-Marxism and the Middle East,* edited by Faleh A. Jabar, 91–107. London: Saqi Books.

al-Jabiri, Muhammad 'Abid [al-Jabri, Mohammed 'Abed]. 1984. *Takwin al-aql al-'arabi* (The Formation of Arab Reason). Beirut: Dar al-tali'ah.

———. 1985. "Ishkaliyyat al-asala wa al-mu'asara fi al-fikr al-'arabi al-hadith wa al-mu'asir: sira tabaqi am mushkil thaqafi?" (The Problematic of Authenticity and Contemporaneity in Modern and Contemporary Arab Political Thought: A Class Struggle or Cultural Problem?). In *al-Turath wa tahaddiyya al-'asr fi al-watan al-'arabi: al-asala wa al-mu'asara* (The Heritage and the Challenges of the Age in the Arab World: Authenticity and Contemporaneity), edited by al-Sayyid Yasin, 29–58. Beirut: Center for Arab Unity Studies.

———. 1989. *Ishkaliyyat al-fikr al-'arabi al-mu'asir* (Problematics of Contemporary Arab Thought). Beirut: Center for Arab Unity Studies.

———. 1990. *al-'aql al-siyasi al-'arabi* (The Arab Political Reason). Beirut: Center for Arab Unity Studies.

———. 1993. "Ishkaliyyat al-dimuqratiyya wa al-mujtama' al-madani fi al-watan al-'arabi" (The Dilemmas of Democracy and Civil Society in the Arab Nation). *al-Mustaqbal al-'arabi* 168:4–15.

———. 1994. *al-Dimuqratiyya wa huquq al-insan* (Democracy and Human Rights). Beirut: Center for Arab Unity Studies.

———. 1996. *al-Din wa al-dawla wa tatbiq al-shar'ia* (Religion, the State and the Application of Islamic Law). Beirut: Center for Arab Unity Studies.

———. 1999a. *Arab-Islamic Philosophy: A Contemporary Critique.* Austin: Center for Middle Eastern Studies, Univ. of Texas.

———. 1999b. " 'Clash of Civilizations': The Relations of the Future?" In *Islam, Modernism and the West: Cultural and Political Relations at the End of the Millennium,* edited by Gema Martín Muñoz, 65–80. London: I. B. Tauris.

al-Janhani, al-Habib, and Sayf al-Din 'Abd al-Fattah Isma'il. 2003. *al-Mujtama' al-madani wa ab'adahu al-fikriyya* (Civil Society and Its Intellectual Dimensions). Damascus: Dar al-fikr.

Johnson, James Turner. 1992. "Does Democracy Travel? Some Thoughts on Democracy and Its Cultural Context." *Ethics and International Affairs* 6:41–55.

Joseph, Suad. 1996. "Gender and Citizenship in Middle Eastern States." *Middle East Report* 198:4–10.

———. 2002. "Gender and Citizenship in the Arab World." Paper presented in Amman, Jordan, at the United Nations Development Program/Maroc 20/20 Mediterranean Development Forum, Apr. 8.

Kallab, Ilham. 1992. "al-Munaqashat" (Debate). In *al-Mujtama' al-madani fi al-watan al-'arabi wa dawruhu fi tahqiq al-dimuqratiyya* (Civil Society in the Arab World and Its Role in the Realization of Democracy), edited by Sa'id Bin Sa'id, 336. Beirut: Center for Arab Unity Studies.

Kamal, 'Abdallah. 1994. "al-Ikhwan: al-makasib wa al-khasa'ir fi azmat al-muhamin" (The Brotherhood: Gains and Losses in the Lawyers' Crisis). *Ruz al-yusuf,* Mar. 20.

Kandil, Amani. 1999. "Women and Civil Society." In *Civil Society at the Millennium,* edited by Kumi Naidoo, 57–68. West Hartford, Conn.: CIVICUS.

———. 2002. "Women in Egyptian Civil Society: A Critical Review" (Arabic and English). *al-Ra'ida* 19, nos. 97–98:30–37.

Kandil, Amani, and Sarah Ibn Nafisa. 1995. *al-Jam'iyyat al-ahliyyah fi misr* (Civil Groups in Egypt). Cairo: al-Ahram Center for Strategic Studies.

Karamanou, Anna. 2002. "Women, the Target of Fundamentalists" (English and Arabic). *al-Ra'ida* 19, nos. 97–98:4, 6.

Karatnycky, Adrian. 2002. "Muslim Countries and the Democracy Gap: The 2001 Freedom House Survey." *Journal of Democracy* 13, no. 1:99–112.

Karru, Muhammad. 1992. "al-Muthaqqafun wa al-mujtama' al-madani fi tunis" (Intellectuals and Civil Society in Tunisia). In *al-Thaqafa wa al-muthaqqaf fil al-watan al-'arabi* (Culture and the Intellectual in the Arab World), edited by Riyadh Qasim, 333–49. Beirut: Center for Arab Unity Studies.

al-Kawari, 'Ali Khalil. 2000. "Mafhum al-dimuqratiyya al-mu'asira" (The Contempoary Concept of Democracy). In *al-Mas'al al-dimuqratiyya fi al-watan al-'arabi* (The Question of Democracy in the Arab Region), edited by Center for Arab Unity Studies, 56. Beirut: Center for Arab Unity Studies.

Kawtharani, Wajih. 1988. *al-Sulta wa al-mujtama' wa al-'amal al-siyasi, min tarikh al-wilayat al-'uthmaniya fi bilad al-sham* (Power, Society and Political Practice, from the History of the Ottoman State in Greater Syria). Beirut: Center for Arab Unity Studies.

———. 1992. "al-Mujtama' al-madani wa al-dawla fi al-ta'rikh al-'arabi" (Civil Society and the State in Arab History). In *al-Mujtama' al-madani fi al-watan al-'arabi wa dawruhu fi tahqiq al-dimuqratiyya* (Civil Society in the Arab World and Its Role in the Realization of Democracy), edited by Sa'id Bin Sa'id, 119–31. Beirut: Center for Arab Unity Studies.

———. 1995. *Mashru' al-nuhud al-'arabi, aw azmat al-intiqal min al-ijtima' al-sultani ila al-ijtima' al-watani* (The Project for an Arab Resurgence, Or the Crisis of Transformation from a Sultanic Praxis to a National Praxis). Beirut: Dar al-tali'ah.

————. 1998. Interview with author. Beirut, Lebanon. Feb. 4.

Kazim, Musa. 2002. *"The Principles of Consultation and Liberty in Islam* and *Reform and Review of Religious Writings."* In *Modernist Islam, 1840–1940: A Sourcebook,* edited by Charles Kurzman, 175–80. New York: Oxford Univ. Press.

Kedourie, Elie. 1992. *Democracy and Arab Political Culture.* Washington, D.C.: Washington Institute for Near East Policy.

————. 1994. *Democracy and Arab Political Culture.* London: Frank Cass Publishers.

Kemal, Namik. 2002. "And Seek Their Counsel in the Matter [Qur'an, sura 3, verse 159]." In *Modernist Islam, 1840–1940: A Sourcebook,* edited by Charles Kurzman, 144–48. New York: Oxford Univ. Press.

Keynes, John Maynard. 1965. *General Theory of Employment, Interest, and Money.* New York: Harcourt, Brace.

Khadduri, Majid. 1970. *Political Trends in the Arab World: The Role of Ideas and Ideals in Politics.* Baltimore: Johns Hopkins Univ. Press.

Khalaf Allah, Muhamammad Ahmad. 1950. *al-Fann al-qisasi fi al-Qur'an al-karim* (The Art of Narrative in the Qur'an). Cairo: Maktaba al-nahda al-misriya.

Khalil, Hilmi. 1985. *al-Muwallad fi al-'arabiyya: dirasa fi numuw al-lughat al-'arabiyya wa tatawwuruha ba'd al-islam* (The Hybrid in Arabic: A Study of the Growth and Development of the Arabic Language after Islam). Beirut: Dar al-nahda al-'arabi.

Korany, Bahgat. 1994. "Arab Democratization: A Poor Cousin?" *PS: Political Science & Politics* 27, no. 3:511–13.

Koselleck, Reinhart. 1972. "Einleitung." In *Geschichtliche Grundbegriffe: Historisches Lexikon zur politisch-sozialen Sprache in Deutschland.* Vol. 1, edited by Otto Brunner, Werner Conze, and Reinhart Koselleck, xii-xxvii. Stuttgart: Ernst Klett Verlag.

————. 1985. *Futures Past: On the Semantics of Historical Time.* Cambridge, Mass.: MIT. Press.

————. 1988. *Critique and Crisis: Enlightenment and the Pathogenesis of Modern Society.* Oxford, UK: Berg.

————. 1994. "Some Reflections on the Temporal Structure of Conceptual Change." In *Main Trends in Cultural History: Ten Essays,* edited by Willem Melching and Wyger Velema, 7–16. Amsterdam: Rodopi.

Kotb, Sayed. 1980. *Social Justice in Islam*. Translated by John B. Hardie. New York: Octagon Books.

Kurzman, Charles, ed. 1998. *Liberal Islam: A Source Book*. New York: Oxford Univ. Press.

———, ed. 2002. *Modernist Islam, 1840–1940: A Sourcebook*. New York: Oxford Univ. Press.

Kurzman, Charles, and Michaelle L. Browers. 2004. "The Reformation Analogy." In *An Islamic Reformation?*, edited by Michaelle L. Browers and Charles Kurzman, 1–17. Lanham, Md.: Lexington Books.

Labib, al-Tahir. 1992. "Gharamshi fi al-fikr al-'arabi" (Gramsci in Arab Thought). In *Qadaya al-mujtama' al-madani al-'arabi fi daw utruhat gharamshi* (The Issue of Civil Society in Light of Gramsci's Notebooks), edited by Amina Rashid, 62–74. Cairo: Center for Arab Studies.

Lambton, Ann K. S. 1988. *State and Government in Medieval Islam*. Oxford, UK: Oxford Univ. Press.

Lane, Edward William, and Stanley Lane-Poole. 1968. *An Arabic-English Lexicon*. Beirut: Librairie du Liban.

Lapidus, Ira M. 1984. *Muslim Cities in the Later Middle Ages*. Cambridge, UK: Cambridge Univ. Press.

Laroui, Abdallah. 1976. *The Crisis of the Arab Intellectual: Traditionalism or Historicism?* Berkeley: Univ. of California.

———. 1977. *The History of the Maghrib: An Interpretive Essay*. Princeton, N.J.: Princeton Univ. Press.

Larson, Gerald James. 1988. "Introduction: The Age-Old Distinction Between the Same and Other." In *Interpreting Across Boundaries: New Essays in Comparative Philosophy*, edited by Gerald James Larson and Eliot Deutsch, 3–18. Princeton, N.J.: Princeton Univ. Press.

Lawyers Committee for Human Rights. 1996. *Beset by Contradictions: Islamization, Legal Reform and Human Rights in Sudan*. New York: Lawyers Committee for Human Rights.

Lee, Robert D. 1997. *Overcoming Tradition and Modernity: The Search for Islamic Authenticity*. Boulder, Colo.: Westview Press.

Lerner, Daniel. 1958. *The Passing of Traditional Society: Modernizing the Middle East*. Glencoe, Ill.: Free Press.

Lewis, Bernard. 1964. *The Middle East and the West*. Bloomington: Indiana Univ. Press.

————. 2001. *"Hurriyya," Encyclopedia of Islam*. CD-Rom edition v.1.1. Leiden: Brill.

Li, Chenyang. 1999. *The Tao Encounters the West: Explorations in Comparative Philosophy*. Albany: State Univ. of New York Press.

Lüsebrink, Hans-Jürgen. 1998. "Conceptual History and Conceptual Transfer: The Case of 'Nation' in Revolutionary France and Germany." In *History of Concepts: Comparative Perspectives,* edited by Iain Hampsher-Monk, Karin Tilmans, and Frank van Vree, 115–28. Amsterdam: Amsterdam Univ. Press.

Maalouf, Amin. 1992. *Leo Africanus*. New York: New Amsterdam.

Mahdi, Muhsin. 2001. *Alfarabi and the Foundation of Islamic Political Philosophy*. Chicago: Univ. of Chicago Press.

Majed, Ziad. 1998. " 'Civil Society' in Lebanon." *Kettering Review,* Fall, 36–43.

Mardin, Serif. 1995. "Civil Society and Islam." In *Civil Society: Theory, History, Comparison,* edited by John A. Hall, 278–300. Cambridge, Mass.: Polity Press.

Marshall, T. H. 1963. *Class, Citizenship and Social Development*. New York: Doubleday.

Martin, Robert W. T. 1997. "Context and Contradiction: Toward a Political Theory of Conceptual Change." *Political Research Quarterly* 50:413–36.

al-Masri, Sanaʿ. 1998. *Tamwil wa al-tatbiʿ: qissat al-jamʿiyyat ghayr al-hukumiyya* (Funding and Normalization: The Story of NGOs). Cairo: Dar sina lil-nashr.

Mawdudi, Abu-l-ʿAla. 1982. "Political Theory of Islam." In *Islam in Transition: Muslim Perspectives,* edited by John J. Donohue and John L. Esposito, 252–60. Oxford, UK: Oxford Univ. Press.

MEED, Middle East Economic Digest. 1992. "Islamists Open New Front with Foda Killing." June 19, 9–11.

Mehta, Uday Singh. 1999. *Liberalism and Empire: A Study in Nineteenth-Century British Liberal Thought*. Chicago: Univ. of Chicago Press.

Melching, Willem, and Wyger Velema. 1994. *Main Trends in Cultural History: Ten Essays*. Amsterdam: Rodopi.

Mernissi, Fatima. 1992. *Islam and Democracy: Fear of the Modern World*. Reading, Mass.: Addison-Wesley.

Messarra, Antoine Nasri. 1995. *al-Mujtamaʿ al-madani wa al-tahawwul al-dimuqrati fi lubnan* (Civil Society and Democratic Transformation in Lebanon). Cairo: Ibn Khaldun Center for Development Studies.

————. 1998. Interview with author. Beirut, Lebanon. Feb. 3.

Migdal, Joel S. 1988. *Strong Societies and Weak States: State-Society Relations and State Capabilities in the Third World*. Princeton, N.J.: Princeton Univ. Press.

Mill, James. 1975. *The History of British India*. Chicago: Univ. of Chicago Press.

———. 1994. *Principles of Political Economy; and Chapters on Socialism*. Oxford, UK: Oxford Univ. Press.

Moaddel, Mansoor, and Kamran Talattof, eds. 2002. *Modernist and Fundamentalist Debates in Islam*. New York: Palgrave.

Moghadam, Valentine M. 2002. "Citizenship, Civil Society and Women in the Arab Region" (English and Arabic). *al-Ra'ida* 19, nos. 97–98:12–21.

Montesquieu, Charles-Louis de Secondat. 1973. *Persian Letters*. London: Penguin Books.

———. 1977. *The Spirit of Laws*. Berkeley: Univ. of California Press,

Moussalli, Ahmad S. 1995. "Modern Islamic Fundamentalist Discourses on Civil Society, Pluralism and Democracy." In *Civil Society in the Middle East*. Vol. 1, edited by Augustus Richard Norton, 79–119. Leiden: Brill.

———. 1999. *Moderate and Radical Islamic Fundamentalism: The Quest for Modernity, Legitimacy, and the Islamic State*. Gainesville: Univ. Press of Florida.

———. 2001. *The Islamic Quest for Democracy, Pluralism, and Human Rights*. Gainesville: Univ. Press of Florida.

Murray, James Augustus Henry, ed. 1933. *The Oxford English Dictionary*. Oxford, UK: Clarendon Press.

Mustafa, Sahkir, ed. 1974. *Azmat al-tatawwur al-hadari fi al-watan al-'arabi* (The Crisis of Civilizational Development in the Arab World). Kuwait: Univ. of Kuwait.

Mustafa, Yusri. 1996a. "Gharamshi wa al-munathamat al-'amaliyya" (Gramsci and Labor Organizations). *al-Yasar* 79:54–55.

———. 1996b. "al-Mujtama' al-madani fi fikr gharamshi" (Civil Society in Gramsci's Thought). *al-Yasar* 72:67–81.

———, ed. 2002. *al-Mujtama' al-madani wa siyasat al-ifqar fi al-'alam al-'arabi* (Civil Society and the Impoverishment Policies in the Arab World). Cairo: Markaz al-buhuth al-'arabiya, and Tunis: El Taller.

al-Mutawakkil, Muhammad al-Malak. 1992. "Commentary on Baqir al-Khabar Paper." In *al-Mujtama' al-madani fi al-watan al-'arabi wa dawruhu fi tahqiq al-dimuqratiyya* (Civil Society in the Arab World and Its Role in the Realization of Democracy), edited by Sa'id Bin Sa'id, 588–93. Beirut: Center for Arab Unity Studies.

al-Nabhani, Taqi al-Din. 1961. *al-Shura fi al-islam* (Consultation in Islam). Leaflet, n.p., June 25.

———. 1965. *al-Dimuqratiyya, nizam kufr* (Democracy, a Heretical System). Leaflet, n.p., Mar. 14.

al-Nadim, 'Abdullah. 1983. "The Merits of Shura (Parliamentary Government)." In *Modern Arab Thought: Channels of the French Revolution,* edited by Ra'if Khuri, 129–31. Princeton, N.J.: Kingston Press.

Nafi, Basheer M. 2000. "The Arab Nationalists and the Arab Islamists: Shadows of the Past, Glimpses of the Future." *Middle East Affairs Journal* 6, nos. 1–2:109–27.

al-Najjar, Baqir. 1992. "al-Mujtama' al-madani fil misr wa al-sudan" (Civil Society in Egypt and Sudan). In *al-Mujtama' al-madani fi al-watan al-'arabi wa dawruhu fi tahqiq al-dimuqratiyya* (Civil Society in the Arab World and Its Role in the Realization of Democracy), edited by Sa'id Bin Sa'id, 565–87. Beirut: Center for Arab Unity Studies.

Najjar, Fauzi M. 1996. "The Debate on Islam and Secularism in Egypt." *Arab Studies Quarterly* 18, no. 2:1–21.

Nakamura, Hajime. 1975. *Parallel Developments: A Comparative History of Ideas.* Tokyo: Kodansha.

al-Naqqash, Farida. 1996. "Mujtama' madani am mu'arida yasariyya?" (A Civil Society or a Leftist Opposition?). *al-Yasar* 71:78–79.

al-Nasr, Khalid. 1983. "Azmat al-dimuqratiyya fi al-watan al-'arabi" (The Crisis of Democracy in the Arab World). In *al-Dimuqratiyya wa al-huquq al-insan fi al-watan al-'arabi* (Democracy and Human Rights in the Arab World), edited by 'Ali al-Din Hilal, 25–61. Beirut: Center for Arab Unity Studies.

Nasr, Seyyed Hossein. 1979. "Decadence, Deviation and Renaissance in the Context of Contemporary Islam." In *Islamic Perspectives: Studies in Honour of Mawlana Sayyid Abul A'la Mawdudi,* edited by Khurshid Ahmad and Zafar Ishaq Ansari, 35–42. Leicester, UK: Islamic Foundation.

Nasr, Vali. 2003. "Lessons from the Muslim World." *Daedalus* 132, no. 3:67–72

Negus, Sanna. 2000. "A Chosen Identity." *Cairo Times* 3 (Jan. 20–26): 25.

Norton, Augustus Richard, ed. 1995. *Civil Society in the Middle East.* Vol. 1. Leiden: Brill.

———, ed. 1996. *Civil Society in the Middle East.* Vol. 2. Leiden: Brill.

O'Donnell, Guillermo, and Philippe C. Schmitter. 1986. *Transitions from Au-*

thoritarian Rule: Tentative Conclusions about Uncertain Democracies. Baltimore: Johns Hopkins Univ. Press.

Oz-Salzberger, Fania. 1995. *Translating the Enlightenment: Scottish Civic Discourse in Eighteenth-Century Germany.* Oxford, UK: Oxford Univ. Press.

Parel, Anthony, and Ronald C. Keith. 1992. *Comparative Political Philosophy: Studies under the Upas Tree.* Newbury Park, Calif.: Sage.

Pelczynski, Z. A. 1988. "Solidarity and 'The Rebirth of Civil Society' in Poland, 1976–81." In *Civil Society and the State: New European Perspectives,* edited by John Keane, 361–80. London: Verso.

Plato. 1992. *Republic.* Translated by G. M. A. Grube. Indianapolis, Ind.: Hackett.

Pocock, J. G. A. 1996. "Concepts and Discourses, a Difference in Culture?: Comment on a Paper by Melvin Richter." In *The Meaning of Historical Terms and Concepts: New Studies on Begriffsgeschichte,* edited by Hartmut Lehmann and Melvin Richter, 47–58. Washington, D.C.: German Historical Institute.

Poulantzas, Nicos. 1973. *Political Power and Social Classes.* London: Sheed and Ward.

Pratt, Mary Louise. 1992. *Imperial Eyes: Travel Writing and Transculturation.* London: Routledge.

Putnam, Robert D. 1993. *Making Democracy Work: Civic Traditions in Modern Italy.* Princeton, N.J.: Princeton Univ. Press.

———. 2000. *Bowling Alone: The Collapse and Revival of American Community.* New York: Simon and Schuster.

al-Qaradawi, Yusuf. 1977. *al-Hulul al-mustawradah wa kayfa janat 'ala ummatina* (How Imported Solutions Disastrously Affected our Community). Cairo: Maktabat wahbah.

Rahman, Fazlur. 1970. "Revival and Reform in Islam." In *The Cambridge History of Islam,* edited by P. M. Holt, Ann Katharine Swynford Lambton, and Bernard Lewis, 632–56. Cambridge, UK: Cambridge Univ. Press.

Rashid, Amina. 1992a. "Limatha gharamshi?" (Why Gramsci?). In *Qadaya al-mujtama' al-madani al-'arabi fi daw utruhat gharamshi* (The Issue of Civil Society in Light of Gramsci's Notebooks), edited by Amina Rashid, 9–11. Cairo: Center for Arab Studies.

———, ed. 1992b. *Qadaya al-mujtama' al-madani al-'arabi fi daw utruhat gharamshi* (The Issue of Civil Society in Light of Gramsci's Notebooks). Cairo: Center for Arab Studies.

Reichardt, Rolf, and Eberhard Schmidt, eds. 1985–. *Handbuch politisch-sozialer*

Grundbegriffe in Frankreich, 1680–1820 (A Handbook of Political and Social Concepts in France, 1680–1820). Munich: R. Oldenbourg.

Richter, Melvin. 1973. "Despotism." In *The Dictionary of the History of Ideas.* Vol. 2, edited by Philip P. Wiener, 1–18. New York: Charles Scribner's Sons.

———. 1986. "Conceptual History *(Begriffsgeschichte)* and Political Theory." *Political Theory* 14:604–37.

———. 1995. *The History of Political and Social Concepts: A Critical Introduction.* New York: Oxford Univ. Press.

———. 2001. "A German Version of the 'Linguistic Turn': Reinhart Koselleck and the History of Political and Social Concepts *(Begriffsgeschichte)*." In *The History of Political Thought in National Context,* edited by Dario Castiglione and Iain Hampsher-Monk, 58–79. Cambridge, UK: Cambridge Univ. Press.

Riedel, Manfred. 1972. "Bürger, Staatsbürger, Bürgertum." In *Geschichtliche Grundbegriffe: historisches Lexikon zur politisch-sozialen Sprache in Deutschland* (Basic Concepts in History: A Dictionary on Historical Principles of Political and Social Language in Germany). Vol. 1, edited by Otto Brunner, Werner Conze, and Reinhart Koselleck, 672–724. Stuttgart: E. Klett.

———. 1975. "Gesellschaft, bürgerliche." In *Geschichtliche Grundbegriffe: historisches Lexikon zur politisch-sozialen Sprache in Deutschland* (Basic Concepts in History: A Dictionary on Historical Principles of Political and Social Language in Germany). Vol. 2, edited by Otto Brunner, Werner Conze, and Reinhart Koselleck, 719–800. Stuttgart: E. Klett.

Rippin, Andrew. 1990. *The Contemporary Period.* Vol. 2 in *Muslims: Their Religious Beliefs and Practices.* London: Routledge.

Robinson, F. C. R. 2001. *"Madjlis." Encyclopaedia of Islam,* CD-Rom edition v.1.1. Leiden: Brill.

al-Sa'adawi, Nawal. 1992. "Ma al-'amal? : halaqa niqashiyya" (What Is to Be Done? A Discussion Circle." In *al-Mujtama' al-madani fi al-watan al-'arabi wa dawruhu fi tahqiq al-dimuqratiyya* (Civil Society in the Arab World and Its Role in the Realization of Democracy), edited by Sa'id Bin Sa'id, 836–38. Beirut: Center for Arab Unity Studies.

Sadowski, Yahya. 1997. "The New Orientalism and the Democracy Debate." In *Political Islam: Essays from Middle East Report,* edited by Joel Beinin and Joe Stork, 33–50. London: I. B. Tauris.

al-Sadr, Ayatullah Baqir. 1982. *Introduction to Islamic Political System.*

Translated by M. A. Ansari. Accra: Islamic Seminary/ World Shia Muslim Organization.

Said, Edward. 1979. *Orientalism.* New York: Vintage.

Salamé, Ghassan. 1994. Introduction to *Democracy without Democrats? The Renewal of Politics in the Muslim World,* edited by Ghassan Salamé, 1–20. London: I. B. Tauris.

Salem, Paul. 1994. *Bitter Legacy: Ideology and Politics in the Arab World.* Syracuse, N.Y.: Syracuse Univ. Press.

———. 1998. "Deconstructing Civil Society: Lessons from the Lebanese Experience." *Kettering Review,* Fall, 8–15.

Salmawi, Muhammad. 1993. "al-Munazzamat al-nasiriyya wa al-hayat al-siyasiyya fi misr" (The Nasirist Organization and Political Life in Egypt). *al-Mawqif al-'arabi,* Sept.

Salvatore, Armando. 1995. "The Rational Authentication of 'Turath' in Contemporary Arab Thought: Muhammad al-Jabiri and Hasan Hanafi." *Muslim World* 85:191–214.

———. 1997. *Islam and the Political Discourse of Modernity.* Reading, Berkshire, UK: Ithaca Press.

Sarhan, Samir, ed. 1992. *Misr bayna al-dawlat al-diniyya wa al-madaniyya* (Egypt Between a Religious and Secular State). Cairo: al-Dar al-misriyya lil-nashr.

Sayed, Nesmahar. 2002. "Hassan Hanafi: Consolations of Philosophy." *al-Ahram Weekly* 572, Feb. 7–13.

al-Sayyid, Ahmad Lufti. 1963. *al-Muntakhabat* (Anthology). 2 vols. Cario: Dar al-nashr al-hadith.

Schmidt, James. 1986. "A Raven with a Halo: The Translation of Aristotle's Politics." *History of Political Thought* 7:295–319.

Schoenhals, Michael. 1992. *Doing Things with Words in Chinese Politics: Five Studies.* Berkeley: Institute of East Asian Studies, Univ. of California.

Schwedler, Jillian. Forthcoming. *Faith in Moderation: Islamist Parties in Jordan and Yemen.* Cambridge, UK: Cambridge Univ. Press.

Seligman, Adam B. 1992. *The Idea of Civil Society.* Princeton, N.J.: Princeton Univ. Press.

Shahrur, Muhammad. 1990. *al-Kitab wa al-qur'an: qira'a mu'asira* (The Book and the Qur'an: A Contemporary Reading). Damascus: al-Ahli lil-taba'a wa al-nashr wa al-tawzi'.

Shams al-Din, Shaykh Muhammad Mahdi. 1994. "Hiwar hawl: al-islam wa al-'almaniyya wa al-shura wa al-dimuqratiyya wa al-shari'a wa al-mujtama' al-madani" (Debate over Islam, Secularism, Consultation, Democracy, Islamic Law and Civil Society). *Minbar al-hiwar* 9, no. 34:5–33

Sharif, Mahir. 1997. "From Marxism to Liberal Nationalism: A Transformation in Palestinian Marxism." In *Post-Marxism and the Middle East,* edited by Faleh A. Jabar, 67–77. London: Saqi Books.

al-Shiyshani, Murad Batl. 2002. " 'Qadhiya nazariya fi dirasat mafhum al-mujtama' al-madani': muqariba islamiyya" ("A Theoretical Issue in Studying the Concept of Civil Society": An Islamic Approximation). *Shu'un khalijiyya* 29:19.

Shukr, 'Abd al-Ghaffar, ed. 1997. *al-Jam'iyyat al-ahliyya wa azmat al-tanmiyyat al-iqtisadiyya wa al-ijtima'iyya fi misr* (Civil Groups and the Crisis of Economic and Social Development in Egypt). Cairo: Arab Research Center.

Shukri, Ghali. 1992. "Ishkaliyyat al-athar al-marja'i lil-muthaqqaf wa al-sulta" (The Problem of the Referential Framework for the Intellectual and Power). In *al-Thaqafa wa al-muthaqqaf fil al-watan al-'arabi* (Culture and the Intellectual in the Arab World), edited by Riyadh Qasim, 49–79. Beirut: Center for Arab Unity Studies.

Sivan, Emmanuel. 1990. "The Islamic Resurgence: Civil Society Strikes Back." *Journal of Contemporary History* 25:353–64.

Skinner, Quentin. 1973. "The Empirical Theorists of Democracy and Their Critics: A Plague on Both Their Houses." *Political Theory* 1, no. 3:287–306.

———. 1989. "Language and Political Change." In *Political Innovation and Conceptual Change,* edited by Terence Ball, James Farr, and Russell L. Hanson, 6–23. Cambridge, UK: Cambridge Univ. Press.

Smith, Adam. 1976. *An Inquiry into the Nature and Causes of the Wealth of Nations.* Oxford, UK: Clarendon Press.

Society of the Muslim Brothers. 2002. "Boycotting the 1997 Election in Jordan." In *Modernist and Fundamentalist Debates in Islam,* edited by Mansoor Moaddel and Kamran Talattof, 301–8. New York: Palgrave.

Springborg, Patricia. 1992. *Western Republicanism and the Oriental Prince.* Austin: Univ. of Texas Press.

———. 1993. "The Origins of Liberal Institutions in the Ancient Middle East." In *Economic and Political Liberalization in the Middle East,* edited by Tim Niblock and Emma Murphy, 26–40. London: British Academic Press.

al-Sulami, Mishal Fahm. 2003. *The West and Islam: Western Liberal Democracy Versus the System of Shura.* London: Routledge.

Tahtawi, Rifaʿa Rafiʿ. 2004. *An Imam in Paris: Al-Tahtawi's Visit to France (1826–1831)*. Translated by Daniel L. Newman. London: Saqi.

Tamari, Salim. 1992. "Left in Limbo: Leninist Heritage and Islamist Challenge." *Middle East Report!*start 179:16–21.

Tamimi, Azzam S. 2001. *Rachid Ghannouchi: A Democrat within Islam*. Oxford, UK: Oxford Univ. Press.

Taylor, Charles. 1995. *Philosophical Arguments*. Cambridge, Mass.: Harvard Univ. Press.

Telhami, Shibley. 2001. "Where Are the Arab World's Moderate Voices?" *Los Angeles Times*, Oct. 19, B15.

Tessler, Mark. 2003. "Do Islamic Orientations Influence Attitudes Toward Democracy in the Arab World? Evidence from Egypt, Jordan, Morocco and Algeria." *International Journal of Comparative Sociology* 43, nos. 3–5:229–49

Tibi, Bassam. 1986. "Islam and Modern European Ideologies." *International Journal of Middle East Studies* 18:23.

———. 1995. "Culture and Knowledge: The Politics of Islamicization of Knowledge as a Postmodern Project? The Fundamentalist Claim to De-westernization." *Theory, Culture and Society* 12:1–24.

Tizini, Tayyib. 2001. *Min thulathiya al-fasad ila qadaya al-mujtamaʿ al-madani* (From the Triad of Corruption to the Issue of Civil Society). Damascus: Dar jifra lil-dirasat wa al-nashr.

Tolson, Jay. 2001. "Struggle for Islam." *U.S. News & World Report*, Oct. 15, 22–26.

Traboulsi, Fawwaz. 1998. Interview with author. Beirut, Lebanon. Feb. 3.

Tribe, Keith. 1989. "The *Geschichtliche Grundbegriffe* Project: From History of Ideas to Conceptual History—A Review Article." *Comparative Studies in Society and History* 31:180–84.

al-Tunisi, Khayr al-Din. 1967. *The Surest Path: The Political Treatise of a Nineteenth-Century Muslim*. Translated by Leon Carl Brown. Cambridge, Mass.: Harvard Univ. Press.

Turabi, Hasan. 1971. *al-Salat: ʿimad al-din* (Prayer: The Pillar of Religion). Beirut: Dar al-qalam.

———. 1983. "The Islamic State." In *Voices of Resurgent Islam*, edited by John L. Esposito, 241–51. Oxford, UK: Oxford Univ. Press.

———. 1984. *Tajdid usul al-fiqh al-Islami* (The Renewal of Islamic Jurisprudence). Jiddah: al-Dar al-suʿudiyya.

———. 1987. *Qadaya al-hurriyya wa al-wahda wa al-shura wa al-dimuqratiyya*

(Issues of Freedom, Unity, Consultation and Democracy). N.p.: al-Dar al-su'udiyyah lil-nashr.

———. 1991. *Women in Islam and Muslim Society.* London: Milestones Publishers.

———. 1993. *Tajdid al-fikr al-Islami* (The Renewal of Islamic Thought). Rabat: Dar al-qarafi lil-nashr wa al-tawzi'.

Turabi, Hasan, and Arthur L. Lowrie. 1993. *Islam, Democracy, the State and the West: A Roundtable with Dr. Hasan Turabi, May 10, 1992.* Tampa, Fla.: World and Islam Studies Enterprise.

Turner, Bryan. 1974. *Weber and Islam: A Critical Study.* London: Routledge.

———. 1994. *Orientalism, Post-Modernism and Globalism.* London: Routledge.

Tütsch, Hans E. 1958. "Arab Unity and Arab Dissensions." In *The Middle East in Transition: Studies in Contemporary History,* edited by Walter Z. Laqueur, 12–32. New York: Frederick A. Praeger.

al-'Umari, Akram Diya'. 1983. *al-Mujtama' al-madani fi 'ahd al-nubuwwa: khasa'isuhu wa tanzimatuhu al-ula-muhawalah li-tatbiq qawa'id al-muhaddithin fi naqd al-riwayat al-tarikhiyya* (Medinan Society in the Period of the Prophet: An Attempt to Apply the Rules of Hadith in Criticizing the Historicist Viewpoint). Medina: al-Jami'at al-islamiyya.

United Nations Development Programme. 2003. *Arab Human Development Report 2003.* New York: Regional Bureau for Arab States.

Urry, John. 1981. *The Anatomy of Capitalist Societies: The Economy, Civil Society, and the State.* London: Macmillan.

U.S. Department of State. 2000. "Country Reports on Human Rights Practices for 1999." Bureau of Democracy, Human Rights, and Labor, http://www.state.gov/www/global/human_rights/1999_hrp_report/overvi ew.html.

Van Gelderen, Martin. 1998. "Between Cambridge and Heidelberg: Concepts, Languages and Images in Intellectual History." In *History of Concepts: Comparative Perspectives,* edited by Iain Hampsher-Monk, Karin Tilmans, and Frank van Vree, 227–38. Amsterdam: Amsterdam Univ. Press.

Viorst, Milton. 1998. *In the Shadow of the Prophet: The Struggle for the Soul of Islam.* New York: Anchor Books.

Walzer, Michael. 1991. "The Idea of Civil Society: A Path to Social Reconstruction." *Dissent* 38:293–304.

Walzer, Richard. 1963. "Aspects of Islamic Political Thought." *Oriens* 16:40–60.

Weber, Max. 1958. *The Religion of India: The Sociology of Hinduism and Bud-dhism.* Glencoe, Ill.: Free Press.

———. 1993. *The Sociology of Religion.* Boston: Beacon Press.

Wedeen, Lisa. 1999. *Ambiguities of Domination: Politics, Rhetoric, and Symbols in Contemporary Syria.* Chicago: Univ. of Chicago Press.

Williams, Raymond. 1985. *Keywords: A Vocabulary of Culture and Society.* New York: Oxford Univ. Press.

Wittfogel, Karl August. 1957. *Oriental Despotism: A Comparative Study of Total Power.* New Haven, Conn.: Yale Univ. Press.

Yasin, Bu 'Ali. 1999. "al-Muthaqafun al-'arab: min sulta al-dawla ila al-mujtama' al-madani" (Arab Intellectuals: From the Power of the State to Civil Society). *'Alam al-fikr* 27, no. 3:45–67.

Yasin, al-Sayyid, ed. 1985. *al-Turath wa tahaddiyya al-'asr fi al-watan al-'arabi: al-asala wa al-mu'asara* (The Heritage and the Challenges of the Age in the Arab World: Authenticity and Contemporaneity). Beirut: Center for Arab Unity Studies.

Zahran, Farid. 1997. *al-Nashat al-ahli, aw al-mujtama' al-madani fi misr* (The Kinship Activity, or Civil Society in Egypt). Cairo: Markaz al-mahrusah lil-buhuth wa al-tadrib wa al-nashr.

Zaki, Moheb. 1995. *Civil Society and Democratization in Egypt, 1981–1994.* Cairo: Ibn Khaldun Center for Development Studies.

Zghal, Abdelkader. 1985. "Why Maghrebi Peasants Do Not Like Land Reform." In *Arab Society: Social Science Perspectives,* edited by Nicholas S. Hopkins and Saad Eddin Ibrahim, 322–35. Cairo: American Univ. in Cairo Press.

———. 1991. "The New Strategy of the Movement of the Islamist Way: Manip-ulation or Expression of Political Culture?" In *Tunisia: The Political Econ-omy of Reform,* edited by I. William Zartman, 205–17. Boulder, Colo.: Lynne Rienner.

———. 1992a. "Mafhum al-mujtama' al-madani wa al-tahawwul nahw al-ta'addadiyyat al-hizbiyya" (The Concept of Civil Society and Change to-ward Party Pluralism). In *Qadaya al-mujtama' al-madani al-'arabi fi daw utruhat gharamshi* (The Issue of Civil Society in Light of Gramsci's Note-books), edited by Amina Rashid, 40–61. Cairo: Center for Arab Studies.

———. 1992b. "al-Mujtama' al-madani wa al-sira min ajl al-haymanat al-iy-diyulujiyya fi al-maghrib al-'arabi" (Civil Society and the Struggle for Ideo-logical Hegemony in the Arab Maghrib). In *al-Mujtama' al-madani fi al-watan al-'arabi wa dawruhu fi tahqiq al-dimuqratiyya* (Civil Society in the Arab World and Its Role in the Realization of Democracy), edited by Sa'id Bin Sa'id, 431–66. Beirut: Center for Arab Unity Studies.

Ziyada, Khalid. 1992. "Commentary on Wajih Kawtharani's Paper." In *al-Mujtama' al-madani fi al-watan al-'arabi wa dawruhu fi tahqiq al-dimuqratiyya* (Civil Society in the Arab World and Its Role in the Realization of Democracy), edited by Sa'id Bin Sa'id, 132–37. Beirut: Center for Arab Unity Studies.

Ziser, Eyal. 2001. *Asad's Legacy: Syria in Transition.* New York: New York Univ. Press.

Zoubir, Yahia H. 1999. *North Africa in Transition: State, Society, and Economic Transformation in the 1990s.* Gainesville: Univ. Press of Florida.

Zubaida, Sami. 1989. *Islam, the People and the State: Essays on Political Ideas and Movements in the Middle East.* London: Routledge.

———. 2001. "Civil Society, Community and Democracy in the Middle East." In *Civil Society: History and Possibilities,* edited by Sudipta Kaviraj and Sunil Khilnani, 232–50. Cambridge, UK: Cambridge Univ. Press.

Index